D1603553

EARLY KAMAKURA BUDDHISM: A MINORITY REPORT

Robert E. Morrell

with a Foreword by
Minoru Kiyota

SPIRIT ROCK LIBRARY

ASIAN HUMANITIES PRESS
Berkeley, California
1987

ASIAN HUMANITIES PRESS

Asian Humanities Press offers to the specialist and the general reader alike the best in new translations of major works and significant original contributions to our understanding of Asian religions, cultures and thought.

1987

Asian Humanities Press
Berkeley, California

ISBN 0-89581-849-3
LC 87-70058

Acknowledgement is made to The Japan Foundation for assistance in the production of this book.

EARLY KAMAKURA BUDDHISM

Nanzan Studies in Religion and Culture

James W. Heisig, General Editor

Hans Waldenfels, *Absolute Nothingness: Foundations for a Buddhist-Christian Dialogue.* Trans. by J. W. Heisig. 1980.

Frederick Franck, ed., *The Buddha Eye: An Anthology of the Kyoto School.* 1982.

Nishida Kitarō, *Intuition and Reflection in Self-Consciousness.* Trans. by V. Viglielmo with T. Yoshinori and J. S. O'Leary. 1986.

Winston L. King, *Death Was His Kōan: The Samurai Zen of Suzuki Shōsan.* 1986.

Nishida Kitarō, *Intuition and Reflection in Self-Consciousness.* Trans. by V. Viglielmo with T. Yoshinori and J. S. O'Leary. 1986.

Tanabe Hajime, *Philosophy as Metanoetics.* Trans. by T. Takeuchi with V. Vigliemo and J. W. Heisig. 1986.

for my families
on both sides
of the Pacific

C O N T E N T S

CONTENTS

FOREWORD

R obert Morrell's aptly titled book *Early Kamakura Buddhism: A Minority Report* fulfills three somewhat neglected needs in modern Buddhology. In the first place, its methodology corrects a common weakness in traditional Buddhology. In the second place, it addresses itself to the task of delineating and enfleshing the "minor" or overlooked figures in Kamakura Buddhism, thus deepening our appreciation of the many-faceted development of Buddhism during that period. It identifies the Kamakura "minority" as those Buddhist monks and thinkers who, precisely because they belonged to the rapidly failing aristocratic establishment, are seldom treated in any detail. In the third place, it examines the theme of *mappō*, showing how it separates the "minority" from the "majority" and tracing its ramifications in the development of Kamakura Buddhism.

Buddhologists, following the tradition of 19th century Europe, tend to investigate Buddhist thought textually and doctrinally, locating their conclusions within the appropriate historical context. Generally they select texts from the mainstream of Buddhist thinking. Indologists concentrate their attention upon *Abhidharma, Mādhyamika,* and *Yogācāra* texts, more recently including *Tathāgatagarbha* texts. Sinologists focus their attention on major texts composed in the Six Dynasties Period and depict the interaction between Indian Buddhist ideas and Chinese notions, or they may direct their efforts toward the major domesticated schools of Buddhism during the Sui-T'ang period. Japanologists usually direct their attention to the texts of the major Heian and Kamakura schools. But even though Buddhologists expend these efforts on textual studies, doctrinal evolution cannot be traced merely by examining major texts laid out in a linear sequence. Each text grows from a dialogic response to its own particular problematic and incorporates ideas previously advanced in a variety of other major and minor writings.

Buddhologists also tend to concentrate on major systems of thought. For example, Japanese monastic education has traditionally used Gyōnen's (1240–1321) *Hasshū kōyō* (The Essentials of the Eight Schools) as an introductory text on Buddhism. This text describes the doctrine of the six Nara and the two Heian schools. It was used as the model for Takakusu Junjirō's *The Essentials of Buddhist Philosophy,* and is still commonly used in Japanese universities as an introductory text. There is no denying the importance of this text, particularly if the instructor using it is able to interpret its contents, but its widespread use does indicate a desire to master facts rather than to understand the underlying elan and the socio-historical circumstances that nurtured the surface facts. This *Hasshū kōyō* approach to the study of Buddhism ignores the human complexity of doctrinal history. Buddhist systems of thinking should not be conceived of as fixed and frozen categories, as if they were the content of Abhidharma ideas on true dharmas, or as if they were adequately presented in the Chinese *p'an-chiao* systems.

Similarly the concentration on particular patriarchal lineages often loses sight of the fact that these lineages have been arbitrarily concocted. Even the patriarchs named within a particular lineage scarcely restricted their insights to one lineage of a single master. They were most often influenced by a broad sampling of contemporaries both within their own lineage and outside of it.

Morrell's doctoral dissertation, submitted to Stanford University years ago, was a translation and interpretation of selected sections of the *Shasekishū* of Mujū (1226–1312), a collection of Buddhist anecdotes written in the vernacular of the Kamakura period. Morrell showed perceptive insight in choosing to treat the relatively unknown Mujū who, faithful Buddhist though he was, remained outside the major stream of the development of Buddhist thought. This kind of insight is crucial and necessary in modern Buddhist studies. If Buddhology were to concentrate exclusively on major texts, systems, and personages, it would in effect separate the minority and their interpretation of the Dharma from the living flow of Buddhist history. In the minority report that follows, Morrell has reclaimed just such figures from the history of Kamakura Buddhism and drawn detailed attention to them.

Late Heian to early Kamakura was a period of chaos, dramatically portrayed by Akira Kurosawa in his classic film *Rashōmon*. It was marked by a shift of political power from the aristocratic Fujiwara to the Hōjōs, the Kantō samurai. New agricultural implements and techniques such as iron tools, horse power, and water mills, were introduced and contributed to the growing economic power of the peasants. This in turn eventually triggered the disintegration of the *shōen* manorial system, which had been administered by the Fujiwara and had formed the economic basis for their dominance. The social dynamic in the new period came from the common people, not from the aristocracy, and it was this dynamic that paved the way for the overthrow of the Heian aristocracy and the establishment of the Kamakura Bakufu. The period was also marked by clashes between the old schools of Nara-Heian Buddhism, which served the Heian aristocracy, and the new schools of Kamakura Buddhism, which appealed to the peasants, samurai, and rootless people within the Heian establishment. The former emphasized incantation, magic, elaborate rituals, and ceremonies in order to maintain the prosperity of the aristocracy both in this world and in the world hereafter, while the latter emphasized a type of Buddhism directed to the needs of the people at large, the seeds of which can be traced back to the *Sangyō gisho*, a commentary allegedly composed by Prince Shōtoku on the *Saddharmapuṇḍarīka, Vimalakīrtinirdeśa*, and *Śrīmālādevīsiṃhanāda* scriptures. These three scriptures were seen as articulating respectively the doctrine of universal salvation, the wisdom of a layman, and the wisdom of a laywoman. The mass Buddhist movements which issued from these teachings in Kamakura times have received considerable attention from scholars, for they constitute the "majority" of Kamakura thinkers, in contrast to which Morrell refers to those neglected figures who belonged to the Heian socio-political establishments and the Nara-Heian Buddhist establishment as the "minority" in the early Kamakura period.

The Buddhist crisis theory of the *mappō* prophecy swelled the rising tide of the new schools with its teaching that late Heian signaled the encroachment of the *mappō* period during which it was expected that the world would face wars, epidemics, and famines; that monks, using their robes as a disguise, would be led into lustful deeds and lured by wealth into becoming social parasites; and that the Dharma would be misrepresented. *Mappō* is a term extensively treated in the popular writings of the early 11th century, such as the *Eiga monogatari*. The year 1052 marked the beginning of the *mappō* period and indeed the Hase temple in Heian was burned, the frustrated samurai rose to power, and monk-warriors, employed at various monasteries, took to widespread violence. Wars were waged within the sacred precincts of Heian, human and animal corpses lay side by side, infants longed for and clung to their slain or starved mothers, and bandits and thieves roamed about freely. Chaos ruled the city; greed, hatred, and delusion held sway within peoples' minds. The *mappō* prophecy had suddenly come true in all its stark reality. Men and women from all classes yearned for the gospel of salvation. Itinerant monks of humble station, chanting the scriptures as they traveled about, attracted these people more than did those clothed in royal robes, shut up within the walls of palatial temples, more than those who engaged themselves in the strict observation of the discipline of *vinaya* and the practice of meditation with a selfish view to their own personal enlightenment. Hōnen's Jōdo (Pure Land) faith was the focal point for all the other new schools of Kamakura Buddhism. He taught that in the *mappō* period the only way to salvation consisted in chanting the name of Amida Buddha and aspiring for birth in the Pure Land. The fact that he addressed himself to the poverty-stricken, and ignorant common people, was an epoch-making initiative, assuring him of a following not only among samurai, vicious bandits, and prostitutes, but eventually even among members of the royalty and aristocracy. He was concerned with the salvation of all, regardless of class, occupation, sex, or intelligence. Conscientious young monks, dismayed by the corruption of the established schools and inspired by the lofty idealism of Hōnen, knocked at the door of his cottage and begged for his instruction. Shinran was one of these monks.

The social chaos of late Heian produced an intense religious awakening of a kind not previously experienced by the Japanese. It forced them to find a new faith to cope with the situation that history had mercilessly imposed upon them. Traditional discipline and meditation, as well as the self-powered bodhisattva practices, all of which were the fundamental methods employed by the old schools to realize enlightenment, suddenly lost all relevance. Thus Hōnen claimed that this "holy path" (shōdōmon) produced no merit whatsoever in the mappō period. His emphasis on the contemplation of Amida's Pure Land and the chanting of nembutsu was derived primarily from the Triple Pure Land Sutra interpreted though Shan-tao's Kuan-ching su, a commentary on the Amitāyur-dhyāna-sūtra depicting the "wicked" nature of humankind and providing skill-in-means to save the "wicked." Faith in Amida required the recognition of potential for enlightenment on the part of the wicked, the complete renunciation of self, and faith in the saving power of Amida through the practice of nembutsu. Jōdo faith is based on the complete endorsement of the mappō crisis teaching.

Morrell paints in the background for these developments by presenting portraits of the establishment figures who were upset by the innovations of these new schools and dedicated to the traditional practices. He again shows that the doctrinal issues were embedded in complex historical situations, thus correcting the black-on-white contrast of the Pure Land schools as entirely good and authentic, and the establishment representatives as entirely corrupt and sycophantic.

His book is divided into five chapters and an appendix. The first chapter is an interpretative account of the history of Japanese Buddhism up to the Kamakura period. It is seasoned with a refreshing originality of thought. This chapter establishes the historical framework and interpretation from which he then in the following four chapters examines the Tendai poet, Jien; the Kegon reformer, Myōe, who was a vocal opponent of Hōnen's nembutsu practice; the Hossō monk, Jōkei, who challenged the "other-power" doctrine of Jōdo and attempted to revive the traditional vinaya discipline; and the reviver of Shingon, Kakukai, who interpreted Pure Land from within his Shingon perspective. From a doctrinal perspective the treatment of Jien, Myōe, Jōkei, and Kakukai is most interesting in that all of them, educated monks of unimpeachable character, challenged Hōnen's Pure Land thought: Myōe and Jōkei by claiming that nembutsu practice ignores traditional

vinaya and meditation practice, and Kakukai by interpreting Pure Land not as a
place to be born in after death, but as the "eternal present." Morrell does not take
sides on these issues, but simply presents the case of the established minority,
heavily documenting the argument with textual testimonies that he has skillfully
and laboriously translated.

Though his work is basically textual and historical rather than doctrinal, Morrell
has broken new ground in the study of Japanese Buddhism. He has combined the
discipline of literature and Buddhist studies. He has filled in lacunae left by
traditional Buddhologists. He has zeroed in on minority Buddhist monks and minor
Buddhist texts of the early Kamakura, thus showing that the new schools did not
emerge abruptly and in a vacuum, but gradually and in tandem with a growing
concern for the common people, a concern amply reflected in Buddhist vernacular
literature. The seeds of the new period reported in this "Minority Report" are often
found in poetic language, not doctrinal disquisitions, but the testimony of these
figures cannot be overlooked in reconstructing the history of early Kamakura
Buddhism. They represented an important propelling force in evolving the new
religious awakening by their criticism of Hōnen's thought and practice.

Fall, 1984   Minoru Kiyota
                        University of Wisconsin-Madison

P R E F A C E

I n the latter half of the Kamakura period, after the currents of popular Buddhism had branched off from the main streams of Nara and Heian but had not yet reached flood stage, an obscure monk compiled a collection of anecdotes in order (he said) to illustrate his religious and moral concerns. Mujū Ichien (1226–1312) had an eclectic bent and, although he is included in the sectarian lineage of Rinzai Zen since he became a disciple of Enni Ben'en (1202–1280) late in life, his work provides a useful survey of the varieties of Buddhism as they were perceived in the popular imagination at the time.

During many years of studying Mujū's major literary work, *Sand and Pebbles* (*Shasekishū*, 1279–1283), I have been struck by the differences between Mujū's view of the religious changes that took place during the preceding century, and our own view of them, which of course is shaped by awareness of their subsequent fortunes. Even to one with Mujū's broad interest in the varieties of religious practice, the major religious figures of the time appear to be Myōe, Jōkei, Jien and Kakukai—rather than Dōgen, Shinran and Nichiren, by whom we now tend to define the age. This can remind us that there are at least two sides to every issue, and that those figures in Buddhist history who represented the increasingly discredited Establishment are rarely given fair hearing. They are always on hand (and usually tucked away in footnotes) as stock characters representing the venality and corruption of the aristocratic clergy, fated to be eclipsed by the new truth-seekers bringing a message of hope to the suffering masses.

This imbalance, I felt, might usefully be addressed by a book of sketches which could soften the received caricatures of a few of these traditional figures. An exhaustive "Minority Report" would be even better. But it would run into many volumes and engage the efforts of many specialists. For the present I must settle for a few sketches which here and there may cast a somewhat different light on a familiar issue.

The following chapters were originally conceived as discrete articles, and some have already been published in journals. I have attempted to build every discussion around one or more primary texts of varying lengths, without drawing a distinction between doctrinal and literary works. The notes will guide the reader to sources of additional information. In the index I have included *kanji* for romanized words in the body of the work, especially for those whose original may not be readily guessed. A Table of Translations permits easy access to primary sources scattered throughout the book.

I have tried to provide meaningful English titles for all of the writings mentioned in the translations and in my commentary. As I argued in my *Sand and Pebbles*, since the title of a book would have had a *meaning* for our Kamakura monks instead of being merely an opaque sound, it is only proper that the title should *mean* something in English translation. The names of temples are a different matter. Probably few in the Kamakura period consciously were aware of "Eastern Great Temple" when they used the word "Tōdaiji." (And yet, Mujū writes a *waka* about the Rengeji which turns on the meaning of "lotus flowers.")When we come to the names of cities and towns, it is even less likely that many in historic times thought of "Sickle Warehouse" when they used the word "Kamakura", any more than Pennsylvanians today think of "William Pitt's Town" when they refer to Pittsburgh.

In general I have tried to stay as close as possible to the literal meaning of the original even if this results in a certain clumsiness. The gap between a literal and a literary translation may be as great as the historical and ideational differences between medieval Japan and the modern West. The problem is especially complicated when a system of expression has hardened over the centuries into a technical jargon, as I note again in introducing *Kakukai's Discourse* in Chapter Five. Shall the translator paraphrase, footnote, or simply ignore the problems? Whatever course he chooses, he cannot possibly please everyone. The best I can hope for is that the translations are reasonably accurate.

Since chapters Three to Five and the Appendix were originally published as articles, the book necessarily lacks the integration of a work written as a single piece from beginning to end. But for some readers interested in one or another of my four monks, this may even be an advantage. Zeami's *Kasuga ryūjin* in the Appendix was actually the first in order of appearance.

Working on it, I was reminded how little information about Myōe is available in English; this led me to write what is now Chapter Three, including translations of the *Final Injunctions* (Ikun) and other fragments from the Kamakura period. From Myōe it was but a step to his friend Jōkei, now represented in chapter Four. And then the idea occurred to me that with chapters on a contemporary Tendai and Shingon thinker and a historical introduction, I would have a group of interrelated sketches that might be of interest to students of early Kamakura Buddhism and literature.

Although only one or two names are printed on the title page, a book could never appear without the combined efforts of many others. To all of those who have had a hand in the *Minority Report* I owe a debt of gratitude. James W. Heisig, Jan Van Bragt, and Michael Kelsey of the Nanzan Institute for Religion and Culture have been an invaluable help to me from the first articles in the *Japanese Journal of Religious Studies* to the final manuscript. The Asian Humanities Press then magically transformed the manuscript into a book, and for this I must thank Mukesh K. Jain and Lew Lancaster.

Minoru Kiyota of the University of Wisconsin not only provided me with an excellent Forward but had many helpful suggestions for the chapter on Kakukai. And in the preparation of *Kasuga ryūjin, Monumenta Nipponica's* Michael Cooper was, as ever, a most thoughtful and tireless editor.

Photographs of Myōe's *Calculations on the Distance to India* and of the painting by Jōnin were provided by Benridō Publishers in Kyoto, with the permission of Rev. Hagami Shōchō of the Kōzanji. Yoshikawa Kōbunkan made available the copy and permission to reprint Sumiyoshi Hirozumi's sketch of Jien (Ōteru Seiichi collection) which appears in Taga Munehaya's *Jien* (Jimbutsu Sōsho series 15). We reproduce with the permission of Rev. Sawaki Jōmyō of the Kaijusenji the photograph of the Jōkei sculpture in that temple's collection. And Rev. Washimine Honken of Mt. Kōya's Zōfukuin gave us permission to make and reproduce the photograph of the Kakukai portrait.

The fine collections of the East Asian and Olin Libraries at Washington University in St. Louis have been a priceless resource. And the Graduate School of Arts and Sciences has supported my project with a Faculty Research Grant.

To all of these I express my heartfelt thanks, without implicating them, of course, in my own blunders.

But I owe a special word of appreciation to my wife Sachiko, who has literally and figuratively crossed seas and climbed mountains on our journey to meet Jien, Myōe, Jōkei, and Kakukai.

LIST OF ILLUSTRATIONS

Figure 1. Jien (1155–1225). Sketch attributed to Sumiyoshi Hirozumi (1631–1705).

Figure 2. Myōe (1173–1232). Painting by Jōnin (fl. early 13th c.). (See p. 48 for related text.)

Figure 3. Myōe's *Calculations on the Distance to India* (Tenjiku riteisho, ca. 1205; holograph). Translation on pp. 105-106.

Figure 4. Jōkei (1155–1213). Anonymous sculpture in Kaijusenji collection.

Figure 5. Kakukai (1142–1223). Detail of Edo period scroll in the Zōfukuin collection, Mt. Kōya.

CHAPTER ONE

Antecedents

he Decline of the Law. Every social institution has its cycles of vigor and decline, and the vision of a founder or reformer often pales in the following generation—as the prophets of our modern economic religions have discovered to their dismay. The very success of Soga Buddhism under the guidance of Prince Shōtoku (573–621) and his successors inevitably created the conditions for its own decay, breeding a numerous, undisciplined clergy, often attracted as much to the material as to the spiritual benefits of Buddhism. Although Ganjin's establishment of proper ordination platforms and a formal code of priestly behavior in the mid-eighth century served to curb abuses, in time the altruism of such figures as Gyōgi and En no Gyōja increasingly gave way to the venality of persons like Dōkyō and Gembō. Eventually, the clerical meddling in political affairs became one of the principal reasons for moving the capital from Nara, via Nagaoka, to Heian-kyō in 794.

'Once again a new age began in a spirit of fervor and integrity as Saichō (Dengyō Daishi, 767–822) on Tendai's Mount Hiei and Kūkai (Kōbō Daishi, 774–835) on Shingon's Mount Kōya laid the foundations of a renewed Buddhism which would dominate Japanese religious sensibility for the following four centuries. But as the discipline again became lax and a worldly clergy interfered in the affairs of state, the scene was set for yet another cycle of reform. When the Tendai abbot Ryōgen (912–985) used monk-soldiers (*sōhei*) to settle a dispute with the Gion Shrine in 970, he set a disasterous precedent for his own and other large religious institutions. Honest monks continued to appear, as they have in every generation, but they found it increasingly difficult to find fulfillment within the traditional religious structures. Even before Yoritomo set up the military government at Kamakura in 1192, new movements began to spring up as the old social order disintegrated. (Decline followed this reform also, inviting yet another reform four centuries later at the beginning of the Tokugawa period; but this time Buddhism itself was eclipsed by a state-sponsored Neo-Confucianism and, somewhat later, by a renascent Shintō.)

It is convenient, but sometimes misleading, for students of religion, art, or literature to adopt the periodizations of the political historian for their fields. Certainly political events influence changes in these other human activities; but the break with the past is never as abrupt as a new set of names and dates may suggest. In speaking of the innovations of Kamakura Buddhism, we need not overstate the case, leaving the impression that Eisai, Dōgen, Hōnen, Shinran, and Nichiren instantly swept away not only Tendai and Shingon, but the vestiges of the old Six Nara sects as well. Nor need all of the changes, justified today as the "popularization" of Buddhism, necessarily be seen as improvements. It is only from our vantage point in light of the subsequent success of certain select movements and with our own current biases, that we are able to reconstruct this fluid time with such empathetic clarity. But if we painstakingly try to place ourselves in that time and place as it was experienced by the participants, the hard black lines become shadows, and the caricatures dissolve into something more amorphous, more complex. We know, for example, that Tendai continued to be a major force in Japanese Buddhism well into the sixteenth century, until the great Hiei complex was razed to the ground by Nobunaga in 1571 and Tokugawa Neo-Confucianism was officially sponsored a few decades later. And we find that the Amidism of Ippen, not the sole-practice (*senju*) *nembutsu* movements of Hōnen and Shinran, was the leading Pure Land sect from the mid-fourteenth century through the early sixteenth. Indeed, it can be argued that we should speak of a Muromachi, rather than a Kamakura, Buddhist revival inasmuch as the major movements as we know them today were consolidated only at that time.[1]

The cycle of renovation and decline is a familiar feature of every social institution; but the decline of Heian Buddhism was interpreted by most of those who witnessed it not simply as part of the normal ebb and flow of events, but as an expression of an overarching pattern in history—the Three Periods of the Law (*sanji*, or *shōzōmatsu*). Antecedents of this notion can be traced in Indian Buddhism, but it first became conspicuous in China and had an even greater impact in Japan.[2]

Although there were differences of opinion, in China the Period of the True Law (*shōbō*) was generally understood to have been the interval of 500 years after the death of the historical Buddha, Śākyamuni, during which his followers had the capacity both to understand and to practice the Dharma.[3] According to the calculations of the time, the Buddha left this life in the year 949 B.C. of the Western calendar, so this first period would have continued through 449 B.C. The thousand-year Period of the Imitation Law (*zōbō*), during which there would be understanding of the teaching but deteriorating practice, would then continue through 551 A.D.[4] The year 552 [5] would then be the first of 10,000 years constituting the

Period of the Decline of the Law (*mappō*), during which both understanding and practice would disappear.

The chief proponent of this view in China was Hsin-hsing (Shingyō, 540–594), to whom Jōkei alludes in Article 4 of the *Kōfukuji Petition* (see Chapter Four). His Sect of the Three Stages (Sangaikyō) was short-lived, but provides an instructive parallel to later Japanese developments, on which, however, it had no direct influence; for the sect was not exported to Japan. Hsin-hsing taught that behavior must be appropriate to the times, and for him this meant that the rules of monastic discipline must be strictly observed to the extent of one's capacities. (Six centuries later Jōkei, Myōe, and the exponents of Kamakura Zen would agree with this proposition; but the sole-practice Amidists would assert that nothing was to be achieved by "self-power" during the Latter Days, and Nichiren would also attack the Hinayanist *vinaya* of the Disciplinary (Ritsu) sect—and, by implication, others who supported it such as Jōkei and Myōe—on the ground that it was inappropriate to the age.[6])

The Sect of the Three Stages had a difficult relationship with the other Buddhist schools, and with the secular authorities, because of its claim that it alone maintained the one practice suitable to the period of the Decline of the Law. The sect was harrassed and did not survive the great persecution of 845 (Ch'en 1964, p. 300). In Japan the theory of decline fostered similar attitudes of exclusiveness among the sole-practice Amidists and the followers of Nichiren; Dōgen, who rejected the theory, also advocated exclusive practice, but this was because he had no use for the doctrine of accommodation (*hōben*; Nakamura 1964, pp. 562–573). Although Kūkai's (and thus Kakukai's) Shingon did not subscribe to the theory of decline, it was supported by Tendai, whose second Chinese patriarch, Hui-ssu (Eshi, 515–577) was among the first to clearly define the issue. Moreover, the major scriptural authority on Latter Day thought recognized by the Kamakura clergy was the *Record of the Lamp During the Latter Days* (Mappō tōmyōki; tr. Rhodes 1980), a Heian forgery attributed to the founder of Japanese Tendai, Saichō. And Latter Day thought is conspicuous in the famous *Miscellany of Ignorant Views* (Gukanshō) 1219; tr. Brown and Ishida 1979) by Tendai's Jien.

The major difference between the Japanese view and most of its Chinese antecedents was that it allowed a millennium for each of the first two periods, thus placing the beginning of the Decline of the Law in 1052, a year marked by pestilence, the burning of the Hasedera, and other calamities. More important, perhaps, was the sense that the great flowering of Heian culture was a thing of the past. "Jewel-strewn Miyako" had prospered beyond all reasonable expectation and was arguably the finest city in all the world, at least in terms of its recent literary achievements. During the political supremacy of Michinaga (966–1024) and the Fujiwara clan, the talented women writers of the age—Lady Murasaki, Sei Shōnagon, Izumi Shikibu—had made history. Now, just a few decades later, the world-weary Daughter of Sugawara Takasue was about to compose the last of the great court diaries, the *Sarashina nikki* (ca. 1059). Vivacity had given way to nostalgia. In 1052 Michinaga's son Yorimichi (992–1074) converted his villa at Uji into a Buddhist temple, the Byōdōin, enshrining a magnificent statue of Amida.

The Precepts. The Complete Regulations (*gusokukai*) introduced by Ganjin (Chien-chen, 687–763), founder of the Japanese Disciplinary (Ritsu) sect, were basically basically the 250 rules for monks and the 348 rules for nuns laid down in the *Four-part Vinaya* (Shibunritsu, T. 1428).[7] These were also central for the Chinese Disciplinary school founded by Tao-hsüan (Dōsen, 596–667),[8] and are thought to have been the regulations of the Hīnayānist Dharmagupta[9] school. To administer these precepts in Japan, Ganjin established three ordination platforms, first at Nara's Tōdaiji in 754 and then in the east at the Yakushiji in Shimotsuke province[10] and in the west at the Kanzeonji in Tsukushi (Kyushu).

Nara's control of the ordination procedures was soon challenged by Tendai's Saichō, who asked the court for permission to establish an ordination platform on Mount Hiei to administer the (Mahāyānist) Bodhisattva Precepts (*bosatsukai*), the ten major and forty-eight minor precepts of the *Net of Brahma Sutra* (Bommōkyō, T. 1484).[11] He was strongly opposed by Hossō's Tokuichi (d. 835) and others of the Nara clergy, and permission was granted by the court only after his death in 822. Both sets of regulations continued to attract vigorous support and opposition in late Heian and early Kamakura. The Nara clergy, especially the Hossō sect, supported Ganjin's formulation; but, as already noted, the Hīnayāna precepts were attacked by Nichiren, who saw himself as restoring Saichō's Tendai. Eizon (Shiembō, 1201–1290), restoring founder of the Saidaiji and organizer of the Esoteric Disciplinary sect (Shingon Risshū) administered both the Complete Regulations and the Bodhisattva Precepts (Inoue 1971). It is worth noting that although laxity of behavior within the established sects is often cited as a major reason for the Kamakura-Muromachi reforms, efforts to restore the proper observance of the precepts came first and foremost from *within* these organizations. But these efforts were often denigrated and undermined by the prophets of the new order as inappropriate to the Period of the Decline of the Law.

The beginnings of interest in clerical reform in the late Heian period can be traced to the Hossō monk Jitsuban (d. 1144) of Nakanokawa,[12] who resolved to restore the practice of the precepts after a visit to Ganjin's Tōshōdaiji, which by this time had ceased to function as the nation's model *vinaya* center and was near collapse. Jitsuban was associated with the Kōfukuji, and his major contribution to the cause may have been to inspire Jōkei, who studied there a generation or so later, and who, in addition to being a scholar of Hossō theory, became a leader in the *vinaya* restoration movement. Jōkei opposed the new sole-practice Amidist groups, partly because they denied the need for practice, for good works, during the period of the Decline of the Law (see Chapter Four: *Kōfukuji Petition*, Article 9). Jōkei and his Hossō colleagues are counted among the members of the Disciplinary sect.

CHART 1.

Lineage of the Disciplinary Sect [13]

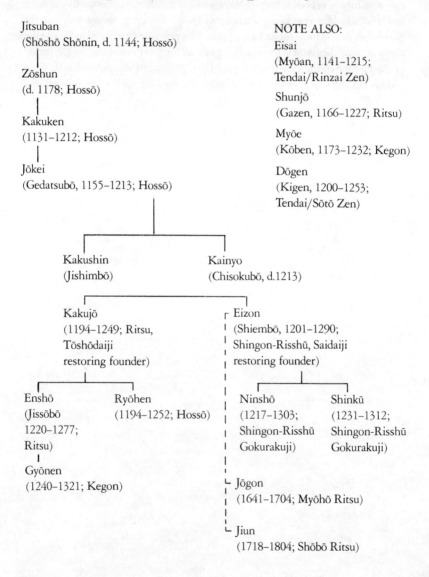

Jitsuban
(Shōshō Shōnin, d. 1144; Hossō)

Zōshun
(d. 1178; Hossō)

Kakuken
(1131–1212; Hossō)

Jōkei
(Gedatsubō, 1155–1213; Hossō)

NOTE ALSO:
Eisai
(Myōan, 1141–1215;
Tendai/Rinzai Zen)

Shunjō
(Gazen, 1166–1227; Ritsu)

Myōe
(Kōben, 1173–1232; Kegon)

Dōgen
(Kigen, 1200–1253;
Tendai/Sōtō Zen)

Kakushin
(Jishimbō)

Kainyo
(Chisokubō, d.1213)

Kakujō
(1194–1249; Ritsu,
Tōshōdaiji
restoring founder)

Eizon
(Shiembō, 1201–1290;
Shingon-Risshū, Saidaiji
restoring founder)

Enshō
(Jissōbō
1220–1277;
Ritsu)

Gyōnen
(1240–1321; Kegon)

Ryōhen
(1194–1252; Hossō)

Ninshō
(1217–1303;
Shingon-Risshū
Gokurakuji)

Shinkū
(1231–1312;
Shingon-Risshū
Gokurakuji)

Jōgon
(1641–1704; Myōhō Ritsu)

Jiun
(1718–1804; Shōbō Ritsu)

After he lived and studied at the Kōfukuji for almost three decades, Jōkei became a recluse (*tonsei*) at the Kasagidera in 1193. But this mountain retreat was too close to the Kōfukuji for him to stay aloof from the religious controversies of his age. Although he had not been abbot of the Hossō headquarters, Jōkei was called upon to draft the *Kōfukuji Petition* (1205) because of his fame as a scholar. In 1208 he retired to the Kaijusenji, a short distance from the Kasagidera; and it was around this time that he composed the following statement urging the restoration of the practice of Ganjin's regulations.

The Venerable Gedatsu's Written Vow for the Restoration of the Precepts
(Gedatsu Shōnin kairitsu saikō gammon) [14]

After the death of the Tathāgata, preceptors *(shi)* were designated to administer the regulations; and who, among the seven groups of disciples, [15] did not look to them for guidance? The *Vinaya in Ten Sections* [16] states: "When various bhiksus abandoned the practice of the precepts, reciting only the sutras and commentaries, [17] the World Honored One vigorously reproved them. The Law of the Buddha remains in this world only to the extent that the precepts are observed." The number of statements to this effect in the scriptures are beyond knowing. However, it is an inevitable fact of life that in time the observance of the regulations will gradually decline. Like the rest, we are spiritually dull: we neither study the precepts nor do we observe them.

After the Eight Sects [18] were defined in our country, among those who differ on the interpretation of the Three Learnings [19] are two sects [Hossō and Kusha]which our [Kōfukuji] temple has transmitted since antiquity. The congregations living in the eastern and western Golden Halls of this temple observe these precepts. With Priest Ganjin as its founder [in Japan], and with the *vinaya* of the Dharmagupta school as its basic teaching, its followers, after receiving the garment of precepts, have specifically been known as the Disciplinary Sect (Risshū). There are gradations among its ten major and lesser mentors [who preside at the ordination of the postulant] [20], and the highest rank that can be achieved is that of Preceptor (Kai wajō). However, the Law of the Buddha in these Latter Days is not free from considerations of fame and profit (*myōri*). It takes courage to make the old precepts the basis of religious practice. In olden times the conferring of the precepts at various temples was to realize the elimination of illusion (*shijū no en*). To perform well at our Great Vimalakirti Assembly [21] was to achieve a level of liberation (*shusshin no kai*). [22]

Now that neither of these is to be attained, what is to be done? Just as the leaders of our two mountains (i.e. the eastern and western halls of the Kōfukuji) honor these attainments, so also, indeed, do the [Tendai] followers of the One Vehicle,[23] for they are medicine for all the world. As a spiritual refuge (*kie*)for society, they are not without benefit.

To pursue the single path of the rules and regulations (*kairitsu no ichidō*)[24] is a great rarity today compared with what was done in antiquity. It is no use to lament the fact, since decline is a function of the times; or is it perhaps that the practice of the rules and regulations no longer conforms to the spirit of the country? So it seems to me, but I cannot speak for others.

The initiation into the precepts in every one of the Seven Great Temples[25] of the Southern Capital [Nara], especially by the ten mentors of the two halls [of the Kōfukuji], is carried out in compliance with imperial order, and the procedures are strictly observed. They are administered properly by three mentors and seven witnesses. The bhikkus may be unworthy and the procedures not strictly according to the Teaching, but if only one or two among the recipients comprehend the Dharma, this would be a considerable blessing, and how could it be futile to support them? Should there be none to succeed them, what will we do about the future? This concerns not only the decline of a single sect, but will be the sorrow of the entire order consisting of the four groups of monastic disciples.[26] Even if the encouragement to maintain the precepts is only for a short time, my colleagues of the old schools of learning in the two halls should put an end to their wearisome enmities and solicit support to perpetuate it.

To be the constant support of those who pursue this new learning, encouraging them to speak of it and to know of it by instruction—be it only a single line from the code of precepts (*kaihon, prātimokṣa*) or one item of doctrine—this is vitally essential for the times and will be a great benefit to the world. Once we hear these things, however faintly,what difficulty will there be to again revive the precepts and hand them down indefinitely, with no lack of scholars or books at both the main [Kōfukuji] and at affiliated mountain temples?[27]

I only hope that the bodhisattvas and sages who have always dwelt in this World-to-be-Endured (*shaba; sahā*)and the various devas and good deities will look kindly on this foolish vow of mine and protect the destiny of the Buddha's Law.

This is the written vow recorded by the late venerable teacher [Jōkei], author of the prayer *(ganshu)*. It was offered up on the occasion of the Kōfukuji's sponsoring a conference recently during the Shōgen era [1207–1210] in order to express his esteem for the Disciplinary sect so that a practice hall might be constructed and its writings might be copied.

Written by Kainyo[28]

It may have been around this time that Jōkei assembled six monks for an experiment to determine the feasibility of a return to the early regulations. Mujū Ichien (1226–1312) has this to say in his *Sand and Pebbles* seven decades later:

> . . . the late venerable Gedatsu of Kasagi selected six men of quality to maintain the fast and study the regulations. Perhaps because the times were not right, none of them followed the strict procedures. However, there was one who studied the precepts and observed the fast during the summer retreat.[29] He gave up the observances after the retreat was over; but recently there have been many among the scholars who have raised the desire for enlightenment and who observe the precepts.
>
> Among these six men was one who broke the fast and maintained many young temple-pages *(chigo)* in the monks' quarters. For food he would send them out to the Saogawa River to catch fish. While one was cooking a live fish, it jumped out of the pot. Whereupon the monk's favorite page washed it off and returned it. The monk applauded him saying that it was well for young boys not to be too fastidious about such small matters. Another monk asked how the monastic rules classified such an act and was told that it was a lesser offense *(ha'itsudai)*[30] in the Hīnayānist regulations and a major offense *(harai)*[31] according to the Bodhisattva precepts.
>
> The divorce between theory and practice has long been common throughout the country. The decline of Buddhism will come from within, from those who use it for fame and profit but do not practice it.[32]

Needless to say, such efforts at reform were doomed to failure from the start as long as people were utterly demoralized by the sense that they were living in the period of the Decline of the Law: if nothing *could* be done, then surely nothing *would* be done. We see the same malaise in others besides Jōkei who hoped to ameliorate, for a time at least, the inevitable downward course of events. The lament (SZS XIX:1222; see Chapter Two) of Tendai's Jien while he was in retreat at the Mudōji in 1178 is in the same spirit as the waka attributed to Jōkei in Tachibana Narisue's *Stories Old and New* (1254):

Gedatsubō's Refusal to Discuss Points of Doctrine in the Sacred Writings [33]

Once after Gedatsubō had become a recluse, he happened to be at the residence of the Tsubosaka Bishop [Kakuken, 1131–1212] to take a medicinal bath. As he was waiting inconspicuously for his turn, a certain individual who was in the same room brought up some points of doctrine in the sacred writings. Gedatsubō remarked that those matters were concealed from them, and he was asked what he meant by this. In answer, Gedatsubō replied with this verse:

Inishie wa	In ancient times
Fumimishikadomo [34]	They saw where they were walking,
Shirayuki no	But now along the path
Fukaki michi ni wa	Covered deep in white snow
Ato mo oboezu	We find not even tracks. [35]

Jōkei's friend Myōe (Kōben, 1173–1232) expresses the same concern for the restoration of the precepts, and the same pessimism about its possibility, in his *Final Injunctions* (Ikun, 1235; see Chapter Three for translation). Yet Myōe, the leading critic of the single-practice Amidist movement, has only praise for Eisai (1141–1215; Tendai/Rinzai Zen), not for his innovative technique of meditation, but for establishing centers where a strict monastic discipline was observed (*Ikun*, item 41).

Probably the most successful of those who defended the precepts was Eizon (Shiembō, 1201–1290; see chart 1), founder of the Esoteric Disciplinary sect. He not only restored Nara's Saidaiji, but spread his message throughout the country (Inoue 1971, pp. 77–103). The account of a brief stopover in 1262 at Nagoya's Chōboji, where he lectured on the discipline and initiated some thirty monks and 200 laymen into the Bodhisattva precepts, is described in his *Back and Forth to the Kantō Region*. [36] Eizon's disciple, Ninshō (Ryōkan, 1217–1303), became head of Kamakura's Gokurakuji in 1261 and was a leading prelate at the seat of the new military government. He is also remembered as the object of Nichiren's attack after praying unsuccessfully for rain a decade later (Petzold 1978, pp. 107–109). The relative success of the Esoteric Disciplinary movement may partly have been the result of its affiliation with Shingon, which, as we have noted, was not dominated by Latter Day thought and its inhibitions.

Finally, we must take note of the Tōdaiji scholar Gyōnen (Jikambō, 1240–1321), in the lineage of the Tōdaiji tradition of the Kegon sect [37] through his teacher Sōshō (1202–1292), and in the Kairitsu (or Shibunritsu) tradition through Enshō (Jissōbō, 1220–1277; see Chart 1). Gyōnen's most famous writing is the *Essentials of the Eight Sects* (Hasshū kōyō, 1268), a compendium of sectarian principles still useful to scholars today. Other works include the *Tōdaiji Enshō Shōnin gyōjō* (acts of the Venerable Enshō of the Tōdaiji), a biography of his teacher which is also the source of some of the few details we have concerning Jitsuban (Inoue 1971, pp. 77–78); and the *Mirror of Essentials of the Garland World of the Dharmas* (Kegon hokkai gikyō, 1295; Kamata and Tanaka 1971, pp. 227–301). Among the earliest surviving manuscripts of Japanese Buddhist liturgical music (*shōmyō*) is a holograph by Gyōnen called "The Song of Upāli" (Ubaribai). The barber Upāli, one of Śākyamuni's ten major disciples, was called upon to recite the rules of the Buddhist Order at the First Council in Rājagrha several months after his teacher's death. This became the *Vinayapiṭaka* (Ritsuzō) among the "Three Baskets" (Tripiṭaka) of early Buddhism. The text of the song in the Tōdaiji manuscript expresses Gyōnen's zeal for the restoration of monastic discipline:

> We prostrate ourselves before the Buddhas
> And Dharma and the communities of monks.
> Now I expound the rule of the *vinaya*
> That the right law may remain forever. . . [38]

Non-exclusive Amidism. The enormous success of the popular Kamakura-Muromachi movements which advocated the Sole Practice of Calling the Name of Amida Buddha (*senju nembutsu*) may lead us to view Amidism in China, as well as that which flourished in Japanese Tendai and Shingon, as antecedents which only dimly comprehended the teaching realized in its fullness by Hōnen, Shinran and Rennyo. But to Jien, Myōe, Jōkei, and Kakukai, the new movements were a perverse repudiation of an old, well-established tradition of worship of the Buddha Amida which had developed within the accommodating framework of the Mahāyāna. They were a step backwards, not forward.

Some see the beginning of the Chinese Pure Land sect (Ch'ing-tu Tsung, Jōdoshū) at A.D. 402, when Hui-yüan (Eon, 334–416) and a group of 123 followers vowed to be born in Amitābha's Western Paradise. Although many details of this event are open to question, Hui-yüan is "sometimes regarded as the first patriarch of the Pure Land sect" (Ch'en 1964, p. 108). He stressed the visual representation of

Amitābha through concrete objects of worship, and fostered the practice of conjuring up the image of the Buddha as described in the *Visualization of Amida Sūtra* (Hanjusammaikyō, T. 418; the Pratyutpanna-samadhi-sūtra.[39] *Nen-butsu* for Hui-yüan meant "to think about," "to remember", "to meditate" on Amida—the *invocation* of the Name being merely a facet of this. Eight centuries later Jōkei would argue for this same interpretation in Article 7 of his *Kōfukuji Petition* (see Chapter Four).

Hui-yüan is not included among the patriarchs recognized by the Pure Land sects established by Hōnen and Shinran. Hōnen himself did not draw up a list, but he did refer to the Five [Chinese] patriarchs of the Pure Land tradition (*Jōdo gosozō*)[40]—T'an-luan, Tao-ch'o, Shan-tao, Huai-kan (Ekan, late 7th c.), and Shao-k'ang (Shōkō, d. 805). Other Jōdo sect systems include Aśvaghoṣa (Memyō, ca. 100–ca. 60 B.C.) and T'an-luan's teacher, Bodhiruci (Bodairushi, 6th c.) (Matsunaga 1976, II, p. 312, n. 17). Best known, however, is the list of Seven Eminent Monks (shichi kōsō)[41] extolled by Shinran in his *Hymn to the True Faith in the Nembutsu* (Shōshin[nembutsu]ge; Seiten 1978, pp. 135–156; DeBary, et al. 1969, pp. 335–339) and in his *Hymns on the Pure Land* (Jōdo wasan; Seiten 1978, pp. 158–200):

> Nāgārjuna (Ryūju, ca. 150–250)
> Vasubandhu (Seshin, Tenjin; 5th c.)
> T'an-luan (Donran, 476–542)
> Tao-ch'o (Dōshaku, 562–645)
> Shan-tao (Zendō, 613–681)
> Genshin (Eshin, 942–1017)
> Genkū (Hōnen, 1133–1212)

It is worth noting that Shan-tao, the last of the recognized Chinese patriarchs and the major influence on the Kamakura reformers, was separated from them in time by half a millennium. He was active in the period that the early "Nara sects" were introduced to Japan, and it is a remarkable accident of history that a Pure Land school was not among them. Faith in the Buddha Amida was known in Japan as early as the days of Prince Shōtoku (573-621), and the famous Taima Mandala (ca. 763) depicts Amida's Western Paradise according to Shan-tao's interpretation of the *Sutra of Meditation on Amida Buddha* (Kammuryōjukyō, T. 365; Okazaki 1977, pp. 42–60). But this early devotion to Amida was generally associated with rites for the dead,[42] and it well may have been that the Pure Land faith could not develop in Japan

. . . until such a time as it could become generally recognized as a means of individual salvation, rather than a method of putting the dead to rest. It also had to wait the proper historical moment when dissatisfaction with the existing world would demand a higher affirmation (Matsunaga 1974, I, p. 114).

Nevertheless, the Chinese patriarchs were already promoting Amidism as a means of individual salvation, and we may well assume that a Pure Land sect would have found a Japanese following at least as large as any of the Six Nara Sects had one of Shan-tao's disciples introduced it to Japan as an autonomous institution. A distinct Pure Land sect did flourish in China (Ch'en 1964, pp. 338–350, 402), but faith in Amida was also widely incorporated among the practices of most other sects, including T'ien-t'ai and Ch'an (Zen). Thus the Ch'an monk Yung-ming Yen-shou (Yōmyō Enju, 904–975), noted for his attempts to harmonize the dominant Ch'an and Pure Land schools, compiled the *Mirror of Sectarian Differences* (Tsung Ching Lu, Sugyōroku; T. 2016), a work later promoted in Japan by Rinzai's Enni Ben'en (Shōichi, 1202–1280) of the Tōfukuji. Chinese Amidism was non-exclusive, but when its characteristic doctrines were later interpreted in the light of the Latter Day (*mappō*) thought, the sole-practice view emerged.

A peculiarity of Kamakura's sole-practice (*senju*) movements was that they were not introduced from China in a direct teacher-disciple transmission. Hossō's Dōshō (628–700) sat at the feet of Hsüan-tsang (Genjō, 600–664), Saichō received the Tendai teaching from Tao-sui (Dōsui, 8–9 c.), Kūkai was initiated into the Shingon mysteries by Hui-kuo (Keika, 746–805), and centuries later Eisai and Dōgen were the immediate disciples, respectively, of Hsu-an Huai-ch'ang (Koan Eshō, 12th c.) and T'ien-t'ung Ju-ching (Tendō Nyojō, 1163–1228)—and so forth. But Hōnen and Shinran traced their spiritual lineage to Chinese and Indian Patriarchs who had lived centuries earlier; their immediate antecedents were the Amidists of Japanese Tendai, notably Genshin, in reaction to whom they defined their own position.

Amidism in Japanese Tendai. In 788 Saichō (Dengyō Daishi, 767–822) established the Enryakuji on Mt. Hiei with a statue of the Buddha Yakushi, carved by himself, as the central object of worship. (The verse credited to him on this occasion, SKKS XX:1921, was given an allusive variation by Jien in SZS XVII:1134; see Chapter Two.) After his trip to China, 804–805, Saichō promulgated an eclectic form of Tendai which, in addition to the Lotus teaching systematized by Chih-i (538–597), incorporated elements of esotericism (*mikkyō*), Zen, Ritsu, Amidism, and Shintō.

Tendai's Three Great Works (*sandaibu*) consist of Chih-i's commentaries on the Lotus Sutra—the *Profound Meaning of the Lotus*[43] and *Textual Commentary on the*

Lotus Sutra[44] as well as a manual for meditation called the *Great Cessation and Insight* (Moho chih-kuan, *Maka shikan*; T. 1911). The second of three methods of meditation formulated by Chih-i is the "perfect and sudden" (*endon shikan*); and this must be preceded by one of four preliminary methods of concentration (Hurvitz 1963, pp. 318-322), the second of these being the Constantly Walking Samadhi (*jōgyō zammai*). Chih-i explains that:

> . . . This method is described in the *Visualization of Amida Sutra*, where it is understood as Buddha-imaging (*Butsuryū*) . . . In deep concentration the appearances of the Buddhas in the ten directions are conjured up before one's very eyes as a person with clear vision might see the stars on a bright night, and so in like fashion does one see a great number of Buddhas in the ten directions. Accordingly, we give this the name, "Buddha-imaging" . . . [This method rectifies the three aspects of human behavior: body, voice, and thought.] During ninety days while the body walks constantly, the practitioner without letup recites the name of Amida Buddha while constantly meditating upon him in his heart. He may recite and meditate concurrently, meditate first and then recite, or recite first and then meditate—but it must be continuous. To invoke [A]mida alone is as meritorious as invoking the Buddhas in the ten directions; and to concentrate solely on [A]mida is the focus of this method. The important thing is that each step, each sound, and each thought are entirely Amida Buddha. (*Maka shikan* 1:2:1; Sekiguchi 1966, I, pp. 77–78)

After Saichō's disciple, Ennin (Jikaku Daishi, 794–864) returned in 847 from his study in China, he constructed on Mt. Hiei the Jōgyōzammaiin for the practice of this form of concentration which, we must remember, did not involve the desire for birth in the Western Paradise characteristic of the Kamakura Pure Land movements. The repetition of Amida's name is also called "*in-zei Nembutsu* after the repetition of Nembutsu in a singsong tone" (Hori 1968, p. 95). Ennin is credited with initiating Tendai's school of liturgical music (*shōmyō*; Harich-Schneider 1973, pp. 312–315), and it is perhaps no accident that those who later continued this liturgical tradition were frequently prominent in the Pure Land movement, with its practice of vocalizing the Holy Name: Genshin, Yōkan (1054–1132) and Ryōnin (1072–1133).

The popular evangelist Kūya (or Kōya) Shōnin (Kōshō, 903–972)[45] was the first to carry the part shamanist-part Tendai Pure Land practices to the masses, "beating his bowl" (*hachi-tataki*) throughout the land to express his joy at the promise of birth in Amida's paradise by virtue of the *nembutsu*. This scene is vividly represented in the fine Kamakura sculpture of Kūya[46] belonging to the Rokuharamitsuji (originally, Saikōji, the "Temple of the Western Light"), which he founded in 951. With bowl suspended before him, a small hammer in one hand and a staff in the other, he chants the *nembutsu*, represented by six small images of Amitābha issuing from his mouth.

The *shami* Kūya renounced his lineage and did not discuss his parents; some say he belonged to the imperial house. His voice constantly invoked the Buddha Amida, so that he was known to the world as Amida's Holy Man (*hijiri*). Others called him the Holy Man of the Marketplace (*ichi hijiri*) because he practiced Buddhism while living among the people in the city. If he chanced on an impassible road, he would clear the way; if there were no bridge, he would build one; and if he saw that a well was needed, he would dig one. And so he acquired the name, Amida's Well Man.

At Mineaidera[47] in the Iihono district of Harima province was a complete collection of the scriptures (*issaikyō*).Whenever Kuya encountered a difficult concept, a golden being (*kinjin*)would appear to him in a dream constantly to instruct him. Now between the provinces of Awa and Tosa is an island called Yūshima[48] with a figure of Kannon which, according to tradition, has great miraculous powers. Here the holy man (*shōnin*) burned incense on his arms[49] and remained for seventeen days and nights without moving or sleeping, while the sacred image radiated shafts of light (*kōmyō*) visible even when the eyes were closed. A certain metalsmith who was returning home with a quantity of gold in the front folds of his garment approached the holy man. "The sun has set, the road is long," he remarked, "and I am afraid." To which the holy man replied that he should meditate (*nen*) on the Buddha Amida. Along the road the artisan encountered a robber as he had feared, and in his heart he quietly fixed his thoughts on the Buddha as the holy man had instructed. The robber approached, and then withdrew with the remark:"It's the Holy Man of the Marketplace."

In the western part of Kyoto lived an old nun who was the former wife of the Vice-Governor (Suke) of the Yamato region, Tomo no Norimoto.[50] She had devoted her life to the *nembutsu* and took the holy man as her spiritual adviser. She had had one of the holy man's surplices mended, and when it was finished she called her maidservant. "My spiritual adviser is going to die today. Take this to him quickly," she ordered.

When the maidservant returned and told of the holy man's demise, the nun showed no surprise or emotion, to the bewilderment of those who saw her. On the day of the holy man's decease, he sat upright facing the western direction, wearing a white robe and offering incense. "Many Buddhas and Bodhisattvas have come to welcome and to lead me to paradise (*raigō injō*)," he remarked to his disciples. When he had stopped breathing, they again offered up incense. At this moment music was heard in the sky and an exquisite fragrance filled the room. Ah truly, the holy man at last exhausted the benefits of the sacred teaching and went forth to Supreme Bliss (*gokuraku*).

Prior to the Tengyō era [938–946][51] contemplation on the name of Amida (*nembutsu zammai*) was rarely performed in the regular practice halls and assemblies. How much more so was it neglected by ordinary petty men and foolish women! But after the holy man arrived, he himself intoned the name and caused others to do so as well, and the *nembutsu* became popular. This holy man truly had the power to convert ordinary people.[52]

This sketch of Kūya's activities appears in the *Accounts of Japanese Born into Paradise* (Nihon ōjō gokurakuki, ca. 983) by the Chinese classical scholar, Yoshishige Yasutane (ca. 931–1002). In 964 Yasutane had organized a Meeting to Encourage Learning (Kangaku-e) consisting of some twenty Tendai monks and scholars at the state university (Daigakuryō). Held for about twenty years during the 3rd and 9th months, the meetings included lectures on the *Lotus Sutra*, composition of poetry with lines from the sutra as topics, meditation (*nen*) on Amida, the invocation of his name, and elegant repasts (*seien*). Yasutane is remembered today for his *Record of the Pond Pavilion* (Chiteiki, 982), the model for Kamo no Chōmei's celebrated *Account of My Hut* (Hōjōki, 1212).[53] In 986 Yasutane took the tonsure and the religious name Jakushin, and went to live in the [Shu]ryōgon'in at Yokawa on Mt. Hiei, where his mentor Genshin is said to have composed the *Essentials of Salvation* (Ōjōyōshū, 985). The eccentric Yasutane[54] exemplifies the increasing lay participation in the Pure Land movement, a feature of Heian society reflected in the novels, poetry, diaries and histories[55] of the literary flowering during the eleventh century.

Yasutane's spiritual guide, Genshin (Eshin, 942–1017) was younger than the scholar and outlived him. He and Kakuun (953–1007) were both disciples of Ryōgen (Jie Daishi, 912–985), and both stand at the head of the two major traditions of philosophical Tendai (*kengyō*), as distinguished from its esoteric (*taimitsu*) component. Genshin's Eshin school stressed the "original enlightenment" (*hongaku*) inherent within all sentient beings; Kakuun's Danna school focused on the "practical enlightenment" (*shikaku*; i.e., "enlightenment having a beginning" in time) to be realized through religious exercises. Both views are complementary and differ not in substance but in emphasis: *hongaku* is to be realized by means of practice, and *shikaku* is possible only because we uncover what is already present. Each school later subdivided into four subgroups to make up eight schools of Tendai scholasticism. [56]

Both Genshin and Kakuun accommodated meditation on Amida to their systems of thought. But the *Essentials of Salvation* [57] made Genshin a celebrity and, as we have noted, one of two Japanese Pure Land patriarchs—the other being Hōnen—recognized by Shinran and his followers. Genshin argued that faith in Amida and in the *nembutsu* were sufficient for birth in the Pure Land, if not for complete enlightenment. His depictions of the pleasures of paradise, and especially of the torments of hell, had a profound influence on the art and thought of his age. He begins with the admonition to "Abhor and Depart from this Defiled World" (*onriedo*), a theme which will appear later in Jien's poetry. [58]

But Genshin did not deny the value of other practices or the need for good works. For *him*, at least, and for others of limited capacity in the Latter Days, faith in Amida seemed to be the best and perhaps only possible method. But he allowed that other means might be appropriate for other people, in accordance with the traditional Mahāyāna principle of accommodation (*hōben*). Like Shingon's Kakukai a few centuries later (see Chapter Five) he could allow for variability in the "creative mythological imagination."

It should be noted here that Amida is set forth [by Genshin] in a representative capacity as a convenient concrete example of what would be equally true of any other of the countless Buddhas that throng the universe. The important thing is to have one of them to fix one's mind upon, and Amida was regarded as the best of all for this purpose (Coates and Ishizuka 1925, p. 38).

Genshin not only provided a theoretical basis for popular Amidism but was perhaps the first to experiment with expressing his religious ideas in ordinary Japanese instead of in the more prestigious but less accessible Chinese. The shortest of three surviving vernacular tracts (*kana hōgo*) states his position simply and concisely, much in the manner of Hōnen's later *One-Page Testament* (Ichimai kishōmon).

The Yokawa Tract (Yokawa hōgo) [59]

For all sentient beings it is a great satisfaction to escape the Three Evil Paths and to be reborn as a human. However gross one's physical condition may be, can it ever be inferior to that of the animal? One's house may be poor, but one is better off than the hungry ghosts. One's heart's desire may not be realized, but this cannot be compared to the torments of hell. The difficulties of this world are mere trivial annoyances, and the sorry state of those not numbered among human kind leads us to seek the path to enlightenment. For these reasons we should delight in having been reborn as a human. Our faith may be shallow, but by virtue of the depth of the Original Vow, if we but rely on it, we shall assuredly be born in Amida's Pure Land (*ōjō*). Our recitation of the Buddha's name may be listless; yet if we but say it, great will be the merit acquired toward our being welcomed at the time of death (*raigō*). For these reasons we should delight at having encountered the Original Vow.

Delusive thinking (*mōnen*) has ever been a basic trait of the unenlightened person (*bombu*). He experiences no other state of mind. But when at the time of death he performs the *nembutsu*[60] fully aware that he is a deluded unenlightened creature, he will be vouchsafed a welcome by Amida and will sit upon a lotus pedestal. Then indeed will he abandon his delusive thinking, and the mind of enlightenment (*satori no kokoro*) will be manifest. The *nembutsu* which emerges from within delusive thinking is pure as the lotus untainted by mud; and there can be no doubt that the devotee will be born in the Pure Land.

Rather than abhor our delusive thinking, we should deplore the shallowness of our faith. Deepening our sense of purpose, we should constantly invoke the name (*myōgō*) [of Amida Buddha].

Ryōnin (Kōjōbō, 1072–1132) is the late Heian bridge, via Eikū (d. 1179), to Hōnen. In retrospect he is credited with having founded, in 1124, the Nembutsu branch of Tendai (Hori 1968, p. 122), which later flourished as the Yūzūnembutsu sect. His authority was a direct revelation from Amida in 1117. This is Narisue's account in *Stories New and Old* (Kokonchomonjū, 1254).[61]

The Venerable Ryōnin of Ōhara Promulgates the All-Permeating Nembutsu
From age twenty-three the Venerable Ryōnin of Ōhara completely abandoned worldly fame and profit and had a profound longing for the Land of Supreme Bliss (*gokuraku*). Without ceasing day or night, he singlemindedly uttered and meditated on (*shōnen*) the holy name and took no rest. At forty-six,[62] having persisted for twenty-four years, he dozed off one summer day—not as the result of flagging spirits but through the agency of the Buddha. Amida appeared in a dream and spoke to him, and this is what he recorded:

"Your religious practice is most extraordinary. In all the three thousand realms within this Jambudvipa (Ichiembudai) world there is no one like you; you are without peer. However, to attain birth in the Pure Land immediately after death is very difficult. This is because my land is a region of total purity, a land for those who cultivate the roots of merit (*zengon*) of the Mahāyāna. It is difficult for those with few karmic affinities to be born there; and even those who, like yourself, engage in religious exercises must pass through many lives before the karmic conditions are suitable for their birth in paradise. So perhaps I should teach you the rapid method to achieve this birth—the so-called Nembutsu of Perfect Harmonization (*ennyū nembutsu*). The actions of one are for the sake of all, and thus its benefits are widespread. The desire for such birth already produces the cause so that the effect is easy to attain;and already the effect of divine response is that this permeates (*yūzū*) the entire world. The permeation of the action of one person causes the birth in paradise of all."

Amida Nyorai's revelation to me was virtually like this. I had no time to record the details, and so this is only a rough sketch of what happened.[63]

> The ninth day of the sixth month,
> Tenji 1 (1124)
> Ryōnin, Child of the Buddha
> within the Single Vehicle

Afterwards, while promulgating his teaching, he recorded the names of 3,282 converts on his membership list.[64]

Early one morning a vigorous monk in a blue robe appeared saying that he wished to enter his name on the list, and after inspecting the record book, he withdrew. Ryōnin sensed something strange, as being neither dream nor reality. Upon examining the record, he found this statement left behind by the monk's brush: "I request that you recite the *nembutsu* a hundred times every day. I am Bishamonten of Kurama Temple, and I have come to protect those who would establish good karmic affinities (*kechien*) through the nembutsu." (The names of 512 people were entered on the list at this time.)

At the end of the Hour of the Tiger [3–5 a.m.] on the fourth day of the first month in Tensho 2 [1132] while Ryōnin was passing the night reciting the *nembutsu* at Kurama Temple, he was startled in a dream by the sight of his own form like an apparition in the sky, which spoke to him: "I [Bishamon] have assumed your form; and Brahma and the others who protect the True Law would add their names to your *nembutsu* list. I will protect you like a shadow following an object. All will benefit by entering into this karmic relationship, even including the gods."

When he awoke from his dream, Ryōnin found a document before him. Lord Brahma and the various groups of heavenly beings, the kings who reign beneath these heavens, the Nine Major Stars[65] in the firmament, the twenty-eight constellations,[66] and all the spirits, gods and buddhas within the entire universe down to the smallest particle of dust—all without exception entered their names for the hundred repetitions. It was an unheard of, uprecedented, occurrence.

Among the 3,282 who had earlier entered their names on the nembutsu list the dates and times were indicated when sixty-eight of these would be born in the Pure Land.

Then in the same month the holy man, in his sixty-first year, finally attained his cherished desire of birth in the Pure Land, having known the time of his death seven days in advance. At the moment of his death his body became light as a goose feather, and other marvels are reported.

The Preceptor Kakugon of Ōhara heard the holy man speak to him in a dream. "I have achieved my goal and abide in the highest form of the highest grade of birth in the Pure Land," [67] he said. "And this has been entirely by virtue of the All-permeating *nembutsu*."

Ryōnin was also noted for his contributions to Buddhist liturgical music. In 1095 he restored the Raigōin, which had been founded by Ennin, as the center for the Ōhara school of Tendai *shōmyō*. [68]

CHART 2.

Kamakura Innovators in the Tendai Lineage

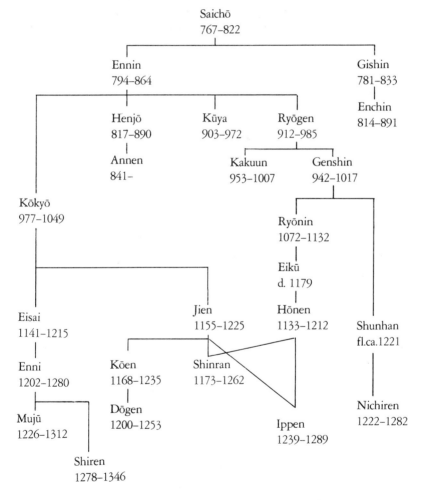

Saichō
767–822

Ennin
794–864

Gishin
781–833

Henjō
817–890

Kūya
903–972

Ryōgen
912–985

Enchin
814–891

Annen
841–

Kakuun
953–1007

Genshin
942–1017

Kōkyō
977–1049

Ryōnin
1072–1132

Eikū
d. 1179

Eisai
1141–1215

Jien
1155–1225

Hōnen
1133–1212

Shunhan
fl.ca.1221

Enni
1202–1280

Kōen
1168–1235

Shinran
1173–1262

Mujū
1226–1312

Dōgen
1200–1253

Ippen
1239–1289

Nichiren
1222–1282

Shiren
1278–1346

Adapted from Tada et al., *Tendai hongakuron*, pp. 594–595.

It does no disservice to the accomplishments of the Kamakura reformers to treat their opponents also as men of integrity with sincere religious convictions. As often as not, the strongest opposition came from those who were attempting to restore the proper observance of the precepts and from those who had reasonable reservations about the growing parochialism and decline in morality. The common caricature of an enervated, corrupt clergy pandering to a frivolous aristocracy and attacking the new movements merely because it feared a loss of power and prestige prevents us from coming to grips with the genuine religious issues of the time. We need to replace straw men with real people.

CHAPTER TWO

Tendai's Jien as Buddhist Poet

The most prominent representative of the Tendai world-view, which dominated Japanese religious thought during the period of transition between Heian and Kamakura, when the popular movements which would supersede it were just taking shape, was the prelate, poet, and historian, Jien (1155–1225). He was a man of many parts; and an exhaustive examination of his life and work would virtually constitute a history of this transitional period in the nation's thought and social institutions. Highly born into a branch of the Fujiwara family from which the leading officials of the land were appointed, Jien was destined to play an influential role in the clerical affairs of his age, after having made an early decision to take holy orders. Four times he was appointed Chief Abbot (*Zasu*) of the Enryakuji, headquarters of the Tendai sect, from whose tutelage emerged those who would radically restructure Japanese Buddhism: Hōnen (1133–1212), Shinran (1173–1262), Eisai (1141–1215), Enni (1202–1280), Dōgen (1200–1253) and Nichiren (1222–1282).

His political role as a defender of the Kujō family line complemented his clerical activities. Brother and close supporter of Fujiwara (Kujō) Kanezane (1149–1207), Jien made his most important contribution to this cause by composing an innovative history of Japan, the *Miscellany of Ignorant Views* (Gukanshō, 1219; tr., Brown and Ishida 1979), the first attempt to view Japanese history as the manifestation of certain preordained principles. Jien argued that Kujō Yoritsune (1218–1256), Kanezane's great-grandson, was destined by the gods to rule Japan in the emperor's name as *shōgun* in order to fend off for a time the inevitable disintegration of social institutions during the period of the Decline of the Law (*mappō*) (Brown and Ishida 1979, pp. 1, 443).

Jien was also a prolific and respected poet. His private compilation of verse, the *Collection of Gleaned Jewels* (Shūgyokushū)[69], includes some 6000 items, mostly *waka*; and even this mammoth work omits many of his contributions to the imperial anthologies and poetry contests. Emperor Go-Toba (1180–1239; r. 1183–1198), major patron of the poetic activities of his time, praised Jien as "inferior to no other accomplished poet in his finest poems" (Brower 1972, p. 36).

Jien's prominence in poetic, political, and religious circles allows his poetry to be viewed from each of these perspectives: as pure literature (Brower 1972, pp. 36–37, 56–62); as allegory, often with a social reference (Kubota 1979, pp. 1–78), and as the expression of religious conviction.

Here I shall focus on Jien as *Buddhist* poet with a view to defining the Buddhist elements in the common literary discourse of the age, elements which modern scholars tend to ignore in favor of nature imagery and secular concerns. We can safely assume that the doctrinal complexities venerated in the scholarly treatises and commentaries of Heian and Kamakura were no more widely understood than are the philosophical classics of our own day. But when we find an idea in the poetry, whose center of support was the court, not the monastery, it must have attained a level of common acceptance, at least among the literate class, for such notions are only slowly absorbed into the literary tradition. While Buddhism was introduced into Japan at least by 538, the *Collection for Ten Thousand Generations* (Man'yō-shū, ca. 759) shows few traces of Buddhist influence, and specific doctrinal themes do not appear in the imperial anthologies much before the *Collection of Gleanings* (Shūishū, ca. 1005–11). The *Later Collection of Gleanings* (Goshūishū, 1086) for the first time specifies a group of *waka* as "Poems on Śākyamuni's Teachings" (*shakkyōka*), although only among the Miscellaneous Poems of Book 6. The *Collection of Golden Leaves* (Kin'yōshū, 1124–27) and the *Collection of Verbal Flowers* (Shikashū, ca. 1151–54) both contain Buddhist poems, but again, only among the miscellanea of Book 10. In the *Collection of a Thousand Years* (Senzaishū, ca. 1188) compiled by Fujiwara Shunzei (Toshinari, 1114–1204) we find for the first time an entire book (XIX, 54 *waka*) devoted to "Poems on Śākyamuni's Teachings" (Hori 1955; Morrell 1973).

Among some 254 poems[70] by Jien which various editors selected for inclusion throughout the last fifteen imperial anthologies beginning with the *Senzaishū*, thirty-three appear under "Poems on Śākyamuni's Teachings." These are a convenient representative specimen of Jien's work by which we may examine him as a Buddhist poet. They are not an arbitrary sampling, for each item was carefully selected by Shunzei, Teika and later editors to represent Jien at his best. This chapter, then, will center on the *shakkyōka* of Jien in these anthologies. But first it will be necessary to sketch the religious and social context which nurtured them.

As on a Darkling Plain. Both Tendai's Jien and Hossō's Jōkei (Gedatsubō, d. 1213) were born in 1155, just as the disturbances of the Hōgen (1156) and Heiji (1159) periods were about to plunge the nation into decades of civil instability that would eventually sweep away the old order, replacing it with new social and religious institutions. An immediate result of the conflict was that major questions of political policy were now in the hands of the Taira military clan, with Kiyomori (1118–1181) at its head. A few decades later the Minamoto would reemerge as victors from the Gempei War (1180–85), with Yoritomo (1147–1199) establishing his military government at Kamakura in 1192. Although Jōkei's grandfather, the infamous Shinzei (Fujiwara Michinori, d. 1160) had supported Kiyomori during the Heiji Disturbance, he did not live to share the spoils, and his twelve sons were banished, among them Jōkei's father, Sadanori. Jōkei became a priest in 1165 and later studied at Nara's Kōfukuji, the Fujiwara clan temple, where he met Jien's brother, Kanezane, possibly on the occasion of the temple's rededication after its restoration in 1193 (see Morrell 1983, p. 9). It is probable that Jien and Jōkei were acquainted, but they tended to move in different circles.[71]

The political complexities of the Hōgen and Heiji Disturbances are formidable. But since Jien's family and religious associates were warp and woof of the closely-knit social class in which they occurred, we must at least take note of the broad outline of the conflict. In the following chart the two main factions in the dispute can roughly be linked up in two columns, those on the right being the victors.[72]

CHART 3.

Jien, Jōkei and the Hōgen-Heiji Disturbances

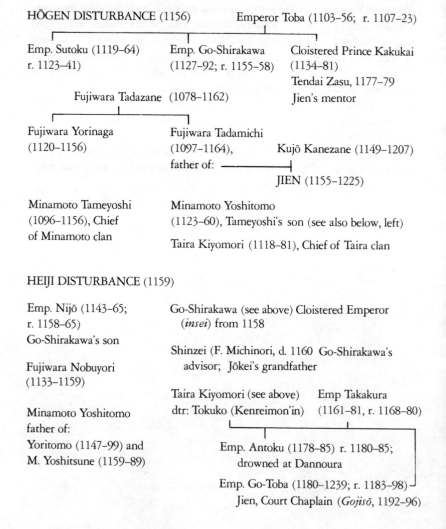

HŌGEN DISTURBANCE (1156)   Emperor Toba (1103–56; r. 1107–23)

Emp. Sutoku (1119–64)   Emp. Go-Shirakawa   Cloistered Prince Kakukai
r. 1123–41)   (1127–92; r. 1155–58)   (1134–81)
    Tendai Zasu, 1177–79
    Fujiwara Tadazane (1078–1162)   Jien's mentor

Fujiwara Yorinaga   Fujiwara Tadamichi
(1120–1156)   (1097–1164),   Kujō Kanezane (1149–1207)
    father of: ───────────┤
    JIEN (1155–1225)

Minamoto Tameyoshi   Minamoto Yoshitomo
(1096–1156), Chief   (1123–60), Tameyoshi's son (see also below, left)
of Minamoto clan
    Taira Kiyomori (1118–81), Chief of Taira clan

HEIJI DISTURBANCE (1159)

Emp. Nijō (1143–65;   Go-Shirakawa (see above) Cloistered Emperor
r. 1158–65)   (*insei*) from 1158
Go-Shirakawa's son
    Shinzei (F. Michinori, d. 1160 Go-Shirakawa's
Fujiwara Nobuyori   advisor; Jōkei's grandfather
(1133–1159)
    Taira Kiyomori (see above)   Emp Takakura
Minamoto Yoshitomo   dtr: Tokuko (Kenreimon'in)   (1161–81, r. 1168–80)
father of: └─────────┬─────────┘
Yoritomo (1147–99) and   Emp. Antoku (1178–85) r. 1180–85;
M. Yoshitsune (1159–89)   drowned at Dannoura
    Emp. Go-Toba (1180–1239; r. 1183–98) ┘
    Jien, Court Chaplain (*Gojisō*, 1192–96)

Jien's father, Tadamichi, was an official at the highest level of the imperial government. Like his own father, Tadazane, he had been both regent (*sesshō/kampaku*) and Chancellor (*Daijō Daijin*),[73] having held the former position from 1121 until 1158. He took the tonsure in 1162 and died two years later, when Jien was ten.[74] After the death of his mother, Lady Kaga, when Jien was two, he was raised by the widow of one Fujiwara Tsunesada. His adoptive mother had taken orders and was known as the Nun Yama'i, or, in Jien's more familiar expression, "the Nun who Raised the Little Monk" (Shōsō Yōiku no Zenni; Taga 1959, p. 10). At her death she bequeathed four manors to Jien, whose yearly proceeds later financed commemorative services for the repose of her soul.

In 1165, the year after his father died, Jien went to live at the Shōren'in the Awataguchi district of Kyoto. This famous residence of Chief Abbots (Zasu) of Mt. Hiei's Enryakuji traces its origins to a hermitage called Shōrembō built by the founder of Japanese Tendai, Saichō (Dengyō Daishi, 767–822) at the Eastern Pagoda on Mt. Hiei. Subsequently it was moved to Kyoto, the better, perhaps, for Tendai's chief representative to keep his hand in the affairs of the government. Under Gyōgen (1097–1155), forty-eighth *Zasu* of the Enryakuji, the Shōren'in was restored as a court-appointed temple (*monzeki*), whose abbots were princes of the blood or other highly-placed members of the aristocracy. When Jien went to live at the Shōren'in, it was administered by Cloistered Prince Kakukai (1134–81), a son of Emperor Toba and later (1177) Chief Abbot of the Enryakuji. The young novice took the religious name (*hōmyō*), Dōkai. Some sixteen years later, around 1181, he adopted the name, Jien. Later in life he was also known as the Archbishop of Yoshimizu (e.g., Brower 1972, p. 36), in reference to his residence at the Yoshimizubō (Manaka 1974, pp. 28, 77–79). Then in 1237 he was awarded the posthumous title, Jichin, by which he is identified in the later imperial anthologies.

Dōkai took the tonsure in 1167 at age thirteen. His high social standing guaranteed that from his teens Jien would run the gamut of honorary clerical ranks: Master of the Abhiṣeka Ceremony (Isshin Ajari) and Eye-of-the-Law (Hōgen) at sixteen (1170), Seal-of-the-Law (Hōin) at twenty-seven (1181), Provisional Archbishop (Gonsōjō) at thirty-eight (1192), and Great Archbishop (Daisōjō) at forty-nine (1203). And to complement these *ranks*, Jien over the years held a number of administrative *offices*. He was Court Chaplain (Gojisō) to Emperor Go-Toba from 1192 to 1196, as well as Chief Abbot (Zasu, Chōri, Bettō, etc.) of several temples, including the Shitennōji (Naniwa), the Byōdōin (Uji), and, of course, the Enryakuji on Mt. Hiei.

We should not quickly conclude from this that Jien was merely another clerical social climber, whose breed had by now seriously undermined public confidence in the Tendai establishment. Jien spent his early years as a monk at several retreats; and when he did return to the arena of social action, his conscientious behavior permits us to suppose that he was in the world but not of it. The bodhisattva ideal of compassionate action *within* the world is, after all, basic to Mahāyāna thought; and the advice of Jien's brother, Kanezane, to Jōkei had been that if competent monks retired from the world, this would only be a further sign of the decline of the Buddha's Law (Morrell 1983, p. 10). Kanezane was close to Jien and no doubt challenged him with the same argument.

Many of Jien's Buddhist poems reveal his sense of responsibility as a spiritual leader of the most influential religious institution of the day. When Fujiwara Teika (1162-1241) compiled his *One Verse Each by a Hundred Poets*, (Hyakunin isshu, ca. 1237), the basis of the still-popular New Year's card game, he had access to at least the 6000 poems by Jien which survive today. And the one he chose to represent his friend and fellow-poet, now dead for more than a decade, expresses this social concern. It is an early verse among the Miscellaneous Poems of his father Shunzei's *Collection of a Thousand Years* (Senzaishū, ca. 1188):

Ōkenaku	Unworthy am I,
Ukiyo no tami ni	But my black-dyed sleeves shelter
Oou kana	People in this floating world
Waga tatsu soma ni	From this hall of timbers
Sumizome no sode	Hewn from the mountain.

Seal-of-the-Law Jien[75]

But before assuming the clerical duties from which it would virtually have been impossible for him to escape, Jien had several opportunities to pursue his own private religious exercises. In 1174, at age 20, he went into seclusion at the Efumidera in Ōhara for a hundred-day retreat involving study and practice centered on the *Lotus Sutra*. The following year he moved to the Mudōji on Mt. Hiei to begin a Thousand-day Retreat (*sennichi nyūdō*) which he did not complete until 1178. It was during this period that his mentor, Kakukai, became Chief Abbot of the Enryakuji while attempting to remain aloof from the political conflicts between, and among, the "scholars" (*gakushō*) and the common monks (*dōshū*; see Brown and Ishida 1979, pp. 405-406). This was the occasion for Jien's single entry among the *Senzaishū* Poems on Śākyamuni's Teachings. (He has seven *waka* in other categories.)

When dissension arose on Mt. Hiei between the common monks and scholars and the scholars were all dispersed [1178], I was about to complete my Thousand-day Mountain Retirement (*sennichi no yamagomori*). I was grieved that the tradition of the ascetics (*hijiri no ato*) was about to be lost. It was winter. On a morning when the snow was falling, as I remained in seclusion in my mountain retreat, I sent this to priest Son'en:

Itodoshiku	"Ever more
Mukashi no ato ya	Will the traditions of old
Taenan to	Be lost . . ."
Omou mo kanashi	A saddening thought
Kesa no shirayuki	In the white morning snow.

Seal-of-the-Law Jien [76]

The Reply

Kimi ga na zo	But your name
Nao arawaren	Will still be known
Furu yuki ni	Even as the traces
Mukashi no ato wa	Of the ancient practices
Uzumorenu tomo	Are buried in falling snow.

Priest Son'en [77]

Of course, Jien's contemporaries would not have seen this versifying as in any way incompatible with his ascetic exercises. In both China and Japan poetry was exempt from the moral condemnation directed at prose fiction, doubtless because it was viewed as the direct expression of emotion, not a pastime depending on deliberate, and often unedifying, fabrications. The moralists who condemned Lady Murasaki for trafficking in falsehoods (in spite of her very plausible defense of fiction based on the Māhāyanist doctrine of Accommodation) were not at all offended by the many religious figures whose names fill the pages of collections of Chinese and Japanese poetry beginning with the *Kaifūsō* (Yearnings for the Ancient Chinese Style) and the *Man'yōshū* in the middle of the eighth century. Moreover, in late Heian the practice of poetry was increasingly viewed even as a means to religious realization rather than merely a harmless diversion or literary accomplishment: the Way of Poetry was identical with the Way of the Buddha (*kadō sunawachi butsudō*).

Although Fujiwara Shunzei himself seldom employed the term, *yūgen* ("mystery and depth"), he is largely responsible for the poetic ideal to which it refers, an ideal apparently inspired by the Tendai meditation practices prescribed in the *Great Cessation and Insight* (Maka shikan, T. 1911) of Chih-i (538–597), the great philosopher of Chinese T'ien T'ai (Konishi 1952, pp. 12–20: Manaka 1974, pp. 18–25). Shunzei's *Poetic Styles Past and Present* (Korai fūteishō, 1197, rev. 1201) is the first major statement of this attempt to join the practice of poetry to the practice of Buddhism. From about the same time come the frequently-cited comments by Shunzei as judge of *The Personal Poetry Contest of the Venerable Jichin* (Jichin oshō jikaawase), a selection of Jien's poems probably edited by him and his nephew, the accomplished poet Fujiwara Yoshitsune (1169–1206) around 1199.[78] Although circumstances suggest that Jien would have every reason to be involved in a Buddhist rationalization of poetic practice, the details are unclear. The story in the *Collection of Sand and Pebbles* (Shasekishū, 1279–83) of Jien's meeting with the great poet, Saigyō (1118–90), is suggestive, but probably apocryphal (Watanabe 1966, p. 251):

> After Priest Saigyō became a recluse, the innermost meaning of the Tendai *mantras (shingon)* was transmitted to him. When Abbot Jichin of Yoshimizu asked Saigyō to reveal this to him, he replied: "To begin with, become adept at poetry. If you don't grasp the meaning of poetry, you will not understand the meaning of the *mantras.*" It is said that after Jichin became adept at poetry, Saigyō revealed this to him.

Of course, such "meaning" is to be understood experientially rather than through concepts and verbal explanations, as Mujū goes on to explain. A poetry of "too few words" (cf., Brower and Miner 1961, pp. 265, 269–70) is entirely consistent with the Buddhist insistence on the limitations of concepts. Be this as it may, our concern here is with the thematic material of Jien's poems rather than with the psychological attitudes involved in their composition and appreciation.

Teika's choice. Jien became Chief Abbot of the Enryakuji for the first time in 1192 but lost the position four years later when his brother, Kanezane, was ousted as Chancellor (Daijō Daijin). He was reappointed in 1201, but was out again the following year. Also in 1201 Ex-Emperor Go-Toba made Jien a Fellow (*yoriudo*) in the newly-established Bureau of Poetry (Wakadokoro) with ten others, including Shunzei, Teika, Kanezane's son Yoshitsune, and Priest Jakuren (ca. 1139–1202). Jien was not among the six, headed by Teika, who were chosen from this committee to edit the *New Collection of Ancient and Modern Times* (Shinkokinshū, 1206, with later revisions); but in the number of poems included in the collection he is overtaken only by Saigyō, 94 to 91. Eight of these are to be found in the group of sixty-three *shakkyōka* comprising Book XX. Since the first four appear fairly early in the set, they can be introduced conveniently with the poems that precede them, allowing us to observe the principles of "association and progression" (see Brower and Miner 1961, pp. 319–29) by which Go-Toba, Teika and their colleagues organized their choices:

Poems on Śākyamuni's Teachings

Nao tanome	Although your pain
Shimeji ga hara no	Be as the burning moxa grass
Sasemogusa	On Shimeji's fields,
Waga yo no naka ni	Still trust in me while yet
Aran kagiri wa	I remain in this world.[79]
	[SKKS XX: 1917]

Nani ka omou	Whatever do you covet?
Nani to ka nageku	And what is it that troubles you?
Yo no naka wa	For this world is no more
Tada asagao no	Than dew upon the blossoms
Hana no ue no tsuyu	Of the morning glory.
	[SKKS XX: 1918]

These two verses have been handed down to us as poems
by the Kiyomizu Kannon

The Venerable Chien made a pilgrimage to Mt. Daisen.[80] At
daybreak when he was planning to leave, he heard this verse [by the
bodhisattva Jizō][81] in a dream

Yamafukaku	Here I stay
Toshifuru ware mo	Deep within the mountain
Aru mono wo	Year after year—
Izuchi ka tsuki no	So like the setting moon,
Idete yukuran	Whither would you go?
	[SKKS XX: 1919]

At hearing the rustle of reed tassles at Mitsu-no-dera[82]
in Naniwa

Ashi soyogu	How long will I
Shiose no nami no	Continue to bob across
Itsu mado ka	This floating world
Ukiyo no naka ni	Like the salt-filled waves
Ukabiwataran	That rustle the reeds?
	Gyōgi Bosatsu
	[SKKS XX:1920]

At the time of building the Central Hall on Mt. Hiei[83]

Anokutara	O Buddhas
Sammyaku sambodai no	Of unexcelled enlightenment!
Hotoke tachi	Bestow your grace
Waga tatsu soma ni	Upon this hall of timbers
Myōga arasetamae	Hewn from the mountain.

Dengyō Daishi
[SKKS XX:1921]

Poem composed at the time he went to China

Nori no fune	Going forth am I
Sashite yuku mi zo	On this boat of the Law:
Moromoro no	May the various
Kami mo hotoke mo	Gods and Buddhas
Ware wo misonae	All look after me!

Chishō Daishi[84]
[SKKS XX: 1922]

On a pillar at the Lecture Hall of a certain ancestral temple[85] insects
chewed away the wood to create this poem

Shirube aru	Now is your time
Toki ni dani yuke	To be blessed with a guide;
Gokuraku	So go forward,
Michi ni madoeru	Bewildered men of this world,
Yo no naka no hito	Along the path to paradise.[86]

[SKKS XX: 1923]

Composed while in seclusion at Hand-organ Cave[87]
on Mitake Peak

Jakumaku no	In the stillness
Koke no iwato no	At this moss-covered rock door,
Shizukeki ni	Without a single sound,
Namida no ame no	No day lacks a rain of tears
Furanu hi zo naki	Falling in gratitude.[88]

Venerable Nichizō
[SKKS XX: 1924]

Composed while considering what would be the correct state of mind
during one's final moments

Namu Amida	Praise to Amida!
Hotoke no mite ni	And though the end of the cord[89]
Kakuru ito no	Suspended from the hand
Owari midarenu	Of the Buddha be unravelled,
Kokoro to mo ga na	Would that my heart be not so.

Venerable Hōen[90]
[SKKS XX:1925]

Topic Unknown

Ware da ni mo	If it is my lot
Mazu gokuraku ni	To precede others in being born
Umarenaba	In Amida's Paradise,
Shiru mo shiranu mo	Then whether I know them or not,
Mina mukaeten	I will come to guide all man there.

Bishop Genshin[91]
[SKKS XX:1926]

On seeing the water of Turtle Well at the Tennōji[92]

Nigorinaki	Scooping up
Kamei no mizu wo	The unsullied water
Musubiagete	At Turtle Well,
Kokoro no chiri wo	I thereby rinse
Susugitsuru kana	The dust from my heart.

Jōtōmon'in[93]
[SKKS XX: 1927]

When topics were assigned to various people on the twenty-eight
parts of the *Lotus Sutra*, this was composed on the sentiment
of the Devadatta Chapter

Watatsuumi no	In an instant
Soko yori kitsuru	Coming up from the depths
Hodo mo naku	Of the ocean,
Kono mi nagara ni	Her body as it then was
Mi wo zo kiwamuru	She did indeed stretch to the limit.[94]

The Hosshōji Lay Priest and
Former Regent Chancellor[95]
[SKKS XX: 1928]

On the sentiment of the chapter on "Fortitude"[96]

Kazu naranu	What distress
Inochi wa nanika	Can I feel in this life
Oshikaran	Of insignificance?
Nori toku hodo wo	For I bear my adversity
Shinobu bakari zo	That I may preach the Law.

Major Counselor Tadanobu[97]
[SKKS XX: 1929]

Composed while attending an Enlightenment Lecture at the Urin'in
("Cloud Grove Temple")[98] when the Fifth month arrived

Murasaki no	Across the grove
Kumo no hayashi wo	Of purple clouds I look:
Miwataseba	Bead-flowers
Nori ni afuchi no	Blossom to remind me
Hana sakinikeri	Of my meeting with the Law.

Higo[99] [SKKS XX: 1930]

When [Higo] was reciting the *Nirvana Sutra*,[100] someone wrote the
following poem and showed it to her:

Chiru hana ni	In strewn petals
Ike no kōri mo	Even the ice on the lake
Tokenu nari	Has dissolved:
Hana fukichirasu	Scattering blossoms in the wind,
Haru no yo no sora	This sky of a night in spring.

She recalls replying in her dream with this verse:[101]

Tanikawa no	Valley stream:
Nagare shi kiyoku	So clear is its flowing
Suminureba	That the bright image
Kumonaki tsuki no	Of the unclouded moon
Kage mo ukabinu	Floats upon it.[102]

[Higo] [SKKS XX: 1931]

From some poems on "Personal Grievances" *(jukkai)*

Negawaku wa	Would that I might
Shibashi yamiji ni	Linger yet a while here
Yasuraite	On this dark path
Kakage ya semashi	To hold forth a light,
Nori no tomoshibi	The Lamp of the Law.[103]

Former Great Archbishop Jien
[SKKS XX: 1932]

Toku minori	To hear the expounded Law
Kiku no shiratsuyu	I rise at night like the white dew
Yoru wa okite	On the chrysanthemums,
Tsutomete kien	Determined to devote myself
Koto wo shi omou	Till morning carries me away.[104]

[SKKS XX: 1933, SGS 3004]

Gokuraku e	Supreme Bliss[105]
Mada waga kokoro	By my heart not yet reached,
Yukitsukazu	I plod with the step
Hitsuji no ayumi	Of sheep to slaughter—
Shibashi todomare	But just wait a while!

[SKKS XX:1934, SGS 3927]

Composed on the meaning of the phrase, "There is the Dharma of only One Vehicle," from the chapter on "Expedient Devices," while reciting poems on the twenty-eight chapters of the *Lotus Sutra*[106]

Izuku ni mo	"Where is the Law
Waga nori naranu	Not subsumed in my Law?"—
Nori ya aru to	I ask the wind blowing
Sora fuku kaze ni	In the midst of space,[107]
Toedo kotaenu	But there is no reply.

Former Great Archbishop Jien
[SKKS XX: 1942]

On the phrase, "He conjures up a great city," in the "Parable of
the Conjured City" chapter [108]

Omou na yo	Do not imagine
Ukiyo no naka wo	That you are finally free
Idehatete	Of this floating world!
Yadoru oku ni mo	Within every stage of understanding
Yado wa arikeri	Is yet a further stage.

[SKKS XX 1943, SGS 6965]

On the phrase, "Some dwell on the ground from which there is no
turning back," in the "Discrimination of Merits" chapter [109]

Washi no yama	Except for those who tread
Kyō kiku nori no	The Way of the Law which now
Michi narade	We hear on Eagle Mount, [110]
Kaeranu yado ni	There are none who reach the stage
Yuku hito zo naki	From which there is no turning back. [111]

[SKKS XX: 1944]

On the phrase, "The recollection of him [Kannon] in thought does
not pass away in vain," in the Chapter on "The Gateway to Everywhere
[of the Bodhisattva He Who Observes the Sounds of the World] [112]

Oshinabete	I had thought
Munashiki sora to	That all was vain
Omoishini	As empty sky,
Fuji sakinureba	But when the wisteria bloomed
Murasaki no kumo	There were purple clouds. [113]

[SKKS XX: 1945, SGS 5031]

On the meaning of the phrase, "Inwardly concealing their
bodhisattva-conduct" in the chapter on the "Receipt of Prophecy by
Five Hundred Disciples" [114]

Inishie no	Even at that retreat
Shika naku nobe no	On the Plains where the deer
Iori ni mo	Cried long ago,
Kokoro no tsuki wa	The moon of [Pūrṇa's] [115] heart
Kumorazarikeri	Was unclouded in understanding.

[SKKS XX: 1951]

In his old age Teika (1162–1124] compiled the *New Imperial Collection* (Shinchokusenshū, ca. 1234), the last of the imperial anthologies in what is defined as the Mid-Classical Period (1100–1241; Brower and Miner 1961, pp. 231–337). Jien is represented by twenty-eight items. In passing we may note that Yoshitsune's son (and thus Jien's grandnephew), Kujō Michiie (1193–1252), the "Former Regent Lay-priest of Kōmyōbuji," was a poet of considerable merit and also has twenty-eight poems in the collection. Father of Yoritsune (1218–56), who became *shōgun* after Sanetomo's assassination, Michiie was the patron of the Rinzai Zen pioneer, Enni Ben'en (1202–1280), and the financial backer of the Tōfukuji (Collcutt 1981, pp. 41–48).

In any case, Jien's contribution to the *New Imperial Collection* includes the following four *shakkyōka*.[116]

On conducting a Service of Thanksgiving for the Buddha's Relics[117]

Kyō no nori wa	The Law we hear today
Washi no takane ni	Is the afterglow of that sun
Ideshi hi no	Which concealed itself
Kakurete nochi no	After coming forth on the summit
Hikari narikeri	Of the Mount of the Eagle.[110]
	Former Great Archbishop Jien
	[SCSS X: 596]

Satoriyuku	Clouds of illusion
Kumo wa takane ni	As we go to enlightenment
Harenikeri	Have left the summit:
Nodoka ni terase	Shine on tranquilly,
Aki no yo no tsuki	Moon of an autumn night![118]
	[SCSS X: 597, SGS 6855]

On the Buddha Circle, while composing poems on the Five Circles[119] of the Diamond Assembly

Ima wa ue ni	At the moment
Hikari mo araji	There seems to be no light
Mochizuki to	In the firmament;
Kagiru ni nareba	But with [Buddha as] full moon
Hitokiwa no sora	What a spectacular sky!
	[SCSS X: 598, SGS 4366]

On the essential meaning of incalculable time

Iru chiri no	Ah, we see it!
Tsumorite takaku	The moon which has come forth
Naru yama no	From within the mount
Oku yori ideshi	Grown high by the pile
Tsuki wo miru kana	Of settling dust. [120]

[SCSS X: 599]

The Later Imperial Anthologies. In 1251 Teika's son, Tameie (1198–1275) compiled the *Later Collection Continued* (Shokugosenshū), the first anthology of the Late Classical Period (1241–1350; Brower and Miner 1961, pp. 337–421). Jien had been awarded the posthumous name, Jichin, in 1237; and it is by this title that he will henceforth be identified. The poems selected for this and later anthologies reflect the changing tastes of Tameie and his successors.

While composing poems on the Ten Worlds [121]

Samazana ni	We are created
Wakuru katachi mo	In a variety of forms
Makoto ni wa	In these worlds.
Hitotsu hotoke no	But in truth there is only
Satori narikeru	One Buddha Enlightenment

Former Great Archbishop Jichin
[ShokuGSS X:607]

Kaeriidete	Lodged in my heart,
Nochi no yamiji wo	O moon upon the mountain rim!
Terasanamu	Would that you might
Kokoro ni yadoru	Light the darkened way
Yama no ha no tsuki	Left behind by your retreat.

Former Great Archbishop Jichin
[ShokuGSS X: 613, SGS 3745]

Composed on a Visit to the Tennōji

Naniwazu ni	At Naniwa Bay
Hito no negai wo	Are people's hopes fulfilled
Mitsu shio wa	Like the full tide
Nishi wo sashite zo	Heading west to the sea;
Chigiri okikeru	And so I have made my pledge. [122]

Former Great Archbishop Jichin
[ShokuGSS X: 621]

Among the poems composed for the Hie Jūzenji Shrine [123]

Nori ni aite	To encounter
Yo ni arigataki	The Law is the best tidings [124]
Tayori ari	In all the world;
Kokoro ni iite	But it speaks to the heart
Hito ni kataraji	And not publicly.

Former Great Archbishop Jichin
[ShokuGSS X: 625, SGS 4564]

Yamakaze ni	Note well how
Nori no tomoshibi	The mountain wind blows away
Ketade miyo	The defiling dust,
Kegasu chiri wo ba	But without extinguishing
Fukiharau to mo	The lamp of the Buddha's Law.

[ShokuGSS X:626]

Collection of Gleanings Continued (Shokushūishū, ca. 1278)

Ika ni shite	How could it be
Miyako no hoka no	That I became one who remained
Kusa no io ni	Even for a short time
Shibashi mo tomaru	At some grass hermitage
Mi to nariniken	Outside the capital? [125]

[ShokuSIS XIX: 1349,
SGS 4877]

"And if in this way it is taught by turns" 126

Tsutaiyuku	At the mountain well,
Isoji no sue no	Handed down to the last
Yama no i ni	Of fifty persons,
Minori no mizu wo	We scoop up and experience
Kumite shiru kana	The water of the august Law.

Former Great Archbishop Jichin
[ShokuSIS XIX: 1361, SGS 2714]

Ika ni sen	What is to be done
Sono mochizuki zo	Since that full moon was overcast
Kumorinuru	By the smoke
Tsuru no hayashi no	Of the midnight pyre
Yowa no keburi ni	In the Grove of Cranes? 127

[ShokuSIS XIX: 1365, SGS 4729]

New Later Collection (Shingosenshū, 1303)

On "Abhorring and Departing from this Defiled World" 128

Mina hito no	The very thought
Saranu wakare no	Of all those painful farewells
Omou koso	Which none can avoid
Ukiyo wo itou	Is itself enough to engender
Kagiri narikere	Distaste for this floating world.

[SGSS IX: 702]

Collection of Jeweled Leaves (Gyokuyōshū, ca. 1313–14)

On the phrase, "Broadly Proclaim and Propagate it,"
in the "Medicine King" Chapter 129

Nori no hana	There is no abode
Chiranu yado koso	Where the blossoms of the Law
Nakarikere	Are not scattered!
Washi no takane no	The mountain wind blows
Yama oroshi no kaze	Down from Eagle Peak.

[GYS XIX: 2657, SGS 4961]

Collection of a Thousand Years Continued (Shokusenzaishū, ca. 1320)

Among a hundred poems offered to the Hie Shrine [130]

Tōrubeki
Michi wa sasuga ni
Aru mono wo
Shirabaya to dani
Hito no omowanu

Would that people
Did not wonder to themselves:
"If only we could
Anticipate the way ahead
Through which we must pass."

[ShokuSZS X: 1007, SGS 4532]

Later Collection of Gleanings Continued (Shokugoshūishū, ca. 1325–26)

Topic Unknown

Nori no kado ni
Kokoro wo irete
Omou kana
Tada ukiyo wo ba
Izubekarikeri

To insert my heart
Through the gate of the Law,
How I do deliberate!
But I have only to remove it
From this floating world.

[ShokuGSIS IX:1267, SGS 3264]

Collection of Elegance (Fūgashū, 1344–46)

Among fifty poems composed on "Abhorring and Departing from this Defiled World" [131]

Ukiyo kana
Yoshino no hana ni
Haru no kaze
Shigururu sora ni
Ariake no tsuki

This floating world:
Among the blossoms at Yoshino,
The spring winds;
In the misty skies of autumn,
The moon at daybreak.

[FGS XVIII: 2069, cf., SGS 5978]

Mukashi yori
Washi no takane ni
Sumu tsuki no
Iranu ni mayou
Hito zo kanashiki

Since antiquity
The moon which lights the peak
Of Eagle Mount [132]
Has not waned—and how sad
That we remain deluded.

[FGS XVIII: 2071]

Among Miscellaneous Poems

Saritomo na	Whatever may be,
Hikari wa nokoru	Still there is light for us
Yo narikeri	In our remaining world: [133]
Sora yuku tsukihi	Sun and moon crossing the skies,
Nori no tomoshibi	And the Lamp of the Buddha's Law.

[FGS XVIII: 2075; cf. ZKT 1345]

Among poems on Śākyamuni's Teachings

Hannyadai ni	The Lotus Sutra
Osame okiteshi	Stored at Wisdom Heights
Hokkekyō mo	Even surpasses
Yumedono yori zo	In reality the one
Utsutsu ni wa koshi	At the Hall of Dreams. [134]

[FGS XVIII: 2092]

New Collection of a Thousand Years (Shinsenzaishū, 1359)

Among the poems of a hundred-verse sequence on the theme of "A Discourse on the Two Truths" during a visit to the Tennōji

Tonikaku ni	Being still confused
Yukabaya to omou	Over which path, after all,
Michi ni nao	I feel I must follow
Madoeba koso wa	Is itself the very reason
Tōrazarurame	I have not progressed. [135]

[SSZS IX: 820; cf., Taga No. 2987]

Topic unknown [136]

Ika ni sen	"What should I do
Makoto no michi ni	That truly I might enter on
Iru mi zo to	The path of truth?"—
Omoizureba	So I ponder and go forth,
Mata wasuretsutsu	Time and again to lose my way.

[SSZS IX: 856; cf., Taga No. 3010]

New Collection of Ancient and Modern Times Continued
(Shinshokukokinshū, 1439)

"I saw the Buddha Torch-Burner," in the Introductory Chapter
of the Lotus Sutra [137]

Tomoshibi no	If the Buddha shines
Hikari wo sashite	The light of his torch upon us
Kotaezuba	And we do not respond,
Minori no hana wo	Then who can expect to see
Dare ka machimin	The flowers of the august Law?

[SSKKS VIII: 819, SGS 4849]

On the meaning of the phrase, "Illuminates the east"
in the Introductory Chapter [of the Lotus Sutra]

Mukashi wo mo	We see it clearly
Sayaka ni zo miru	Even as it was of old;
Izuru hi ni	For the light we face
Mukō hikari no	In the rising sun
Kumori nakereba	Is undimmed by clouds.

[SSKKS VIII: 842, SGS 4845]

Jien's Lotus Imagery. Predictably, the main literary inspiration for Jien's Buddhist poetry was the *Lotus Sutra* (Myōhōrengekyō, T. 262). We would expect this scripture, the basis for Tendai's exoteric teaching, to be thoroughly known to the sect's leading cleric of the time. But the prominence of *Lotus* imagery in Jien's poems is not really a function of one individual's sectarian commitment. Throughout the Heian period, and for some centuries later, the *Lotus Sutra* occupied a central position in the literary and religious world of ideas. The new movements of the Kamakura period gradually eroded its prestige, but its arguments and images were not supplanted overnight in the popular mind. Beginning with Hōnen (1133–1212) the Pure Land movements shifted attention to the *Larger Pure Land Sutra* (Muryōjukyō, T.360), the *Amitabha Sutra* (Amidakyō, T. 366), and the *Sutra of Meditation on Amida Buddha* (Kammuryōjukyō, T. 365). Zen emphasized the *Diamond Sutra* (Kongōkyō, T. 235) and others of the *prajñāpāramitā* class, along with the *Garland* (Kegonkyō, T.278, 279, 293), *Vimalakirti* (Yuimakitsukyō, T. 475) and *Lankāvatāra* (Nyūryōgakyō, T. 671) sutras. For Nichiren (1222–1282) and his followers the *Lotus Sutra* did retain its importance, but perhaps more as an object of veneration through the invocation of its title (*daimoku*) than as a text for explication and study.

CHAPTER THREE

Kegon's Myōe as Popular Religious Hero

Myōe Shōnin (Kōben, 1173–1232) lived at the beginning of an age of religious renewal and innovation. Hōnen (1133–1212) was advocating the Sole-practice Calling upon the Name of the Buddha, and now founded the Jōdo sect in 1175. Eisai (1141–1215) returned in 1191 from his second trip to China to propagate the meditation practices of Rinzai Zen. After the battle at Dannoura six years earlier, the Minamoto established a center of political power in Kamakura which would shape the direction of the nation's social, religious, and cultural life with the court in Kyoto. The belief was widespread, although not universally accepted, that the world was well into the period of the Decline of the Law. New methods appropriate to the times were required, as Hōnen, Eisai and Myōe realised. They were succeeded by a flood of reformers, notably Dōgen (1200–1253), Nichiren (1222–1282) and Shinran (1173–1262), who was born the same year as Myōe but outlived him by three decades.

Myōe's ambition was to rejuvenate Kegon, the most prominent of the old Six Nara Sects with its headquarters at the Tōdaiji. After being ordained a priest in 1188, he devoted himself both to the study of Kegon theory and the practices of Buddhist esotericism (*mikkyō*), eventually developing his own synthesis known as *gonmitsu*. In 1206, when Myōe was in his thirty-fourth year, he was commissioned by retired Emperor Go-Toba to restore the Kōzanji on Mount Toga-no-o. In time the temple flourished (although the main hall of worship, the Kondō, was not completed until 1219), and Myōe won respect for his sanctity and dedication. But his movement lacked popular support and in the end was no more successful in extending Kegon's appeal beyond a small group of Buddhist thinkers than similar efforts earlier. The doctrines of Hua-yen (Kegon) had been influential in Shingon and Zen thought, but they were too abstruse to arouse widespread enthusiasm.

In spite of the failure of his movement, Myōe was personally one of the great figures of his time. His writings on Kegon, many of which are extant (see Tanaka

1961, pp. 237–249), had little effect on the development of Japanese Buddhism, whatever intellectual originality they may reveal. The Myōe *legend,* however, provided a literary and religious image of a model priest to an age in which the worldliness of the clergy was widespread. This legend does not reveal the serious scholar of esotericism and Kegon philosophy that we know Myōe to have been in real life. It does, however, show us an uncompromising idealist who would accept no easy answers even during the period of moral decline in the Latter Days of the Law. This legend offered the hope that even in these degenerate times there were still a few who understood and practiced the original discipline. In the spirit of Tennyson's Ulysses, Myōe might have said:

> . . .and though
> We are not now that strength which in old days
> Moved heaven and earth, that which we are, we are—
> One equal temper of heroic hearts,
> Made weak by time and fate, but strong in will
> To strive, to seek, to find, and not to yield.

We shall here examine the legendary Myōe as he is revealed in four well-known writings of the Kamakura period. The quasi-biographical material presented in the first three writings may serve as an introduction Myōe's lengthy *Final Injunctions,* translated in full at the end of the chapter.

The earliest record (second to be presented below) is a brief entry at the end of Book 10 (*shakkyōka*) of the *New Imperial Collection* (Shinchokusenshū), a poetry anthology compiled by Fujiwara Teika (1162–1241) about 1234, within two years of Myōe's death. Myōe was a poet of some distinction. His favorite topic was the moon (Kawabata 1969, pp. 41–43; 68–74), and his waka appeared in several imperial anthologies as well as in a private collection, the *Venerable Myōe's Waka* (Myōe Shōnin wakashū), completed in 1248 by his disciple Kōshin. Unlike his elder contemporary, the quasi-recluse Kamo no Chōmei (1155– 1216), Myōe did not move in the fashionable poetic circles of his day, but seems to have come to Teika's attention late in his life. This eminent scholar-poet notes in his diary, *Journal of the Full Moon* (Meigetsuki), that in 1229 his wife and children visited Kōzanji to hear Myōe lecture on the precepts (Kamata and Tanaka 1971, p. 476).

The Kamakura record next in order of composition—the longest and final item to be translated here—is the *Final Injunctions of the Venerable Myōe of Toga-no-o* (Toga-no-o Myōe Shōnin ikun), a collection of aphorisms assembled by the disciple Kōshin between 1235 and 1238. Several texts of the *Ikun* have come down to us, and the translation is based on the popular version appended to the

1665 (Kambun 5) two-volume xylograph of the *Biography of the Venerable Myōe of Toga-no-o* (Toga-no-o Myōe Shōnin denki), which has frequently been reprinted, both in Tokugawa and in modern editions.

The first of the accounts presented here is the 1254 depiction of a saintly but eccentric Myōe by Tachibana Narisue in his *Stories Old and New* (Kokonchomonjū), a collection of anecdotes intended as a sourcebook of paintable themes. Narisue was a painter, and the demands of the artist for an interesting visual arrangement tend to bend sober facts into caricature. Although *Kokonchomonjū* appeared only two decades after Myōe's death, he is already treated as an icon.

The latest of the Kamakura accounts considered here (third in order of presentation) is more realistic, even though the legend has had an additional quarter of a century to develop. Mujū's *Sand and Pebbles* (Shasekishū, 1279–1283) shows us the exemplary recluse and elaborates on the aphorism opening the *Final Injunctions*, which came to represent Myōe's teachings in the popular mind: "Do what is appropriate" *(arubeki yō wa)*.

Eccentric, Wonderworker, and Would-be Traveler. Every legend must have an admixture of fact to be credible, and this is also true in the case of Myōe. After the deaths of his parents, Myōe went in 1181 to live at the temple Jingōji on Mt. Takao, northwest of Kyoto. The abbot of this temple was Myōe's maternal uncle, the Shingon priest Jōgaku, with whom he took the tonsure in 1188. (Myōe's original religious name was Jōben; he adopted the name Kōben much later in life, around 1210.) Jōgaku had been closely associated with Mongaku, the notorious monk who instigated Yoritomo's revolt.

The fragment of the legend from *Stories Old and New* (Kokonchomonjū II:2:64; Nagazumi and Shimada 1966, pp. 98–102) states that Mongaku met Myōe at the temple Ninnaji and took him as a disciple. Now it is indeed true that Myōe studied at this temple in his youth, and that such a meeting of these two eminent priests would provide a suitable subject for a painting, but the legend unfortunately does not appear to be based on the historical record. Neither are the subsequent anecdotes about Myōe and the carpenters and his association with Kōon corroborated by the authoritative biography, the *Acts of Venerable Myōe of Kōzanji* (Kōzanji Myōe Shōnin gyōjō), written by Myōe's colleague and disciple, Kikai (d. 1250; Tanaka 1961, pp. 216–217). In short, the Myōe we are about to see is already half fiction.

*About the Venerable Kōben who was an Extraordinary Man, and How
the Kasuga Deity Prevented his Going to India*
In his youth Kōben was raised by the Kita-no-In no Omuro.[139] Priest
Mongaku saw the child during a visit [to the Ninnaji] and noted that he was no
ordinary person. "You must let me have this youth to be my disciple," said
Mongaku; and he took the boy with him.

When Kōben had become a priest and was living on Mount Takao, he put
his heart and soul into his studies to the exclusion of all else. Mongaku had
decided to rebuild Takao's [Jingōji] and he brought in carpenters, whose
constant milling about distracted Kōben. So he retired into the mountains
taking with him as many sacred texts as he could carry, and he could be seen
there alone, away from all comings and goings. At noon when the carpenters
had spread out their rations, he would run down from the mountain and
hurriedly gobble up seven or eight portions of food. Then he would return to
his hideaway carrying additional copies of sacred texts and remain there for
two or three days without making an appearance. He would do this once every
couple of days without fail. When Mongaku heard of it he remarked: "This is
not the way a mere mortal behaves; it is the conduct of an incarnate being."

The holy man would read the sacred texts in the dead of night. Now a
priest called Kōon,[140] son of Ōga Motokata, became Kōben's disciple. Kōon,
who waited on his teacher for many years, related that Kōben would inspect
the holy texts in the pitch-black night without even lighting a lamp. "Bring
me a certain writing that is in such-and-such a place," he would say to his
disciples. And then he examined what they brought to him after bumbling
about in the dark. "This isn't the one," he would remark. "It's the writing with
this-and-that passage." Such unusual behavior!

One evening as it began to grow dark the master called to Kōon. "At a
time like this a mountain temple is just the place to attain purity of heart.
Come out and see the moon!" Then they left the building and made their way
up the mountain along the bank of the Kiyotaki River for more than three
kilometers until they came to a large rook, which they scaled. "What an
impressive rock it is," remarked Kōben. "It could have been the foundation
stone for a great monastery. Somehow I have a great fondness for this rock."
Then Kōben, with deep purity of heart, conversed about a variety of matters.

"It seems to be cold." Kōben brought out a straw mat from nowhere and
had Kōon spread it over the rock—a strange and curious business! The site
was named "Meditation Rock" (Jōshinseki), modeled after the boulder at

Wu-chen Temple in China. There is also a pine here called the "Rope-Seat Tree" (Jōshōju) where Kōben took refuge during meditation (*zazen*). [141] On one occasion, around the first of the year when he was engaged in contemplation under this tree, hail fell [and Kōben composed this verse]:

Iwa no ue	On black-dyed sleeves
Matsu no kokage ni	In the shadow of the pine
Sumizome no	Upon the crag,
Sode no arare ya	Hail! A string
Kakeshi sono tama	Of prayer-beads. . . etc.

This is a variation on a poem which Teika included (along with several others not translated here) in the *Shinchokusenshū* two decades earlier. It is introduced with a long headnote:

In a valley west of where [Myōe] was living was a crag which he called Meditation Rock. Also at that place was a pine called Rope-Seat Tree, on whose two branches he would take refuge to sit in meditation. One day in the First Month when the snow was falling, he was practicing meditation (*zazen*) for a short time when the wind blew violently through the pine tree. Gathering up the hail which collected on his black-dyed sleeves, he stood upright on the rock and composed the following verse comparing the hail stones to the "wondrous jewels in the folds of the garment": [142]

Matsu no shita	On black-dyed sleeves
Iwane no koke ni	Here in the boulder's moss
Sumizome no	Beneath the pine,
Sode no arare ya	Hail! A string
Kakeshi shiratama	Of white jewels. [SCSS X:629] [143]

Narisue continues his story of Myōe with an account of his first attempt to visit India. Myōe made his plans during the winter of 1202–1203, and then visited Nara's Kasuga Shrine to take leave of the deity for whom he had special affection. On his way to the shrine sixty deer bowed to the ground on bended knee to pay homage to the holy man. When Myōe returned to his native province of Kii, the Great Deity spoke through a woman he had possessed and asked Myōe not to leave Japan. When the holy man requested a sign that the oracle was indeed from the deity, the woman vaulted up onto a beam of the thatched roof and sat there for three days answering Myōe's questions about the Kegon Sutra, while a fragrant white foam trickled from her mouth!

This is probably the most popular theme in the Myōe legend. With variations it is described, mentioned, or illustrated in the early biographical *Denki*, *Kokonchomonjū, Shasekishū* (1:5), *Kasuga Gongen genki-e* (Illustrated Record of Miracles of the Kasuga Avatars, 1309), *Shingonden* (Lives of Esoteric Masters, 1325) and in *Kasuga ryūjin* (The Dragon God of Kasuga) by the great nō dramatist, Zeami (1363–1443). I have included these variations at length in the preface to the translation of *Kasuga ryūjin* in the Appendix.

The *Kokonchomonjū* account concludes with a description of Myōe's final moments.

The Exemplary Recluse. Mujū Ichien (1226–1312) was six when Myōe died and he did not compose the *Shasekishū* until almost a half century later. By this time the new currents of Kamakura Buddhism were flowing away vigorously from the main stream of Heian's Tendai and Shingon, although their channels were not so well defined as they would appear to later historians.

Mujū eventually associated himself with the Rinzai Zen school of Enni Ben'en (1202–80) but his roots were in traditional Buddhism. In an age in which many of the new movements tended to deny the viability of any form of religious practice other than their own, Mujū defended the traditional principle of skillful means (*hōben*) whereby the Buddha was seen to preach the Law through a variety of doctrines and practices accommodated to the diversity of human needs and biases (Morrell 1985). This principle was sometimes denied indirectly, through a reinterpretation rather than by straightforward rejection: the Buddha might indeed accommodate his teaching to specific needs, but the needs of this *particular age* during the Decline of the Law (*mappō*) can be satisfied only by *one specific method*, the one to which I happen to subscribe.

We can easily see why Myōe's aphorism about suitability would appeal to Mujū. It was, on the one hand, compatible with the traditional principle of accommodation: "the sects and the teachings of monks who have left their homes for various temples on many mountains may differ, but they are all children of Śākyamuni." On the other hand, if a monk wished to behave in a way appropriate to his lot in life, he would observe the priestly regulations. While the laxity of the clergy could be *explained* as an inevitable condition of society during the Decline of the Law, there was also widespread determination that it be *corrected*. And Myōe provided a welcome model. The following is Mujū's account in the *Shasekishū* (3:8; Watanabe 1966, pp.161–63).

The Discourse of the Sage of Toga-no-o

A number of recluses from Mount Kōya made a pilgrimage to Toga-no-o to establish karmic affinities with the venerable Myōe, and sent in word of their arrival. At first they were told that he had a cold and would not hold an audience. But presently Myōe appeared on the heels of his messenger. The group was hustled in and the sage addressed them.

"The way this monk Myōe pampers himself is so gross that he goes about with an attendant. All of you have come a long distance from Kōya to visit this old priest. When you wanted to come in to see me, I acted like an ordinary layman by saying that I had a cold. Even if I had been laid up with a grave illness, I should have agreed to meet with you to discuss the Law of the Buddha. If my condition were any less serious, there could be no conceivable justification for my behavior. I have simply lost sight of *that which is appropriate (arubeki yō)* for a person in my circumstances.

"If I were to write in simple characters what to teach people, after having examined the sacred writings over the many years of my life, it would be the six syllables, 'Do what is suitable.' I teach that which is appropriate according to the ways and methods of what is suitable for the layman, and for the priest, and for the recluse. But in the Latter Days people are confused about what is appropriate. The kings and ministers, those acquainted with the uses of external support, should protect the Law and respect it, not losing sight of the fact that Lord Śākyamuni has entrusted it to their care. That is what is appropriate for the emperor. And other laymen should not act contrary to his purposes.

"The sects and the teachings of monks who have left their homes for various temples on many mountains may differ, but they are all children of Śākyamuni. So once they take their vows, shave their heads and dye their garments, they should abandon desire and cut off attachment, being mindful of the Five Aggregates of which we are constituted and pursuing the Practice of the Three Learnings [morality, wisdom, meditation]. But although they shave their heads, they do not shave their desires; and they dye their clothes but not their hearts. Some assume responsibilities for wife and child, while others buckle on armour. The country is gradually being overrun with monks who act just as the Three Poisons [of covetousness, anger, and delusion] and the Five Desires [for property, sex, food, fame, and sleep] lead then: so that in the end they do not maintain the Five Commandments nor engage in the Ten Good Deeds. They are not mindful of what is appropriate to those who have abandoned the life of the householder.

"The recluse in particular should cast away pride and attachment and obliterate worldly thoughts, training mind and body according to what is appropriate to the teaching of the Law instead of acting like men of the world. To behave as everyone else does truly violates the teaching of the Buddha."

Thus Myōe spoke tearfully on the profound meaning of the Law as what was appropriate for those who had entered upon the Way of release and liberation, and on what was essential in the teaching for this generation, so that the venerable recluses wrung out their black, tear-drenched sleeves. Myōe spoke from the evening of that day throughout the night until morning, then during the following day until they heard the sound of a bell. "What a long time I've been talking," he remarked, and then retired.

It had seemed that the discourse had lasted only a moment. The monks recalled that the Buddha's sermon of sixty short kalpas [144] had seemed to his audience as only half a day long; and they all felt that had they lived at that time and heard him preach, it would have been just like this. Deeply impressed, they returned to Mount Kōya.

A venerable recluse who was observing the post-noon fast was invited to perform a religious service in Kawachi province. It was a wintry day over a seven-league stretch of road, and he was asked to come before noon. This recluse was mounted on a horse which could not move very fast; and, although the day was cloudy and he could not see the sun, it seemed to have been high in the sky for a considerable time.

The monk remarked that the sun seemed to have passed the meridian; but his host replied that it was still before noon, and, with various delicacies, encouraged him to eat. By nature a gourmand, he ate with gusto until he was sated, finishing up with dessert. As he was picking his teeth, he heard the sound of a bell; and when he made inquiry was informed that it was the vesper bell. This can be compared to Myōe's being startled by the vesper bell, but the recluse's diversion by food was downright reprehensible compared with Myōe's forgetting the time while discussing the Law.

When we view the present world using the past as our mirror, we find genuine differences among what prospers and what is rejected. The recluse of old imbued his heart with the Buddha's Law and set aside the myriad matters of the world, while in the present age men abandon the Buddha's Law but do not neglect worldly fame and profit. Under such circumstances they only bear the name of "recluse" (*tonsei*), but do not know its reality. Year after year we can see an increasing number of people who "escape the world" (*tonsei*) simply to get ahead in life and in spite of the fact that they have no religious aspiration at all. In the world they are nobodies with neither fame nor profit, but on entering the gate of the recluse, they now have both! So nowadays perhaps we ought to change the character *ton* in *tonsei* ("to escape the world") and write it with a homonym so as to read *tonsei* ("to covet the world").

Tonsei no	Let us change
Ton wa tokiyo ni	The character *ton* in *tonsei*
Kakikaen	To accord with the times:
Mukashi wa nogare	Of old it meant "to escape,"
Ima wa musaboru	And now it means "to covet."

The Popular Moralist of the "Final Injunctions". Myōe died in 1232 in his sixtieth year, revered by his disciples for his austerity and scholarly achievements. It is reasonable to suppose that the hagiographer Kōshin,[145] a relatively young member of the Kōzanji community, would not have been especially close to the temple's venerable abbot and would have had little contact with him during his lifetime, only coming to know him largely through the stories which circulated after Myōe's death. Three years after the event Kōshin began to write down what he heard attributed to Myōe, fully aware, as he tells us at the outset, that there were probably some errors in people's recollections.

It is the legend that concerns us here, however, and not the accuracy of the account. Kōshin's collection of aphorisms is readily understood, which doubtless accounts for its subsequent popularity. It is not great literature, or even particularly well-expressed as conventional wisdom. It does, however, define the Kamakura religious mood: the sense that the world was clearly in the period of the Decline of the Law, the widespread desire for clerical reform, and the valuation of action above sterile speculation. These are the same concerns which we have seen reflected in the stories about Myōe as a popular religious hero.

One might summarize *Final Injunctions* for the reader, calling attention to its major themes and eliminating redundancies. But the kind of understanding which is only to be realized through direct exposure to a work in its entirety is worth the reader's additional effort. Kōshin's account was widely read in later centuries and it is translated here without embellishment or extenuation. Using the standard 1665 text (Miyasaka Yūshō 1964, pp. 59–75), I have added in brackets the entry numbering used in a modern colloqial rendering (Satō 1971, pp. 457–70) in order to facilitate identification.

Final Injunctions of the Venerable Myōe of Toga-no-o
(Toga-no-o Myōe Shōnin Ikun)

Compiled by Kōshin beginning in the summer of Bunryaku 2 (1235). I collected and wrote down what people told me. There are surely some errors.

[1] We ought to hold fast to this seven-syllable phrase: "That which is appropriate" (*arubeki yō wa*). There is that which is appropriate for the monk and that which is appropriate for the layman, that which is appropriate for the emperor and that which is appropriate for his subjects. Every evil arises because we disregard what is appropriate for us.

[2] I am not one who looks forward to being saved in the afterlife. I simply want to do what is appropriate for me in this life.

[3] One who practices the Way of the Buddha must have an unsullied mind. With their defiled behavior, what can the warrior and his kind expect of life? I cannot imagine that my religious practice would be adequately maintained if I treated the Buddha's Law lightly and followed the crowd to act like everyone else in the world. Even if something is beyond my realization, I should make every effort to reach to the bottom of it (*soko wo kiwamete*),[146] as does the Buddha's wisdom, and to understand. Although I am called a dabbler, since there are many things that I do not understand, this should not distress me. But I should not trifle with the Buddha's law by having a defiled mind. If I do, then it will be impossible for me, just by making the tonsure, to maintain life in this human form.[147] How would I differ from those *dengaku* entertainers known as "Eulalia Priests"?[148]

[4] There is a passage in the *Āgamas*[149] which states exactly what I have maintained for many years: that the fervor of those in antiquity who rejoiced in the Law of the Buddha was like the attitude of people today who covet fame and prosperity. Look it up later.

[5] It does not bother me to hear it said that I follow the lead of others. I have no desire for fame and prosperity; nor have I urged people to solicit subscriptions for statues and sutras. In this spirit I simply feel as much compassion as I am capable of toward the world of sentient beings. It would be pathetic if people thought that even beggars and lepers held me in contempt [for failing to observe the Buddha's teaching].

[6] When one has inner worth corresponding to the donations he accepts from the faithful, then it is a blessing to receive. But if the monk (bhikkhu) who violates the regulations has accrued no merit for the afterlife, then it is certain that his robe will become a net of fire, and the food he has accepted with become molten rings to sear his stomach.[150]

[7] A person may never recite a single scroll of a sutra or mystic spell, nor even once offer incense and pray for his own spiritual benefit. And yet, if he is upright in mind and body and behaves according to what is appropriate [to his lot in life], then all the gods and beneficent spirits will protect him. His aspirations will be naturally realized and his wishes easily attained. Rather than making life difficult, simply be upright without much ado. If a person's mind is subject to anxiety, deception and cupidity, and his behavior is always unsettled and given to willful inpropriety, then even though he were to commission a celebrant of great spiritual achievement to recite a million scrolls of sutras, and though he might construct and venerate a thousand times a hundred million images of the Buddha, his retribution will be the same as for those who recite the scripture with a foul mouth. One who prays with a defiled mind moves ever rapidly toward a bad end, and he will never have his petitions granted.

Doing nothing to correct his state of mind, the fool is entangled in his own willful desires. He has the unreasonable expectation that if he prays, he can obtain anything at all. Engaging the services of a foolish venal monk, he torments himself in mind and body without there being any response to his prayers. And so he merely creates the karma for his fall into hell. What a sad state of affairs!

[8] "When you know something well, you will not be arrogant about it. When you know something well, the very idea of being arrogant will not occur to you. If it does, then you don't really know!" This is a common saying.

[9] For one who would realize his Buddha-Nature, it is like seeing Tōji's pagoda[151] at the start of First Avenue and finally reaching it at Ninth Avenue—a truly gratifying experience!

[10] A person who follows the Buddha's Law must first of all be free of passions and free of attachments. Beyond this, those with a knowledge of religious matters are called "scholars," and those able to elicit response to prayer are known as "adepts" (*gensa*), or "esoteric masters" (*shingonji*); while those with neither scholarly nor devotional abilities are just good-for-nothing monks. But if one has the least fixation on the phenomenal world, he simply cannot be called a follower of the Buddha's Law.

[11] King Prasenajit[152] addressed the Buddha with these words: "My mother has just died. If someone would restore her to life, I would reward him even if it meant giving up country, castle, wife and children, or losing life itself." People today have little to be complacent about, but grief to such an extent is unknown. Everyone is aware of the wide disparity between antiquity and these Latter Days, between that great country and this savage hinderland. How distressing it is!

[12] It is customary in these Latter Days for people to parade their casual knowledge of Buddhism for fame and profit without grasping its essentials. Thus, they neglect the truth of the Two-Fold Emptiness [of persons and things],[153] and do not reveal its intent. If that which is taught by contemporary scholars were the real Dharma, then Buddhism would be the worst of all ideologies. Just consider this: if you take as your mentor a person who does not grasp the essentials of the Teaching, what kind of results can you expect? A deplorable situation indeed.

[13] In my study of Buddhism I have concentrated solely on the problem of how the various Buddhas and Bodhisatvas would practice the Way, so my results are useless for today's scholars. But the Buddha seems to have been gracious toward me. When I put these difficult methods more-or-less into practice, my mind becomes clear and free of impediments.

[14] Ever since I was a child many years ago I have been studying the sacred scriptures solely that I might comprehend the law which the Buddha devised for our salvation. I certainly never wanted to become a scholar that I might be praised by others.

[15] What I should like to have is a teacher, not disciples. People usually prefer to become teachers, rather than to follow others as life-long disciples; but instead of having disciples to train, I wish to train my own mind to attain enlightenment. Moreover, it was because the Buddha venerated all others who were virtuous that he excels all sentient beings and is teacher to the gods and men.[154]

[16]"Nowadays, even those with pretensions as scholars, having learned by rote chapter and verse from the scriptures, no longer comprehend the Ultimate Truth[155] in their hearts." When I made this remark to someone who came to my hut to ask about the teachings of Buddhism, he said nothing but presently became paralyzed with rage.

The *Nirvana Sutra*[156] says: "This is what I would now explain to you— because they do not comprehend the Ultimate Truth in their hearts, they transmigrate for aeons in the painful seas of birth-and-death . . ."

Perhaps the reason he got angry when I said that I have not seen anyone who really comprehends "the Ultimate Truth in his heart" is that for me to make any statement—either that a person knows or does not know, sees or does not see—implies that I myself have plumbed its depths and clarified the issue. But because he became angry, it is evident that the man himself did not understand.

A man everyone knew was a thief stole a pot, and then completely forgot that he placed it on his head. When the owner came to inquire, saying that his pot was missing, the thief denied that he was to blame. "I didn't take it," he said, spreading out his hands. And, indeed, he held the pot neither in his hands nor in his words. He spoke with great sincerity, not realizing that it was perfectly evident to everyone that he was wearing the pot on his head. His saying "I didn't take it" was just like my visitor's attempt to vindicate himself. How tedious.

[17] In antiquity a monk would experience the Truth about Reality (*jissō no kotowari*) and hand this on to his disciples; but in this Latter Age we do not have the wisdom to realize that Truth. Monks have a worldly air and are involved in mundane affairs before all else. Moreover, as a way for the temple to stir up interest in Buddhism, they spend their entire lives worrying about costumes for dancers and folk-music entertainers.[157] Such a scholar-monk who hustled about telling people that he had been made manager of the folk-music performances at a certain temple became quite a topic of conversation. To enter the path of the Buddha is an entirely different matter. The man, who was thought to have made considerable progress in Buddhism, gradually became estranged from the Dharma.

[18] We ought to bear in mind that our behavior day and night is reflected in the crystal mirror of judgment.[158] Nor should we imagine that because something is hidden, that because we keep it secretly in our heart, others will not know of it. All is reflected in this mirror, which is obscured by no clouds. This should teach us compunction.

[19] The layman may conscientiously perform meritorious acts for the sake of the dead; but if he is motivated by fame, profit, or any worldly fixation, he acquires no benefit and exerts himself to no avail. And when priests recite sutras and meticulously chant mystic spells without genuine conviction, when they are lacking in the observance of the regulations and make no effort to improve the three modes of behavior [body, word, and thought] but place great store on good eating and receiving donations, then they provide no help for the dead. Not only that, but by virtue of accepting alms from the faithful under false pretenses, each in his own way will fall into the [three] Evil Paths. This is the amazing way we behave in this Latter Age, benefitting no one. Both clergy and laity should face up to this problem, so as not to suffer grave calamity. It is both a curse and a blessing that as a result of our past actions we have been reborn into this world. We should grieve that our physical bodies have the misfortune to live in an age after the passing of the Buddha; but we should be gratified that our hearts have established affinities with the Buddha's Law.

[20] When the Dharma is dispensed indiscriminately, then it will not have an effect on the action and speech (*shingo*) of the recipient. And when it does not affect action and speech, then, contrary to its purpose, it becomes a poison. Because the Dharma has no single fixed formulation (*musō*), there are those who say: "Well, then. Let's just lie down and do nothing at all!"

[21] The miraculous feats of the eminent priests of old are beyond comprehension, and we set them aside as a special case. But there are those without superhuman abilities but with tremendous dedication who, throwing caution to the wind and willing to chance death, travel to India to engage in various religious austerities. I think this is most splendid and enviable.

[22] In antiquity the foolish benefited from association with the wise. Nowadays, on the contrary, the foolish who associate with those who give the appearance of being profound are only confounded by pedantry and gradually turn away from the truth of the Dharma.

[23] Today there are no exceptionally good people or exceptionally bad ones: everyone is the same and we cannot distinguish the virtuous from the wicked. This is because of the Latter Age in which we live. The years and days pass, and in the end even such distinctions as we have now will fade.

[24] The pity of the Latter Age is that religious practice as prescribed by the Buddha now is secondary to learning. When the scholar has finished perusing all the characters of one work, he wants to go on to the next, simply to add to his store of what he has read. He has no intention of putting the ideas to use, of performing the prescribed religious practice. His heart is drawn to empty words and delusive concepts, and he appears lukewarm toward that which he takes to be the truth. With this example before me, it behooves me to examine my own heart, which has yet to attain Buddhahood.

[25] Choose your mentor cautiously after careful deliberation. The matter is not to be taken lightly, to be decided by parental dictate, the attraction of friends, or happenstance. The *Sutra on Perfect Enlightenment*[159] teaches one to "take as your teacher one who can cure the four ills of religious practice: seeking enlightenment through the performance of works (*sa*), through cessation of mental operations (*shi*), through acceptance of things as they are (*nin*), and through the elimination of the passions (*metsu*). This is explained in detail in the fourth scroll of the commentary[160] on the *Sutra on Perfect Enlightenment*.

[26] There are those whose personal behavior does not conform to the Law prescribed by the Buddha. But although they shamelessly offend against the regulations, people have great respect and confidence in them. We should

not regard this as a commendable state of affairs. In the *Accumulation of Jewels Sutra* the Buddha says: "In the Latter Days of the Law such things will happen because I will permit demonic powers of deception to appear. But the person who maintains Right Views [161] will see me by his side." [162]

[27] Even though all is transient for this body which does not remain long in this world, it is pathetic how we dote on the good opinion of others. Were we to live a thousand or ten thousand years, we should delight only in the good. It is shameful and stupid for one as ephemeral as lightning or morning dew to act badly even once.

[28] When one conducts a religious service, standing in for the Buddha to expound the Dharma, it is shameful to ramble on aimlessly while accepting donations from the faithful. For such priests "expounding the Dharma" *means* "accepting donations"; they have forgotten the Buddha's intention. The *Accumulation of Jewels Sutra* has injunctions against such behavior. In the section on expounding the Dharma, the monk says: "Because He is by the side of the priest who expounds the True Law, it is no different than if the Buddha were actually living in the world." [Cf. item 26]

[29] "How are we to behave?" people ask nowadays, understanding Buddhism as conventionally teaching that we are to leave this world of birth-and-death. But this is no more than the selfish attachment to the Nirvana of the Two Vehicles. [163] When I say that people speak without comprehending the way things are, it may seem that I am conceited; but I am just bemoaning the fact that the Law of the Buddha has declined. When I speak of the Decline of the Law (*hōmetsu*) I do not mean that the Law itself is lacking or deficient, but rather that a certain state of affairs has arisen. This is all explained in detail in *Questions on Manifestation.* [164] Look it up!

[30] The ordinary person does not even realize that he "has a nature" (*ushō*) [with the potential for enlightenment]. But Buddhism uses the idea of "no Buddha nature" (*mushō*) as an entrance to the Way. When we inquire if one can enter the Way with such attachment to self as we indulge in, we find that there is no such teaching in Buddhism. [165]

[31] The man who dwells on the faults of others is himself without virtue. Virtue belongs to those who cherish it, who regard virtue (*toku*) as something to be attained (*toku*). Those obsessed with the faults of others have no room for virtue to reside in themselves.

[32] Who am I to put on the airs of a Master? If the Buddha were still alive, I would not be considered to be even at the level of a novice.

[33] This is my usual advice to those who wish to pursue the religious life.

"What should you do to become a Buddha? How should you act to perfect yourself in the Way? Give up all hankering and transform yourself into a worthless fellow. Acting without any thought of self, simply eat when you are hungry and bundle up when you are cold. If you spend your life like this, then the earth may be hammered into pieces, but the Way of the Buddha will not collapse."

A bystander hearing this remark decides that it must be a good idea to become a worthless fellow. "That's what I'll do," he thinks to himself, proceeding to eat his fill and sleep to excess. Now he spends his time immersed in some passing fancy, or he passes the day in casual chatter without performing an act of the slightest benefit to others. Spending his time from morning till night without for a moment helping his temple, he imagines that he has truly become that worthless fellow who does nothing at all. But in fact he has been transformed into a worthless creature of the animal world. If a person acts like this, he will certainly be numbered among the denizens of hell. How could he possibly attain the fruit of Buddhahood which is Enlightenment?

What I mean by a "worthless fellow" is one who begins by throwing himself body and soul into the practice of the Way. He has no sluggishness of mind and is not moved by fancy to cultivate random thoughts. So his meditation is spontaneous and undisturbed. Acting with such determination day and night, he has no taste for the *nō* theater nor does he seek diversions. [166] He does not consciously think of becoming a Buddha nor does he vow to perfect himself in the Way. Casting aside social advancement, his great desire is to eliminate all hankering and to live having been transformed into a worthless fellow.

[34] It is a terrible thing to have become a monk and to have studied the Way for the purpose of becoming a Buddha; and then to tell yourself: "Don't think you can do it!" With such an attitude you will not attain perfection in the Way. I do believe that I can make people into Buddhas, and I would not lead them astray. If you trust and have confidence in me, then you will believe that these methods [which I prescribe will lead to Enlightenment]. And if you become a worthless fellow (cf.#33), passing your life like this, is this really such a worthless thing to do?

[35] The relationship between teacher and disciple is extremely important in Buddhism. If you do not comprehend the Dharma, then follow a ten-year-old novice who does and hear the Dharma from him, even if you are a hundred years of age.

Forget about praying to Buddha, reading the scriptures, and all the devices of Mahāyāna and Hīnayāna. Just ask your teacher what to do, step by step.

[36] People nowadays think that there is certainly nothing wrong in performing religious exercises other than those established by the Buddha. They are like wolves whose tails are snipped short [so that they can pass as dogs].[167]

[37] When your spiritual adviser is not about, you should follow the counsel of the senior monk present. Everyone should subordinate himself to others in this way. If people do not associate in harmony, how do they differ from tigers, wolves, or poisonous snakes?

[38] It seems that Ānanda's younger sister, who was a nun, became angry with the Venerable Kāśyapa and thereby fell into hell.[168] When we apply the moral of this incident to our own circumstances, we know that also in today's world anger toward a monk produces the karma for rebirth in hell. Unfortunately, we all transgress in this respect without thinking that such behavior is sinful.

[39] Enlightenment (*bodai*) initially is simply a slight stirring within the heart toward the Truth of the Dharma.[169] Although this stirring is still utterly undeveloped, it is inwardly in accord with the Two-fold Emptiness of persons and things (cf., #12), and so the individual will not consider himself to be superior to others. One who strives for integrity receives the protection of the Buddha even in this life. This protection brings him to accord with the truth, to have the power of faith, and to make his heart responsibly pliable toward the good.

[40] Every time you enter the practice hall, imagine that the living Buddha is there; and, in the presence of the living Tathāgata, set straight your aspirations. When you think of an object carved of wood or drawn in a picture as a living being, then it *is* a living being.[170]

[41] For the lone mendicant who energetically pursues the religious life at all costs it is important to seek out an untroubled area and a quiet place for his exercises. But for ordinary practitioners, it is better to form a group whose members mutually censure each others faults and encourage practice. The Buddha himself forbad groups of fewer than four. Practicing quietly in the corner of a room appeals to the slothful, and they try to deceive people by acting as if their hearts were committed to the Way. Their bodies in a peaceful state, they pass their days sleeping. Some build small independent quarters and others partition off an enclosure in which to live. And there they sleep day and night. It is like building your coffin while you are still alive, and

ensconcing yourself therein. If they act this way, when in the world will they ever become Buddhas? It's a pity!

We are born by chance in human form, we have the good fortune to don the surplice and to assume the name of one who enters into the Law of the Buddha and practices the Law. And then to do nothing at all—this is to return to the Three Evil Paths of transmigration! Deploring these conditions, the Venerable Bishop of Kenninji [Eisai, 1141–1215] said that he constructed a string of monastic quarters so that in each of them he could assemble those who had abandoned worldly ties that they might singlemindedly seek Enlightenment, that they might as friends in the faith cast off the myriad attachments and practice the Way. This is just what I think should be done. In addition to the profound merit accruing to these monks who make confession of their sins, they assemble together in one place to mutually improve each other's behavior. When did the Buddha ever instruct us to doze off in the corner of a room? The variety of 80,000 sacred teachings is enormous and there may be such a method; but I have yet to see it.

[42] From the time I was in a group of novices long ago, I have successively used the esoteric methods of Aizen Myōō and the Five Esoteric Bodhisattvas. I never thought of allying myself with some fine scholar, but sought rather to hold firmly to the Buddha Śākyamuni, if only to his representation on a scrap of paper. Had I been alive in the days of the Blessed Śākyamuni, I would have been among the least worthy of his disciples. What a sorry state of affairs that I should now administer a great number of monks and put on the airs of a preceptor, without having attained the virtue of the sages of long ago. This is not right.

Seated in the presence of the Buddha I thought to myself: "Being utterly without promise, what can I hope to accomplish in this life? Had I decided to become a warrior, by virtue of being born into a military family, I should already have been dead after my moment of shame in this short-lived world. But having opted for the religious life, my heart will be undefiled. Perhaps I will become a person of great influence in Buddhism." This is what I thought.

[43] Having by chance entered the religious life, I devote myself to what I have learned not as a useful path to release from delusion, but somehow to promote the miserable business of clerical advancement. And in the end, without any effort on my part, I will become ill; and no matter what I do, I will die. Ah, how are we to behave in this remote land in these Latter Days? I have become petty, a person without anything intelligent to say.

[44] Pride is like a mouse. When we are occupied at the esoteric practice platform, it slips in through the windows of the various houses of learning. I

always speak of the two ways it operates. If I do not know something, but, out of pride, do not ask and learn from another whose ability may be known, then my loss is great. And if I contemptuously talk down to one of lesser ability, what is the advantage? In both instances nothing is gained. Even with meager abilities, if one is judged superior to another, pride quickly arises.

[45] In Śākyamuni's day monks did not drink. The details of the Grave Prohibitions, such as those against killing, stealing and adultery, had not yet been clarified; so there was no way to measure how well one was observing the regulations. And there was not even a code of behavior which reflected the Sacred Teachings.

A person makes progress by refining what he has already learned, and making a start on what he has not yet learned. I should correct my failings by taking the Sacred Teachings as my norm and applying them to myself. This is discussed in detail in *Mandalas Explained*.[171] It is worth looking up.

[46] Observing humans from antiquity to the present, we see that the greedy, the double-dealers with no apparent sense of shame, never become true followers of Buddhism. The Buddha mentioned this in the sutras, and it is also to be found in the commentaries; there is not the least discrepancy between them.

Although I have not consulted the books on physiognomy carried by those who practice the art, I judge a person from his appearance, basing my conjecture on the implications of statements by the Buddha and patriarchs. Eight or nine times out of ten my judgment does not differ from that of the physiognomist. In the past and at present high-minded Buddhists have come from among those with a cultivated disposition. Composing eulogies or having a taste for *waka* and linked verse are not indispensable for the practice of religion; nevertheless, those whose feelings are cultivated by such pursuits are quickly refined by the Buddha's Law, developing wisdom and a most exalted disposition. The man with a vulgar disposition may attain results if he applies himself to the religious exercises. But because of his tendency to view everything in terms of profit, he looks foolish. You would do well to teach the Law of Buddha to those with sincere disposition and gentle refinement from childhood on.

[47] As the years and months advance in these Latter Days, crookedness begins to look straight, and there are few with a sincere disposition. As a result, nothing we do can be brought to perfection.

[48] When I was living at this temple [172] in my youth, I had to wipe away the tears that welled up in spite of myself as I intently watched all the monks come together for prayer. The twelve watches of the day were spent entirely

in diversions. They had no real faith, so that if by chance one of them came before the image of the Buddha, he would not exert himself to pray even for a moment. They were utterly uncouth in the way they carried themselves— their eyes, countenance, hands, their way of sitting, and the manner in which they circumambulated the altar. By behaving this way, they acquired no merit whatever for reciting the sutras and chanting mystic formulas but only brought disquiet to themselves by performing the rites perfunctorily so that others would notice. They did not safeguard the people nor did they require the obligation for the alms received from the faithful. Is there any doubt that they will be reborn as animals? The Buddhist with a sense of responsibility will waste few moments during the twelve watches of the day. At least, don't act as those monks did.

When such monks happen to appear in public, they have no sense of shame about how they look, performing religious ceremonies without sincerity. The ancients called this perfunctory devotion, "the prayer of a mortar going up and down." When you worship, compose your mind and feel that you are in the presence of the living Buddha. Then when you pray: "Praise to the Lord of Great Grace, the Tathāgata Śākyamuni," the various Buddhas and Tathāgatas will guide and respond to you. Through the union of devotee and deity, you will obtain merit and eliminate sinful action. I think that such great robbers and frauds as those priests who go through life without sincere faith are not to be found even among the laity. It is despicable for them to appropriate this Teaching as a livelihood, a Teaching provided by a series of Buddhas coming into the world to bring sentient beings to Buddhahood.

[49] From the single individual at the top of society to his ten thousand subjects beneath, laymen, each according to their station in life, share benefits which result from maintaining a livelihood in the family profession. After a monk abandons the world, he is not to share in such benefits. Even if he receives food and clothing from family and relations, these are just the same as alms donated by the faithful. It seriously violates the principles of Buddhism for a monk to be helped by, or to support, his relatives, simply looking out for his material needs in a faithless and idle manner instead of opening the mind-ground [173] and keeping his behavior unsullied by observing the precepts. When a person seriously violates these principles, he cannot escape the karma for his bad actions, and there can be no doubt that he will fall into hell. Appropriating the Law of the Buddha to his own ends, he administers the temple property saying that he prays for the country, and he accepts donations

saying that he prays for the benefit of the devotee. If he prays and performs esoteric rites with the Three Activities [of body, speech and thought], undisciplined, he simply violates the precepts without compunction from morning till night. As a result, he turns the ceremonial offerings and donations into occasions for violating the Five Commandments and the Ten Grave Injunctions—a deplorable state of affairs even for these Latter Days.

It seems that those who are most deeply deluded are not even aware of their delusion; and that those who are excessively immoral are not self-critical enough to see their own excesses as a great sin. By virtue of having gravely violated the principles of Buddhism, they will surely fall into hell. So when you all consider that you have become priests, even if you are not able to comprehend the Dharma, you should at least behave with concern that you do not lose your human form [for rebirth in a lower level of existence].

[50] We should earnestly awaken our faith in the Three Treasures of Buddhism. Even if we were to hear that it is sinful to rely on the Three Treasures, what could befall us if we were immovable in our faith? When there is something we really want to do, we do it, even though we have heard that a bad act engenders bad results. But everyone believes that [far from being a sinful act], we obtain merit by trusting in the Three Treasures by virtue of the good karma from our having heard the True Law in a previous life. [Why, then, do we not do so?]

[51] By laying a small tree across a narrow stream, we act to relieve another's hardship. Although the help is minimal, our sympathy for others gradually deepens and in due course brings us to unsurpassed enlightenment. Everyone somehow feels that this is so. It is simply an example of the Four Universal Methods (*shishōbōgyō*) of almsgiving, affectionate speech, altruistic conduct, and accommodation to others, which covers all the stages of Bodhisattva activity from beginning to end.

[52] The priest has no other business but to become single-minded, to perfect his religious aspiration, to eliminate occasions for wasting time, and to practice the Way of the Buddha. If he is lazy, he would do better to remove his clerical attire and become a layman, for the sins of such a priest will be grave.

For the most part, no implements are necessary for the practice of the Buddha's Way, which consists simply in waking to the sound of the wind in the pines, taking the bright moon as one's friend, and being earnest in one's comings and goings. If, alone in the practice hall, you clear your heart, what other friends do you need? And even if you were to fall into hell through some misdeed, it seems that Bodhisattvas abide even there for our salvation. Because it is said that from the very beginning there have been Bodhisattvas in hell, the place is not to be feared. One who has the proper determination to follow the Law of the Buddha is fully and immediately aware of what behavior is beyond reproach, and he strives to eliminate even his minor faults.

> I write this on the second day of the sixth month in Katei 4 [1238] at Kōzanji's Akai Shōbō. After making inquiries, I was able to augment the work.
>
> His disciple, the mendicant novice, Kōshin

Myōe thus represents the ideal monk, not the partisan leader. Hōnen's reputation rests firmly on his advocacy of the *nembutsu*, Eisai and Dōgen are primarily associated with Zen meditation practices, and Nichiren is known for his devotion to the *Lotus Sutra*. But Myōe is remembered only incidentally as the would-be reformer of Kegon. In the popular mind of his day he is the perfect recluse, the moralist who tells us that we are to act according to our lot in life, whatever that might be among a variety of possibilities.

CHAPTER FOUR

Hossō's Jōkei and the Kōfukuji Petition

n the autumn of 1205 the scholarly recluse Jōkei (Gedatsubō, 1155–1213), representing the Hossō sect's Kōfukuji in Nara, drafted a petition to the court asking that Hōnen's popular teaching of sole reliance on the Buddha Amida be suppressed. The Pure Land (Jōdo) sect had been initiated three decades earlier when Hōnen (Genkū, 1133-1212) left Kurodani on Tendai's Mt. Hiei for the Ōtani district in Kyoto, where he began publicly to advocate the Sole-practice Calling upon the Name of the Buddha [Amida] (*senju nembutsu*). Jōkei's nine-article petition argued that Hōnen, or at least his followers, were violating basic assumptions which for centuries had been shared by all sects within the Buddhist tradition, and that the flourishing young movement was a clear danger to the state.

It is tempting to dismiss the indictment as another dreary example of the *odium theologicum* latent in every ideological enterprise, and to sympathize with Hōnen's band of religious idealists spreading a message of hope to the common people in the face of a corrupt clerical establishment fearing a loss of prestige. But the reality is not so simple. Hōnen was a scholar whose personal behavior was above reproach; but so also were his two major opponents: Jōkei, and the Kegon reformer, Myōe (Kōben, 1173-1232). Moreover, devotion to the Buddha Amida had long been incorporated within the practices of the traditional Eight Sects [174] of Japanese Buddhism. Why, then, was there such concern over a movement which promised to revive acceptance of the Buddha's Teaching, whose institutions were widely recognized to be in need of reform?

This chapter will focus on Jōkei's perception of the issues as expressed in his *Kōfukuji Petition* (Kōfukuji sōjō). There are other perspectives, amply defended elsewhere. But here I would like to speak for Jōkei. And rather than summarizing or paraphrasing the *Petition*, I wish to present a complete and reasonably faithful translation so that the reader can examine the charges for himself. An extract or summary would have permitted me to skirt a number of treacherous passages, but only a complete translation will serve my purpose. Selection cannot avoid partiality, and what might seem negligible to one reader could easily be crucial for another. I will begin with short sketches of Jōkei the monk and the Pure Land movement which prompted his criticism.

Jōkei's World. Jōkei's grandfather was Fujiwara Michinori (d. 1160), "a clever and unscrupulous man" (Sansom 1958, p. 256), better known to history by his clerical name, Shinzei. Although Emperor Go-Shirakawa (1127–92; r. 1155–58) retained his throne through the Hōgen disturbance of 1156, he abdicated in 1158 to become one of Japan's most powerful retired emperors (*In*) until his death four decades later. An adviser in his early intrigues was Shinzei, who was opposed by Fujiwara Nobuyori (1133–59); these two factions were supported respectively by Taira Kiyomori (1118–81) and Minamoto Yoshitomo (1123–60), father of Yoritomo and Yoshitsune. The Taira clan, with Kiyomori as its head, was victorious in the Heiji Disturbance of 1159, but Shinzei perished in the conflict. He has a prominent role in the *Heiji monogatari* account of the war, and he is the focus of the second of the three famous picture scrolls (*emaki*) portraying these events ("Shinzei"; for a translation see Reischauer 1951, pp. 375–457). (See also Chart 3.)

Three of Shinzei's sons had close ties with Jōkei. The first was his father, Sadanori, who was exiled to the province of Oki in 1159 after an abortive attempt to avoid punishment by taking Holy Orders (Reischauer 1951, pp. 410–11, 429; Nagazumi and Shimada 1961, pp. 196, 213). We do not know what happened to him after this. Another of Shinzei's sons was Kakuken (1131–1212), exiled to Iyo but later (1189) abbot (*bettō*) of the Kōfukuji. Jōkei studied Hossō doctrine with Kakuken and had a close association with him until his death, only a year before Jōkei's. Finally, the popular preacher Chōken (ca. 1125–1205),[175] also one of Shinzei's twelve sons banished in 1159, is known to have participated on at least one occasion in a ceremony with both Kakuken and Jōkei (Tanaka 1971, p. 462). An exhaustive biography of Jōkei would doubtless reveal the influence of many family connections.

Jōkei, also known as Gedatsubō in his priestly life, took the tonsure in 1165, as early as his eleventh year. The details of his youth at the Kōfukuji are sketchy but his later eminence as a scholar suggests that his time was spent in diligent study. Then in 1180 the Taira forces under Kiyomori's son, Shigehira, laid waste to the Kōfukuji in addition to destroying the colossal Buddha at Nara's Tōdaiji. The *Heike monogatari* (V:14; Kitagawa and Tsuchida 1975, pp. 340–44) says thousands of priests and laymen perished in the flames. Jōkei survived; but to have witnessed the destruction of what to him was the very center of Japanese Buddhism was a terrible shock. What more was needed to confirm the fact that the world was well into the period of the Decline of the Law (*mappō*)?[176] For the next decade Jōkei lived at the

An'yōin (The Hall of Peace and Rest),[177] a subtemple of the ravaged Kōfukuji. Restoration of the major structures was not begun until 1189, when the influential (Fujiwara) Kujō Kanezane (1149–1207) came to Nara to initiate the rebuilding of the Golden Hall (*Kondō*).[178] A great dedication service of the restored monastery was held in 1193 (Sansom 1958, p. 332).

It was around this time that Jōkei attracted the attention of Kanezane and others of the nobility, who admired his skill as celebrant and preacher. But his life as a fashionable cleric did not last long. In 1192, after a decade of deliberation, Jōkei decided to adopt the life of a recluse (*tonsei*) at the mountain temple of Kasagidera, about twelve kilometers as the crow flies northeast of the Kōfukuji. The temple's main object of worship is a great stone image of the future Buddha, Maitreya (Miroku Nyorai), to whom Jōkei had a special devotion. Kanezane argued that it was only a further sign of the decline of the Buddha's Law when competent monks withdrew from religious participation in the world. But Jōkei was not to be dissuaded, replying that he had made a vow to the Great Deity at Kasuga, the Shintō shrine adjacent to, and traditionally associated with, Hossō's Kōfukuji and the Fujiwara clan. In his *Kasuga Daimyōjin hotsugammon* (Votive Declaration to the Great Deity of Kasuga), which dates from this time (Tanaka 1971, p. 463), he states that he was waiting expectantly for birth in Maitreya's Tuṣita Heaven, the Paradise of Satisfied Gods;[179] and that until this was attained, he would devote himself to Maitreya's provisional manifestation (*gongen*), that is, the Great Deity of Kasuga.[180] Both Jōkei and his friend Myōe are associated in popular tradition for their unusual devotion to Kasuga.

Jōkei moved to Kasagidera in the autumn of 1193. For some years he had been engaged in a collaborative project to copy the entire six hundred fascicles of Hsüan-tsang's translation of the *Great Perfection of Wisdom Sutra*.[181] We are told that Jōkei himself worked on the section known as the *Perfection of Wisdom in 150 Lines*,[182] completing it at Kasagidera in 1195. To house the collection Jokei built a three-bayed, hexagonal sutra turret in black lacquer. This was consecrated late in 1195, together with a monastic building called Hannyadai ("Wisdom Heights"), and monastic living quarters. His uncle and old mentor, the Kōfukuji abbot Kakuken, was present for the dedication; and it may have been Jōkei's life as a recluse that induced him to resign his administrative post. When his proposal was rejected, he retired to the Tsubosakadera, south of Nara.

It is this time and place which define Jōkei in popular legend. Mujū's *Collection of Sand and Pebbles* (Shasekishū, 1279–83) 1:5 is a short vignette of Jōkei and Myōe (Morrell 1985).

"I regard Myōebō and Gedatsubō as my Tarō and Jirō," declared the Great Deity of Kasuga Shrine. When the two men were once on a pilgrimage to the great shrine, all the deer on Kasuga Plain bent their knees and knelt out of respect for them. . . . [183]

When the venerable Gedatsubō, living at Kasagi in a secluded retreat which which he called Wisdom Heights, invited the deity for a visit, it assumed the form of a child and rode on his shoulders. The god composed this verse:

Ware yukan	I will come,
Yukite maboran	And having arrived will protect
Hannyadai	Wisdom Heights
Shaka no minori no	As long as the Holy Law
Aran kagiri wa	Of Śākyamuni may survive. [184]

Once, in a vacant practice hall at Wisdom Heights, the voice of the deity proclaimed:

Ware wo shire	Know who I am!
Shakamuni butsu no	Now that Śākyamuni Buddha
Yo ni idete	Has appeared,
Sayakeki tsuki no	Think of me as the clear moon
Yo wo terasu to wa	Shining over the land. [185]

It is said that the deity constantly discoursed on Buddhist doctrine. Indeed, how fortunate and enviable the experience of those who actually heard what took place when Śākyamuni was in the world . . .

The *Collection of Sand and Pebbles* also relates Jōkei's visit to Ise Shrine, where he saw in a lotus pond the souls of those who were to be reborn (I:2), and the story of his disciple Shōen (I:6), who visited a hell directly beneath Kasuga plain, where it was revealed to him that the Kasuga Deity of the Third Shrine (Sannomiya) was in fact the bodhisattva Jizō who every morning relieves the suffering of the unfortunate residents (I:6). Both the Shōen episode and Jōkei's invitation to the Kasuga deity are depicted in the *Kasuga Gongen genki-e* (Illustrated Record of the Miracles of the Kasuga Avatars) of 1309. [186]

For a decade and a half Kasagidera was the arena for Jōkei's religious practice. He meditated, wrote, copied sutras, constructed buildings, and performed ceremonies—all as a recluse with the hope of birth in Maitreya's Pure Land. The retreat was far enough away from the traffic of Nara and Kyoto for a life of seclusion, but also close enough for Jōkei gradually to be drawn in, willy-nilly, to these centers of religious and political activity. By 1205, when he drafted the *Kōfukuji Petition*, we find him increasingly involved in public events.

Jōkei was now fifty. During a half century he had witnessed much to dismay the conscientious follower of the Way. He was born just as Heian society was about to be swept away by insurrections and civil unrest. His immediate family fell victim to these in their early stages, and Jōkei took the tonsure while still a child. At the beginning of the Gempei War (1180–85) he saw the great temples of Nara destroyed, followed by five years of brutal conflict. Peace came with the defeat of the Taira at the Battle of Dannoura and the establishment of a military government in Kamakura, but public morale was low and people were sure that bad times still lay ahead as social and religious institutions continued to decline during the final period of the Law. Society was appalled by the laxity of the clergy.

Then in the midst of this malaise a new cult sprang up which claimed that calling on the name of the Buddha Amida was the only religious practice possible in the present degenerate age, and that every other belief and observance was not only useless but counterproductive. The conventional rules of morality need not be observed if salvation could be attained solely by reliance on the Other Power (*tariki*) of Amida. Is it any wonder that Jōkei, Myōōe, [187] and others were alarmed and called for civil intervention, in spite of the fact that doctrinal Accommodation (*hōben*) was an integral part of the Mahāyāna? They could tolerate anything but intolerance.

Hōnen himself evidently did not endorse the extravagant claims of some of his followers. But, after all, he had initiated the movement and was clearly its focus. If he could not, or would not, control those who would undermine the very foundations of the Mahāyāna, then it would have to be done by Imperial Edict. And so, speaking not only for Hossō but for all of the Eight Sects of Buddhism, in the tenth month of 1205 Jōkei drew up the *Kōfukuji Petition*.

In 1208 Jōkei retired to Kaijusenji, several kilometers west-northwest of Kasagidera. The temple, which seems to have been a private villa owned by the current abbot of the Kōfukuji, Gaen, was a spot sacred to Kannon. In his late years Jōkei had a special devotion to Kannon and prayed for birth on Mount Potalaka. [188] Moreover, in the *Kanjin'i shōjōemmyō no koto* (On the Purity and Clarity for Contemplating Mind), dictated from his sickbed in the middle of the first month of 1213, the year he died, Jōkei states that he "believes deeply in the Western Region [of Amida]" (Tanaka 1971, p. 468). Elsewhere he consciously merges devotion to Amida with that directed to Miroku. The name and characteristics of a specific object of worship might differ, but ultimately they were all expressions of the Dharma. Provisional methods might vary, but what is ultimately basic for release from illusion (*shutsuri*) is the experience of Consciousness Only (*yuishikikan*), according to the *Shugyō yōshō* (Essentials of Practice) dictated four days before the *Kanjin'i.*

Professor Tanaka sees Jōkei's characteristic religious stance in the notion of *sange* ("repentance," "penitence," or even "resolution"), [189] that is, the recognition of one's limitations due to the accumulation of karma, and the need for good works to counteract it. In this Jōkei differs from Hōnen's Pure Land movement, in which merely calling on the name of Amida guarantees birth in his paradise.

> Release from illusion depends on one's personal limitations. It isn't that we have not heard the Law, but simply that our hearts do not rise to the occasion. Is this not because there is a disparity between the specific teaching and those who hear it (*ki*)? Because there is a difference between one's aspirations and one's lot in life? I wish to engage in some great-spirited religious endeavor, but my nature cannot support it. And even when I try to perform some trifling act of merit, I cannot depend on my heart to carry it through. I question the sage elders whenever we happen to meet, but I get no reply. . . . (From the *Kanjin'i shōjōemmyō no koto,* cited in Tanaka 1971, p. 469)

Jōkei was also a prolific writer on Hossō theory, but none of this is available in translation. He was the first in a line of distinguished thinkers who created a minor Hossō scholastic revival during the Kamakura period. The school's abstruse idealism never excited the Japanese in spite of its honored place in the Buddhist philosophical tradition from Asaṅga (Mujaku) and Vasubandhu (Seshin) in the 4–5th centuries A.D. through Hsüan-tsang (Genjō, 600–664) and K'uei Ch'i (Kiki, 632–82; also known as Tz'u-en). Jōkei's disciple Kakuhen (1175–1258) was the teacher of Ryōhen (1194–1252), whose *Kanjin kakumusho* (The Compendium [Which Teaches How] to Awaken from the Dreams [of Illusion] by Contemplating the Mind) was once thought to have been written by Jōkei himself. The *Compendium* is today believed to be Ryōhen's work, partly on the basis of minor theoretical differences between the two thinkers (Weinstein 1965, pp. 6–7); but it can still provide us with a sense of the complex conceptual tradition in which Jōkei played a prominent role quite apart from his public activities.

The Sole-practice Calling Movement. In 1175 Hōnen established the (Amidist) Pure Land sect (Jōdoshū) on the ground that the Sole-practice of calling on the Name of the Buddha [Amida] (*senju nembutsu*) was the one method appropriate to the period of the Decline of the Law. Considerable confusion subsequently arose as to whether Hōnen meant that the *nembutsu* was merely the *best* among many or the *sole viable* practice. Earlier Amidist devotion had understood *nembutsu* as "meditation'" (*kannen*) on the Buddha rather than as "invocation of his name" (*shōmyō*; cf., *Petition*, Article 7). Hōnen based his program on three sutras which seemed to support the latter interpretation, as wall as on the authority of a number of prominent Indian, Chinese and Japanese patriarchs, including Vasubandhu,[190] Shan-tao (Zendō, 613–81) and Tendai's Genshin (942–1017). He had lectured on these sutras at Nara's Tōdaiji as early as 1190, while Jōkei was still living at the nearby Kōfukuji. Jōkei may well have attended these sessions, but it is not likely that he was present at the Ōhara Controversy (Ōhara dangi) of 1186, as tradition claims. On this occasion it is said that Hōnen successfully defended his position against the criticism of several learned scholars belonging to the older sects, and that 300 went over to his cause. But some modern historians doubt the importance, or even the historicity of this event. In any case, Jōkei would have had ample opportunity to hear and meet Hōnen, perhaps under the auspices of their mutual friend, Kanezane.

The Three Pure Land Sutras (*Jōdo sambukyō*) chosen by Hōnen as the scriptural basis of his movement are the following:

1. *The Larger Pure Land Sutra.* The *Muryōjukyō*, literally "The Amitāyus Sutra," T. 360, is thought to have been translated into Chinese in A.D. 252 by Sanghavarman. Popularly known as the (Larger) *Sukhāvatī-vyūha* ("Pure Land") *Sūtra*, it relates the career of the Buddha Amida as the bodhisattva Dharmākara (Hōzō), who made 48 vows to save sentient beings. For the Pure Land movement, the eighteenth vow is central:

   "Even when I am able to attain Buddhahood, if sentient beings of the ten quarters, with sincerity and faith, desire to be born in my land by practicing up to ten thoughts [i.e., chanting the name of Buddha Amitāyus] and are not born there, I will not accept supreme enlightenment—only excluding those who commit the five atrocities and abuse the True Dharma." (Kiyota 1978, pp. 256, 274).[191]

2. *The Amitābha Sūtra.* The *Amidakyō*, T. 366, is Kumārajīva's translation (ca. 402) of the (Smaller) *Sukhāvatī-vyūha* ("Pure Land") *Sūtra*. In describing Amida's paradise and recommending the invocation of his name it summarizes the argument of the *Larger Pure Land Sutra*.

3. *The Sutra of Meditation on Amida Buddha.* The *Kammuryōjukyō* (T. 365; *Amitāyur-dhyāna-sūtra*) tells of Śākyamuni's appearance to the imprisoned Queen Vaidehī, whom he instructs in various forms of meditation on the Buddha Amitāyus with the promise that even the worst sinner can attain birth in Amida's Pure Land if he recites Amida's name ten times at the moment of death. This sole reliance on Amida as savior

differs from the visualization of Amida suggested by the sutra's name. (See especially Articles 6 and 7 of the *Petition*.)

At Kanezane's request, as early as 1198 Hōnen had compiled his basic statement of religious policy, the *Senjaku [hongan nembutsu] shū* (Collection of Passages [bearing on the Original Vow of Amida]), which was not made public until after his death in 1212. Hōnen evidently felt that his message would be misunderstood by some of his followers, and that the movement did not always reflect his own thinking. He remarked at the end of the *Senjakushū*: "It is only hoped that once you have graciously glanced at this writing you will hide it in some cavity in the wall and will not leave it before the window, to keep slanderers of the Dharma from falling into evil paths." (Bandō 1974, p. 45) For Hōnen faith was essential, and good works were not only useless but an assertion of egoism and lack of confidence in the Buddha's compassion. To some it seemed to follow that if good actions were not a help to salvation, bad actions were not a hindrance.

Hōnen was aware of the excesses to which his statements seemed to lend support and of the charges brought against his movement because of them. His first major confrontation with the religious establishment came in 1204. Hearing that the Tendai priests on Mt. Hiei had gathered to ask Shinshō, the current abbot, to prohibit the Sole-practice Calling, Hōnen anticipated the action by sending the prelate a Seven-Article Pledge (*Shichikajō kishōmon*) supported by 190 of his disciples, together with his own personal letter of pledge. [192] The Seven-Article Pledge, also signed by Hōnen's radical followers (Jūren, Anraku [=Junsai], Gyōkū), stated that Hōnen's followers should not criticize other religious methods nor ignore the regulations of the *vinaya*. It anticipated many of the objections of Jōkei's Petition of the following year, and we must assume that Hōnen and his disciples signed the document in good faith. But there was a credibility gap between the establishment and the Pure Land movement, in addition to the communication gap between the movement and Hōnen. In the Summary at the end of the *Petition* Jōkei makes the curious charge that at the time of their encounter with the Hiei monks, Hōnen's disciples were telling his lay followers that the Shōnin spoke with forked tongue, and that they should pay no attention to what they might have heard!

Jōkei's *Kōfukuji Petition*, submitted in the tenth month of 1205, would probably have caused little official reaction were it not for a scandal that shook the court the following year. While the Retired Emperor Go-Toba was on a pilgrimage to Kumano in the twelfth month of 1206, Jūren and Anraku, after celebrating a Pure Land service at the Palace, were said to have spent the night with some ladies-in-waiting. After Go-Toba's return Jūren and Anraku were beheaded in the second month of 1207, while Hōnen was defrocked and he and several of his disciples were sent into exile (Coates and Ishizuka 1925, pp. 598–606; Matsunaga 1976, pp. 66–68).

We may be inclined to see Jūren and Anraku as innocent victims of a plot to discredit the *senju nembutsu* movement. However, the poet and historian Jien (Jichin, 1155–1225) did not view the incident in this light. Jien was Kanezane's brother, four times abbot of Mt. Hiei, and he personally befriended Hōnen after his return from exile. But in the *Gukanshō* (Miscellany of Ignorant Views, 1219) Jien sustains the charges against Jūren and Anraku and considers the entire affair to have been handled with leniency.[193]

Be that as it may, Hōnen was exiled to Tosa on the island of Shikoku until the end of 1207, when he was permitted to return to the mainland but not to enter the capital. For the next four years he lived at Kachiodera in Settsu (a suburb of modern Osaka), finally being permitted to return to Kyoto late in 1211, where Jien provided him with living quarters at a small temple in Ōtani. Hōnen died early in 1212.

Hōnen's relationship to the movement he founded is somewhat puzzling. Although he defended the *nembutsu* as "invocation" (*shōmyō*), he himself was given to meditations and visualizations of the Pure Land (Bandō 1974, pp. 40–42). The movement tended to antinomianism, but Hōnen observed the priestly regulations, as even Jōkei seemed to recognize (Article 8); and he did seem genuinely to reject the exclusive attitude of many of his followers. All of which ". . . has led modern critics to maintain that Hōnen was actually not very different from his Tendai predecessors" (Matsunaga 1976, p. 61). In this he may be not unlike his younger contemporary, Eisai (1141–1215), the "founder" of Kamakura Zen (Collcutt 1981, pp. 36–40).

Jōkei's Petition to the Court. Recent scholarship has dispelled any doubts about Jōkei's authorship of the Petition, although no manuscript of the work survives from the Kamakura period. For the text of my translation I have followed the modern printed edition included in Kamata Shigeo and Tanaka Hisao, eds. *Kyū kamakura bukkyō* (Tokyo: Iwanami Shoten, 1971; *Nihon shisō taikei* 15). This is a strict transcription (*tendoku*) into Japanese of the *kambun* original, also attached, whose *teihon* is a 1909 photograph, held by the University of Tokyo Historiographical Institute, of a Temmon 8 (1539) manuscript. The modern editor has corrected this against a Tempō 9 (1838) manuscript held by the Tōdaiji, and a rather different version included in the *Dainihon bukkyō zensho* based on a manuscript of Eishō 18 (1521) (Tanaka 1971, pp. 509-510). I am deeply indebted to Professor Tanaka's scholarship in almost every detail of this study of Jōkei's life and the *Petition*.

THE KŌFUKUJI PETITION
(Jōkei Gedatsu Shōnin's document in the matter of Hōnen Shōnin's exile, with addenda) [194]

Nine Articles of Error
1. The Error of Establishing a New Sect
2. The Error of Designing New Images for Worship
3. The Error of Slighting Śākyamuni
4. The Error of Neglecting the Varieties of Good Deeds
5. The Error of Turning One's Back on the Holy Gods of Shintō
6. The Error of Ignorance Concerning the Pure Lands
7. The Error of Misunderstanding the Nembutsu
8. The Error of Vilifying the Followers of Śākyamuni
9. The Error of Bringing Disorder to the Nation

The Overseers and Superiors of the Kōfukuji
offer this sincere statement to the court
with awe and respect.
A petition
requesting that an Imperial Edict be issued
to rectify the doctrine of Sole-practice
Calling upon the Name of the Buddha long
advocated by the monk Genkū [i.e., Hōnen].

In respectfully calling to your attention the facts of the case, we would remind you that there is a certain monk known to the world as Hōnen who has established a Nembutsu Sect which promotes the Sole-practice (*senju*) exercise. Although what he says resembles what was taught by the ancient sages, his intention is for the most part at variance with their basic thought. In order to concentrate on the substance of his offenses, we have summarized them in nine articles.

Article 1. *The Error of Establishing a New Sect*
Since the Buddha's Dharma has come to the east [from India through

China to Japan] there have been Eight Sects in our land. Some were transmitted by holy men from foreign regions, others by eminent priests of our own country who went abroad to seek their benefits. In those days the illustrious monarchs of old promulgated these sects by decree, and miraculous sites and noted places became widespread, as appropriate to circumstances. But we have never heard of anyone establishing a new sect, opening up another way, since middle antiquity (*chūko*). Is this not because the Buddha's response to human needs was adequate and the Dharma was suited to the times? Generally speaking, the way to establish a new sect is first to distinguish the relative shallowness and depth of its doctrinal path, and to examine carefully what is provisional and what is absolute in the sectarian position, drawing away from the superficial and penetrating to the profound, understanding the provisional while taking refuge in the absolute. Although polemics abound as to which is greater or lesser, before or behind, there is for each person one teaching he cannot leave, one method he cannot go beyond. Searching his own limits, he finds his proper sect. It is like the various currents finding their source in the great sea, or the multitudes paying court to a single individual.

When we designate as a separate sect those who call on the name of the Buddha for birth in his Pure Land, then we reduce all the sacred teachings or our era merely to calling on the name (*shōmyō*) of the single Buddha Amida; and taking refuge in the Three Treasures is no more than birth in the single Western Region [of Amida]! Is Genkū such a great patriarch as to transmit the light of the teaching, the first to found a sect now in these Latter Days? Shall we call him the model for a thousand ages, like [the Hossō sect's] Chihō [fl. ca. 706] of Kudara, or [the Ritsu sect's] Chien-chen [Ganjin, 687–763] of the Great T'ang? Is this one the glory of ten thousand generations, like [Shingon's] Kōbō [=Kūkai, 774–835] or [Tendai's] Dengyō [=Saichō, 767–822] of Mount Hiei? [195] Even if one were to claim that his teaching had been handed down from antiquity and did not just now commence, who would go out to meet this wise man to receive his oral instructions? And then, with a certain amount of religious understanding, go forth to admonish and instruct? Even if he were a man of ability and virtue, it is only proper that he address the court and wait for the imperial permission to preach. It is quite improper to establish a sect privately.

Article 2. *The Error of Designing New Images for Worship*

In a number of places recently people have been trifling with a kind of pictorial representation known popularly as "The Mandala Embracing All and

Forsaking None" (Sesshu fusha mandara).[196] In front of the Tathāgata Amida is a large group of people. The Buddha emits rays of light (*kōmyō*), some of which zig-zag to shine to the side while others go out to return to the point of origin. Around a group of scholars of the exoteric sects and Shingon practitioners are others cultivating their own "roots of merit" (*zengon*), holding various sutras and reciting sacred incantations. But the light shines only on the company of those performing the Sole-practice Calling on the Name of the Buddha. Those who see representations of the hells fear committing sins, but those who see this mandala regret practicing good works. This is generally the tenor of this teaching. And the Shōnin says: "The statement that Amida will embrace all and forsake none who call upon the Buddha's name is in the scriptures.[197] I am entirely without blame."

But it is unreasonable to claim that if a person, in his single-minded practice of other good actions, were never to call upon Amida, he would thereby be excluded from the rays which truly embrace all (*jitsu ni sesshu*). [By his serious commitment he, in effect,] already delights in the Western Paradise and also calls upon Amida. So why should he be alienated from the light rays of great compassion merely because he follows other routes to the same goal?

Article 3. *The Error of Slighting Śākyamuni*

What sensible person does not know that although the various Buddhas of the Three Worlds are impartial in their compassion, the favors and blessings bestowed upon us by the teacher of our epoch [Śākyamuni] are uniquely beneficial? Now the Sole-practice people say: "With our bodies we do not worship other Buddhas and with our voices we do not call upon other Names." This statement about "other Buddhas and other Names" refers to Śākyamuni and the other Buddhas. You Single-practicers—whose disciples are you? Who taught you this name of Amida? Who showed you this Pure Land of Peace and Rest (*an'yō jōdo*)? You are to be pitied that during your life in these Latter Days you should forget the name of our Original Teacher. Neither Buddhamitra nor Dharmapriya[198] committed such a transgression, but they were censured by the sages. Shan-tao says in his writing *In Praise [of Birth in the Pure Land]*:[199]

> Praise to the Three Treasures
> of Śākyamuni and the other Buddhas!
> Now I prostrate myself in veneration.
> Praise to all the Three Treasures

within all worlds innumerable as particles of dust
throughout the regions of space
in the Ten Directions and the Three Worlds!
Now I prostrate myself in adoration.

From this statement the eminent monk's views should be perfectly clear. The community of monks takes refuge in the Buddha—in all of the Buddhas. And if we do not discriminate against the various Buddhas, how much more so should we not slight our Original Teacher [Śākyamuni]!

Article 4. *The Error of Neglecting the Varieties of Good Deeds*

Numerous sectarian positions arise as occasion demands, and we partake of the good ambrosial medicine [of the Buddha's varying teachings] each according to our karmic predispositions. They are all aspects of the True Law which our great teacher Śākyamuni gained for us by difficult and painful labors over innumerable aeons. Now to be attached to the name of a single Buddha is completely to obstruct the paths essential for deliverance. It is not merely the action of a single individual but a warning to the entire nation; not merely a matter of neglect, but something approaching insolence. Meanwhile, groundless rumors arise like clouds and heretical biases well up like springs. Some say that those who recite the *Lotus Sutra* will fall into hell; others state that those who maintain the *Lotus Sutra* as a karmic cause for rebirth in the Pure Land slander the Mahāyāna. And so forth. Hearing such opinions, people who earlier recited the eight or ten scrolls [of the *Lotus*][200] now reject it forever. Moreover, they repent of their former recitation as a sin.[201] Their original exercises, which they now abandon, were habits deeply rooted in past karma; but the *nembutsu*, which they have come to through calculation, has not yet acquired the perfume of sustained practice. Caught in the middle, there are many who raise their eyes to heaven and lament.

Apart from these [who reject the *Lotus*] are others who once took refuge in the *Garland*[202] and *Wisdom*[181] sutras, or who developed spiritual affinities with esoteric [Shingon] or [Tendai] meditation (*shikan*) practices. Now, eight or nine out of ten give them up. As numerous as clods of dirt or sand are those who belittle and ridicule the building of temples and pagodas and the fashioning of sacred images. Lacking in both virtues and wisdom, they have little to hope for in the present or in the future.

The Shōnin is an intelligent man and certainly has no intention willfully to slander the Law! It is simply that among his disciples not a few are fools who are unable to comprehend the situation and so commit these evils. No doubt it is the usual case of some understanding the root of an issue and others only the branches. Long ago when Meditation Master Hsin-hsing [Shingyō Zenji, 541–594] established what was to be done during the Three Stages [of the Law], [203] the bhiksu Hsiao Tz'u [Kyōji] stopped reciting the [*Lotus Sutra* of the] Single Vehicle (*ichijō*). He did not otherwise criticize the Mahāyāna but prohibited the recitation after considering the conditions of the world in those Latter Days. Then Hsin-hsing assumed the form of a great serpent with a large assembly of followers present in his mouth. Hsiao-Tz'u, affected by the poison of a demonic spirit, suddenly prostrated himself under the high dais with his fellow scholars. [204]

To slander the Mahāyāna is the worst of sins. We speak of the Five Grave Offenses [205] but none approaches this in seriousness. Thus, according to Amida's compassionate vows, his "leading and receiving" (*injō*) [206] [into the Pure Land] is far-embracing, but he rejects and will not help "those who speak ill of the True Dharma." [207] Ah, you who prepare yourselves for birth in the Pure Land—on whom then can you rest your hopes [if you continue to slander the Law]?

Article 5. *The Error of Turning One's Back on the Holy Gods of Shintō*

The *nembutsu* followers have long been estranged from the gods. They do not consider the distinction between Reality and its Provisional Manifestations, nor do they pay their respects at the great shrines and imperial sanctuaries. [208] They make such statements as that if one puts his trust in the Shintō deities, he will surely fall into hell, and they put aside the reality of supernatural beings (*kijin*). The Trace Manifestations (*suijaku*) who assume Provisional Forms (*gongen*) are actually the great [Buddhist] Holy Ones, revered by all the eminent priests of antiquity. Dengyō made pilgrimages to the Usa [Hachiman] and Kasuga Shrines, [209] receiving various miraculous omens. Chishō [Enchin, 814–891] went to Mount Kumano and entreated the god Shinra, praying devoutly for the success of his movement. And on the scarf of [the Sanron] priest Gyōkyō [fl.ca. 859] appeared shadows of the Three Sacred Ones [the Buddhist deities Amida, Kannon, and Seishi, while Gyōkyō was praying at the Usa Hachiman Shrine]; [210] and in Kōbō Daishi's picture he drew the likeness of Hachiman. [211] Do none of these measure up to Hōnen? Are these the priests who will fall into the infernal regions? Even more striking is the case of priest Gyōkyō, who on his return to [Nara's] Daianji built a two-storied turret. In the upper story he enshrined an image of

Hachiman, and in the lower he kept all of his scriptures and commentaries. If the gods were not worthy of veneration, then how in the world could he have placed this sacred image above the writings of the Dharma? Priests in this Latter Age respect the secular authorities; how much more so should they venerate the miraculous deities.

Such abuse as this [turning one's back on the Holy Gods of Shintō by the followers of Hōnen] should be stopped.

Article 6. *The Error of Ignorance Concerning the Pure Lands*
When we examine *The Sutra of Meditation on Amida Buddha* we find this statement:

> All ordinary people who wish to be born in this [Pure] Land should cultivate three categories of action (*sangō*). First of all, they should act filially toward their parents and support them, serve (*buji*) their teachers and elders, be of compassionate mind and avoid killing, and perform [the rest of] the Ten Virtuous Actions. Secondly, they should take and observe the Threefold Refuge [in the Buddha, the Dharma and the Sangha], fulfill all moral precepts without neglecting any of the normal rules of behavior. Thirdly, they should raise the desire for enlightenment,[212] be deeply convinced of the principle of cause and effect, and chant [the sutras of] the Mahāyāna.[213]

Moreover, in describing those beings to be born in the highest form in the highest grade (*jōbon jōshō*) among the nine grades, it says that they should "accomplish all the virtuous actions according to the precepts and recite the sutras of the Mahāyāna" (Nakamura 1964, pp. 62–63; Müller 1965, p. 188). Concerning those to be born in the lowest form of the middle grade (*chūbon geshō*), it says that they should be "filial to their parents and support them, besides exercising benevolence and compassion in the world" (Nakamura 1964, p. 68; Müller 1965, p. 194).

Teacher of the Law T'an-luan [Donran, 476–542] is the founder of the Nembutsu [Sect]. Among the five kinds of conditions (*en*) for birth in the highest assembly in the Pure Land, of the fourth he says that we must "cultivate all the virtues." And among the seven conditions for birth in the middle assembly, he speaks of "constructing pagodas and temples," and "feeding the clergy."[214] Meditation Master Tao-ch'o [Dōshaku, d. 645], compiling his writings on the Constant Practice of Meditation on the Buddha (*jōjū nembutsu zammai*), says that "it is because we frequently meditate on the Buddha that we speak of 'constant practice' (*jōjū*), certainly not because we neglect other forms of meditation."[215] And there was no instance in which Priest Shan-tao left unrepaired the pagodas and temples which he happened to see.[216]

Thus, from the sect's three basic scriptures down through its doctrinal interpretations, birth in the Pure Land is abundantly guaranteed to a variety of religious practices. Moreover, T'an Jung (Don'yū)[217] raised bridges, Shan Ch'eng (Zenjō) built roads, Ch'ang Min (Jōmin) repaired halls, Shan Cho (Zenchū) cleaned living quarters, K'ung Jen (Kūnin) collected flowers, An Jen (Annin) burnt incense, Tao Ju (Dōnyo) offered food, and Seng Ch'ing (Sōkyō) sewed clothes. Each by a single concrete good work attained birth in the Pure Land immediately after death. Seng Yü (Sōyu) had a [Hīnayānist] *Scripture of the Tradition* (Agon; Āgama) while Hsing Yen (Gyōen) lectured on the [Mahāyānist] *Summary of the Great Vehicle.*[218] Although one had but a single Hīnayānist sutra and the other differentiated between the commonplace and the sage, [the Buddha] responded to each in his own way and they both did indeed reach the Pure Land. But Priest Tao-chün (Dōshun) ceaselessly performed the *nembutsu* and would not copy the *Great Wisdom [Sutra]*;[219] Buddhamitra[198] would not carve Buddha images while engaged in the sole-practice, oblivious of all else. Both thereby were not in accord with the Vows for the attainment of birth in the Pure Land and were admonished by their superiors. After a long while they rectified their biases and in the end were born in the Western Region.

We should certainly understand that the path to liberation depends neither on the *nembutsu* nor on any other practice but is simply Mind. Although there is a phrase in the *Lotus Sutra* which speaks of "going to the world-sphere of Peace and Rest,"[220] and the *[Great] Wisdom [Sutra]* speaks of "birth in the Pure Land in accordance with the Vows,"[221] we must distinguish between the totality of aspects (*sōsō*) [of Mind] and a single small part (*shōbun*). As long as we say that [Mind] is not to be equated with the specific aspect (*bessō*) which is *nembutsu*, and as long as we do not claim that the *nembutsu* is a fixed karmic cause, then the whole will encompass the specific, the higher will necessarily incorporate the lower.[222] This is truly the way Buddhist reasoning operates. Why should we, by adopting habits familiar to the unenlightened, make the error of losing the impartial path which is the world of the Buddha? Birth in the Pure Land is not attained by the self-power (*jiriki*) of the devotee but simply by relying on the power of Amida's Vow. In other scriptures and other methods there are no special provisions for being received into the Pure Land (*injō*; cf., note 206); no special vow about the

Buddha's welcoming (*raigō*). If the nembutsu people cannot measure up [to the other scriptures and other methods], can they simply, as those who receive Amida's teaching (*shoke*), depend on his coming (*raigō*)? Are they not really a strange lot!

Having encountered the Law handed down by Śākyamuni, we are to observe the practices of the Mahāyāna—this is the essence of the matter. If we do not take refuge in this Holy One [Śākyamuni] we may truly say that we have no affinity with him. If the *nembutsu* is not accompanied by other practices, then we will be lacking in good karma. The two approaches are complementary. How then can those who practice other methods be excluded from reception (*injō*) into the Pure Land? If one may not attain birth in the Pure Land simply because he does not solely concentrate (*sennen*) on the Buddha [Amida], then how could Meditation Master Chih-chüeh [Chikaku] [223] have attained the highest form of the highest grade when he combined his meditations every day with a hundred other practices? In general, the wicked are hard to redeem, but [Amida] is pleased to save them; although difficult to redeem, they will be born with him [in his Pure Land] through the merit of performing some slight good with their voice. Thus we should understand the meaning of the phrase, "by practicing up to ten thoughts [i.e., chanting the name of the Buddha Amitāyus]" (*naishi jūnen*). [224] However, people today neglect the root and go for the branches, rely on the inferior and scorn the superior. How could they be in conformity with the purpose of the Buddha? On the day when an august emperor designates, at the court where he conducts affairs of state, the officials to act in his behalf, he requests service from the wise and the foolish, each according to their abilities, and from families both of high and low status. But to the foolish he does not entrust a position which would not be within their capacity even if they were to apply themselves from morning till night; and a person of low social status cannot advance to the rank of the nobility even if he is diligent in public affairs. In his own country the Great King of Enlightenment dispenses his ranks of Nine Stages [described in the *Sutra of Meditation on Amida Buddha*] at the gate where the wise and the foolish come to his court. His principle of selection is surely that one receives in accord with his performance in observing virtuous behavior in former lives. It would be an excess of stupidity for one to rely entirely on the Buddha's power without taking into account his own condition in life. The mere mouthing of the syllables of the Buddha's name does not bring the fruit of unblemished action to maturity; and to expect birth in the Pure Land after death under such circumstances is a serious misconception.

How can one expect this if he is lacking in morality and wisdom? If one would gradually attain this birth through many lifetimes, do the morally-perfuming (*kunshu*) practices of the Single Vehicle [i.e., Tendai] or the union (*kaji*) [of sentient beings with Mahāvairocana] through the three Teaching-practices (*sammitsu*) [of Shingon] have no power to help? Although we all sink [in this world of birth-and-death], the foolish sink straight down; and although we rise together, the wise quickly float like a bowl [on water]. And those who have both wisdom and practice are as strong as tigers with wings: one can stand up to many, and the Buddha graciously shines his light upon such people.

But from the first these [*nembutsu*] people dismiss such considerations. As long as the sole-practice group recklessly disdains the virtuous behavior [required of us mortals whose good fortune to encounter the Law is as rare as] the sea turtle [encountering a log in the vast sea];[225] and as long as they mistakenly hold to their own wisdom [which is as narrow as that] of a frog in a well [which imagines its limited horizon to be the entire world], we cannot remain silent. And so it has come to the point of our addressing the Throne. If there are foolish priests or laymen who misunderstand the meaning [of the Dharma], whether by making light of the way of birth in the Pure Land, or by excluding the practice of the *nembutsu*, or by not combining this with other exercises—these people will not attain birth in the Pure Land and so will completely fail to achieve their religious objective. They should be placed under an interdiction. And even though such a policy would have the defect of [calling attention to the Sole-practice] *nembutsu*, when the pros and the cons of the matter are weighed, is an Imperial Proclamation not called for?

Article 7. *The Error of Misunderstanding the Nembutsu*

First of all, with respect to the Buddha as object of meditation, we distinguish between name (*na*) and substance (*tai*), and within substance we distinguish between the conditioned (*ji*) and the Absolute (*ri*).

Next, with respect to the subjective ability to meditate, there is verbal articulation (*kushō*) and mental recollection (*shinnen*). Within mental recollection there is close meditation (*ke'nen*)[226] and contemplation (*kannen*); and within contemplation one proceeds from the diffused stage (*san'i*) to the focussed stage (*jōi*), then from tainted (*uro*) to untainted (*muro*). The progression is from shallow to profound, the earlier being inferior and the latter superior.

Now to intone the name of the Buddha with the mouth is neither meditation (*kan*) nor concentration (*jō*). This is the most coarse and shallow of the methods of *nembutsu*. We may say that it is good enough for certain individuals in a worldly state of mind, but how can we avoid such distinctions if we strictly compare the methods? When the sole-practice devotees are faced with these difficulties, they do not consider the issues but simply fall back on the statement: "Among the Forty-eight Vows of Amida, the Eighteenth assures birth in the Pure Land to those who recite the *nembutsu*." But how can they conceal all the other Original Vows and speak of just this one? Even with respect to this one vow, the phrase "by practicing up to ten thoughts [i.e., chanting the name of Buddha Amitāyus] (*naishi jūnen*)" is intended to emphasize the least [among a variety of superior practices]. Taking meditation (*kannen*) as the standard, it incorporates the lesser practice of vocal utterance (*kushō*); and giving prominence to the practice of calling on the Holy Name many times (*ta'nen*), it thus does not neglect the practice of the ten thoughts (*jūnen*) [i.e., the ten invocations of the name of the Buddha].[227]

This exemplifies the depth of the Great Compassion, the great power of the Buddha. To lead people easily and to effect their easy birth [in the Pure Land] there is meditation and also the many-practice calling (*ta'nen*). Thus in the *Meditation Sutra [Amida]* says: ". . . being harrassed by pains, he cannot think of the Buddha . . . [so he should] at least utter the name, 'Buddha Amitāyus.'"[228] Already, apart from the word for "uttering the Name" (*shōmyō*) there is the word for "thinking on the Buddha" (*nembutsu*). We know that to *think* on the Buddha is mental recollection (*shinnen*), contemplation (*kannen*; cf., first paragraph of Article 7). Among what is superior and what is inferior, why should the Original Vow of the Tathāgata set aside the superior and adopt the inferior? How then could priest Shan-tao, on first arousing the desire [for enlightenment (*hosshin*)] and seeing a representation of the Pure Land, have stated: "Certainly only by this method of meditation (*kammon*) can we transcend birth-and-death!" And presently he entered upon that path and could attain samādhi.[229] Certainly we know that the personal practices of this monk included the Sixteen Meditations [described in the *Meditation Sutra*] (*jūroku sōkan*). The word *nembutsu* comprises "seeing" (*kan*) as well as "speaking" (*ku*). Were this not so, would Shan-tao have written a commentary[229] on the *Meditation Sutra* and developed a method for meditation? In both the original sutra and the treatise, why should the character for "meditation" (*kan*) be used in the title? In his explication of the *Meditation Sutra*, Shan-tao states that if one simply employs the Buddha's name, this is an expedient device (*hōben*) to lure a person of small spiritual potential. These are the two sides to the words of this master's explanation:

compassion-wisdom *(jihi chie)* [the absolute whose comprehension defines the Bodhisattva] and [the provisional truth of] helpful aids *(zengyō=hōben)* are not identical. Would those who are the pillars of this religious community impute error to their founder?

Although Shan-tao emphasizes verbal utterance *(kushō)*, he gives the name sole-practice *(senju)* to genuine meditation on the Buddha which is accompanied by the Three States of Mind *(sanshin)*[230] and which is not lacking in the Four Practices *(shishu)*.[231] But if *sen* ("single, sole, special") is merely taken to mean the abandonment of other practices, and if *ju* (practice) merely means moving the mouth and hands, then what we ought to say is that [sole-practice] is a "singularity about which there is nothing special *(fusen no sen nari)* and practice which is no practice at all *(hishu no shu nari)*." And if its followers act with the idea of attaining assured birth in the Pure Land using this adulterated method *(koke zōdoku)* [combining good and bad elements], then how could the sect of Shan-tao serve the superior devotees of Amida? It is fair to say that when these [sole-practice] people speak of the Pure Land, the *nembutsu*, the causality of karma, or birth in the Pure Land, it is difficult to fathom the relative depth of the rivers and lakes [of their arguments], and easy to confuse what is far from what is near in the matter of practice.

If we do not study the nature and characteristics of the various sects, how will we come to know the truth of their methods? In this respect our own Hossō Mahāyāna sect originated from the heart of Blessed Śākyamuni and Maitreya (Jison) and is minutely codified in the scriptures comprised of the basic sutras and the basic commentaries *(honkyō honron)*.[232] In India the Philosopher of a Thousand Parts [Vasubandhu][233] and the Ten Great Bodhisattvas[234] both advocated and opposed commitment to either the phenomenal or the Void [in order to maintain the Middle Way between extremes]. Then also, quite early, Priest Hsüan-tsang [Genjō, 600–664] and the Lord of the Hundred Commentaries [K'uei-ch'i (Kiki, 632–82); also known as Tz'u-en] carried on the tradition without error. Now although the Pure Land devotees have the explanations of Tao-ch'o and Shan-tao, we [in the Hossō sect] do not place our reliance on them. But they too were men of accomplishment in samādhi; and would they have contradicted the words of He-Who-will-be-Buddha-in-His-Next-Life (Isshō fusho) [i.e., Maitreya, founder of Hossō]? Seek for mutual harmonization and do not delight in wanton opposition.

Article 8. *The Error of Vilifying the Followers of Śākyamuni*

The Sole-practice followers say: "The games of go *(iki)* and parcheesi *(sugoroku)* do not violate the sole-practice; neither are the relations between women and priests *(nyobon)* nor the eating of meat hindrances to birth in the Pure Land.[235] Practicing the discipline in this Latter World is as rare as having a tiger in the marketplace.[236] And it is a fearful mistake. A person who has scruples about committing evil is one who does not place his reliance on the Buddha."

Because this kind of rough talk *(sogon)* spreads throughout the land and captures people's thoughts, it becomes an enemy of the Dharma. It is essential that the teaching of birth in Paradise promote the practice of the discipline, the karmic cause for birth in the Pure Land. If you ask why this is so, I reply that, were there no regulations, then it would be impossible to maintain the Six Roots of Merit; and when one permits the doors of the senses [to remain open] at will, then the Three Poisons [illusion, envy, anger] easily arise. When one entangles oneself in the conditions for illusion, then the window for meditating on the Buddha *(nembutsu)* is not serene; and when one muddies the heart with envy and anger, the waters of the Jeweled Lakes *(hōchi)*[237] cannot be clear. Is not the experience of these good karmic states the Pure Land itself? Accordingly, we intently employ the practices of the discipline as the karmic cause for birth in the Pure Land. The writings which set forth the teaching are as I have stated above. It is known to everyone that priests in this Latter Age fail to observe the regulations and violate them. Within the sole-practice [community] are those who do observe the regulations.[238] Their behavior is certainly not what we lament here. Although they may not observe the regulations strictly, and although they may not follow the procedures as explained traditionally, they do have a sense of respect for them, and they lament over the laxity of the times. But in addition to living a life of repentance *(zangi;* cf., *sange)*, they make a point of breaking the regulations and so accommodate the Way to the vulgar mind. Nothing is worse than this to cause the extinction of the Buddha's Law. The movement is popular in the capital and in nearby provinces; and it is said that as far [north] as Hokuriku and the various provinces along the Eastern Sea (Tōkai) and other circuits, monks and nuns of the sole-practice movement successfully propagate these notions. Except by Imperial Edict, how can they be restrained? The purpose of this request is entirely concerned with these matters!

Article 9. *The Error of Bringing Disorder to the Nation*

The Buddha's Law and the Imperial Law are as body and mind: each should see to the well-being of the other, and then the welfare of the state will be assured. In these times the Pure Land movement has begun to arise and the activities of the Sole-practice to flourish. But can we also say that these are times when the imperial power has been restored? Moreover, the Three Learnings [morality, wisdom, meditation] are about to be abandoned and the Eight Sects are declining. Time and again how the government of society is in disarray!

What we wish is that the Nembutsu and the other sects would be as compatible as water and milk, and that the Buddha's Law and the Imperial Law would forever harmonize heaven and earth. But although the various [traditional] sects all believe in meditation on the Buddha (*nembutsu*) and harbor no ill designs against that movement, the Sole-practice followers deeply despise the other sects and will not share the same seat with them. They carry their conduct to this extreme, being as difficult to accommodate as fire and water. If matters were to be as the Sole-practice followers intend, then all other Buddhist activities in the world [literally, "under heaven and within the seas"] would be suspended. If high and low have not yet all taken refuge in this doctrine, and if the life of the Dharma has not yet become obliterated, it is not because external circumstances have hindered it, but because your august sense of purpose is not easily swayed, due to the clarity of your understanding. In these Latter Days, if the Sole-practice people succeed in their campaign, the attitude of the government will be to see the other sects as so much rubbish. And even if it did not come to the point of their actually being banned, the Eight Sects would truly be as if they did not exist! Perhaps we should call to mind King Puṣyamitra's destruction of the great monasteries;[239] or the Hui-Ch'ang[240] suppression of priests and nuns, in response to the advice of foolish ministers and the jealousy of the Taoist clergy.

As for the causes and conditions for the extinction of the Law, we cannot tell what the future will bring. With such considerations in mind, we send up this memorial that your Majesty may take action. If an admonition is not forthcoming at this time, then how will future perplexities be resolved? Buddhism, alas, has had its problems since antiquity; but this common appeal by all the Eight Sects is unprecedented. We respectfully look up to your sage judgment to decide on the relative merits of the case. What we hope and ask for is that Your Imperial Decree will make known your wishes throughout the Seven Circuits and all the provinces calling for the correction of the doctrine of the Sole-practice of calling on the Name of the Buddha as advocated by Genkū. The wish of the community of the World Honored One is that the waters of the Dharma gradually harmonize with the waves of the Sea of Emptiness,[241] and that the subjugating power of the Kings of Wisdom (Myō-ō)[242] may forever clear away the clouds of evil in the winds of the High Mountain (Yao).[243]

This sincere statement presented to the court
with awe and respect
Summary
Submitted to Accompany the Petition

The aforementioned Genkū is biased toward a single religious method and completely rejects the Eight Sects. Since it is the purpose of Temma [the Evil One] to obstruct the Buddhas and Gods, all of the [Eight] Sects are of the same mind in desiring that this matter be handled by Imperial Decree.

Genkū has already proferred a letter of apology (*taijō*),[244] but since this was not sufficient to quell the annoyance, an order of prohibition was issued from the Retired Emperor [Go-Toba]. But the agitation of Genkū's followers was such that it increased their visibility all the more. In particular, after he had taken up his brush to write his pledge (*kishō*) on the day when the monks of Mount Hiei sent a messenger with additional queries, his disciples told his lay followers: "The Shōnin's words are all two-sided and don't go to the heart of the matter. Don't be influenced by what you hear from outsiders!" They made other statements to the same effect. Afterwards there was no change at all in the cleverness of his heretical views. Will the apology this time be the same as the one before? But if one reports falsely to the Emperor, his crime is all the more grievous. Whatever the august wishes of your Majesty might be, how could your loyal subjects not obey?

So what we desire and request is that by virtue of your gracious compassion you will quickly send out an Imperial Proclamation throughout the Seven Circuits and all the provinces to stop the excesses of the Exclusive Sole-practice (*ikkō senju*); and that you will put a stop to the transgressions that may be performed by Genkū and his disciples, and to the heretical tendencies which they have long had to violate the [Buddha's] Law. And we hope that they may come to the true way of the *nembutsu*. Accordingly, we have submitted the above.

The [. . .] day in the tenth month of Genkyū 2 [1205].

CHAPTER FIVE

Shingon's Kakukai on the Immanence of the Pure Land

From ancient times, demons had often harrassed the devotees on Mount Kōya to obstruct their religious practice. Vowing to pacify these evil influences and so protect the Buddha's teaching, Bridge-of-the-Law Kakukai, on the 17th day of the eighth month in Jōō 2 (1223), suddenly sprouted wings, kicked down the door in the gate of the temple where he resided, and flew away into the sky. Shiban (1625–1710), who records this incident in his *Biographies of Eminent Japanese Priests* (Honchō kōsōden, 1702), goes on to say that in his own day Kakukai was still to be seen making his way among the mountains of Kōya (Iwano 1961, p. 228).

Kakukai (Nanshōbō, 1142–1223), after serving as thirty-seventh Superintendent of Shingon's Kongōbuji headquarters from 1217 to 1220, retired to Kōya's Keōin. Historical records less imaginative than Shiban's state that three years later, in his 82nd year, he auspiciously expired while performing the hand gesture of Mahāvairocana, the *mudrā* of the Knowledge Fist (*chiken'in*) expressed by the central Buddha in the Diamond mandala (Saunders 1960, p. 103). He left behind a brief statement of his religious views, the *Bridge-of-the-Law Kakukai's Discourse on the Dharma* (Kakukai hōkyō hōgo) whose precise dating and authorship are uncertain. Apparently a transcription of Kakukai's remarks by a disciple, the work's originality consists largely in its being an early vernacular tract (*kana hōgo*), an attempt to explain theoretical obscurities to a popular audience in the beginning phase of the Kamakura religious reformation. Doctrinally it is little more than a restatement of the traditional Shingon position on the uses of myth, but its timing enhances its significance. The *Discourse* is clearly a response to the new Amidist Pure Land movements which enjoyed phenomenal popularity after Hōnen's advocacy of the Sole-Practice of Calling upon the Name of Amida Buddha (*senju nembutsu*) in 1175. Kakukai argued that the Pure Land—Amida's, Mahāvairocana's Maitreya's, or any other—was to be realized immediately in this defiled world, just as Kūkai (774–835) had taught that we are to attain Buddhahood in this very body (*sokushin jōbutsu*). The Pure Land was to be found in our everyday thought and action, rather than in some geographically remote realm as usually conceived by the popular Pure Land movements of his day, if not by Hōnen (1133–1212) himself. In this brief *Discourse* Kakukai is content to describe his own viewpoint rather than explicitly calling Hōnen's into question, as did the *Kōfukuji Petition* (Kōfukuji sōjō, 1205) of Hossō's Jōkei and the *Attack on the Bad Vehicle* (Saijarin, 1212) of Kegon's Myōe (Bandō 1974).

Here we shall examine Kakukai's *Discourse*, introducing a complete translation with a discussion of several central notions in which it is grounded. But first we must see Kakukai in the context of his age.

Kakukai's Spiritual Lineage. The details of Kakukai's life are sketchy and our sources do not always agree. He was born in Tajima province, the present-day Hyōgō Prefecture which borders the Sea of Japan northwest of Kyoto. Most authorities tell us that he studied with Jōkai (1074–1149), founder of Daigoji's Sambōin school of Tōji esotericism. And since Kakukai was only seven in the year that Jōkai died, he was evidently a precocious child. Whatever doubts we may have about the details, a tentative diagram of the relationships between Kakukai and others of the Sambōin school may at least help to define *his* circle of acquaintances and influences (cf., charts in *Bukkyō daijiten* 1954, VI, supplementary pp. 40–42, and *Mikkyō daijiten* 1970, vol. 1, p. 189; also Miyaska 1964, pp. 10–12.)

Note that Kakukai's colleague, Ikkai, is in the line of transmission to Eizon (Shiembō, 1201–90), founder of the Esoteric Disciplinary (Shingon Ritsu) sect centered at Nara's Saidaiji. A trip east which Eizon made in 1252, stopping along the way for five days at the Chōboji Temple in what is now Nagoya, is recorded in *Back and Forth to the Kantō Region* (Kantō ōgenki; Kokusho Kankōkai 1974, pp. 1–2). Later that same year Mujū Ichien took over the administration of this temple, where he was to remain for the next half century. Circumstantial evidence suggests that throughout his life Mujū had a continuing relationship with Eizon and may well have been initiated by him into the mysteries of the Tōji Sambōin school. In his *Casual Digressions* (Zōtanshū 3:5) of 1305, Mujū mentions that he had gone to [the Shōrakuji on Nara's] Mount Bodai in 1261 to have the practices of that school transmitted to him (Yamada and Miki 1973, p. 110). If his mentor on this occasion was Eizon, this would provide the link between Mujū and Kakukai. A short anecdote recorded in *Sand and Pebbles* (Shasekishū, 1279–83) is a major item of the Kakukai legend repeated in subsequent accounts. Chapter 2:10 is entitled "Karmic Affinities with the Buddha's Law not without Effect."

CHART 4.

Kakukai's Spiritual Lineage

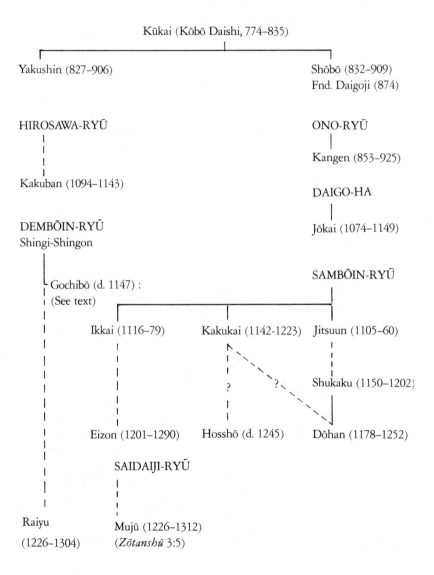

Kūkai (Kōbō Daishi, 774–835)

Yakushin (827–906)

Shōbō (832–909)
Fnd. Daigoji (874)

HIROSAWA-RYŪ

Kakuban (1094–1143)

DEMBŌIN-RYŪ
Shingi-Shingon

Gochibō (d. 1147) :
(See text)

ONO-RYŪ

Kangen (853–925)

DAIGO-HA

Jōkai (1074–1149)

SAMBŌIN-RYŪ

Ikkai (1116–79)   Kakukai (1142-1223)   Jitsuun (1105–60)

?   ?   Shukaku (1150–1202)

Eizon (1201–1290)   Hosshō (d. 1245)   Dōhan (1178–1252)

SAIDAIJI-RYŪ

Raiyu
(1226–1304)

Mujū (1226–1312)
(*Zōtanshū* 3:5)

Kakukai, Superintendent of Nanshōbō on Mount Kōya, had a reputation as a prominent contemporary scholar of the Esoteric Sect. Wishing to know about his earlier existence, he prayed to the Great Teacher [Kūkai] and was shown the circumstances of seven of his former lives. "First of all you were a small clam in the sea west of Tennōji Temple tossed in by the waves. While you were lying on the beach, a small child picked you up and brought you to the front of the Golden Hall where you heard the chanting of the Hymn in Praise of Relics (*Sharisandan*). By virtue of this you were reborn as a dog living at Tennōji who constantly heard the sutras and mystic formulas being chanted. Then you were reborn as an ox; and because of having carried paper used for the copying of the *Great Wisdom Sutra*, you were reborn as a horse. The horse carried pilgrims to Kumano and was reborn as a votive-fire attendant who lit the way for people by always keeping the fires bright. Having gradually become suffused with the karmic activity of wisdom, you were reborn as caretaker of the Inner Chapel (Oku no In), where constantly your ears were moved and your eyes exposed to the practice of the Three Mysteries. And now you are living as Superintendent Kakukai." Having heard of this incident, we can clearly see the value of establishing affinities with the Buddha's Law.

As we view early Kamakura Buddhism from a distance of seven and a half centuries, Kakukai appears as a minor player in the events which would radically alter its institutional structure. But as abbot of the Kongōbuji from 1217 to 1220, he was one of the leading prelates of Shingon, the sect second in influence at the time only to Tendai. Hōnen's Amidist Pure Land movement had grown rapidly since its inception in 1175, but it was still far from being the main stream of Japanese Buddhism which it became in later centuries after Shinran (1173–1262), Ippen (1239–1289) and Rennyo (1415–99). Japanese Zen was only a few decades old, the *Promulgation of Zen as a Defense of the Nation* (Kōzen gokokuron) having been written by Eisai (1141–1215) in 1198, seven years after his return from China with the Rinzai transmission. Dōgen (1200–1253) would return from study on the mainland in 1227; Enni (Ben'en, 1202–80), in 1241. And Nichiren (1222–82) would not found his Lotus Sect (Hokkeshū) until 1253.

In short, early Kamakura Buddhism was still dominated by Tendai and Shingon, with Hossō and Kegon among the old Nara sects still occupying a broad range of the ideological spectrum. In 1205 the *Kōfukuji Petition* called for the suppression of what were perceived as excesses in the Amidist Pure Land movement. Hōnen's *Collection of Passages [bearing on the Original Vow of*

Amida] (Senjaku [hongan nembutsu] shū) was compiled in 1198 but not made public until after his death in 1212, when it was immediately challenged by Myōe's *Attack on the Bad Vehicle.* Moreover, in tallying the events which define these transitional decades between the old and the new order of things in every area of Japanese life and thought, we might note that the *Gukanshō* (Miscellany of Ignorant Views, 1219), the monumental history of Japan by the Tendai prelate Jien (1155–1225), was produced while Kakukai was Superintendent of the Kongōbuji.

Kakukai is said to have had a substantial following in his time, but nothing that could be compared with those of the new Amidism or Zen. Shiban and others tell us that Dōhan (Hongakubō, 1178–1252) on occasion came to Kakukai for instruction, if he was not actually a direct disciple. Dohan had a distinguished career as a promoter of Shingon. His numerous works include the vernacular tract known as *Dōhan's Letter* (Dōhan shōsoku, ca. 1184–1252; Miyasaka 1964, pp. 76–83). Whatever the personal relationships between Kakukai and his Shingon contemporaries may have been, they shared a common tradition of religious thought and practice which continued to influence Japanese Buddhism even after it had been deprived of its earlier prominence by the new popular movements.

Kakukai's World of Ideas. Like every Mahāyānist system of thought and practice, Shingon recognizes the necessary variability of theological explanations. The goal of religious experience ultimately transcends every human formulation, and no one explanation is true to the exclusion of all others, although it may be viewed as more adequate than its competitors. Variations arise because of differences in the abilities of sentient beings to comprehend the Truth that surpasses understanding; and the underlying metaphor for this view is not the one-to-one correspondence, the mirror image, between a physical object and its verbal counterpart, but rather shifting perspectives and varying descriptions as we view an object from several directions. While no description is definitive, the provisional usefulness of varying explanations is not in question. In the words of Kūkai (Kōbō Daishi, 774–835), founder of Japanese Shingon:

> The Dharma is beyond speech, but without speech it cannot be revealed. Suchness transcends forms, but without depending on forms it cannot be realized. Though one may at times err by taking the finger pointing at the moon to be the moon itself, the Buddha's teachings which guide people are limitless (Hakeda 1972, p. 145).

Fully recognizing the viability of other perspectives, Shingon chooses to explain the mechanism of the religious life in terms of the ultimate identity, but phenomenal non-identity, of all sentient beings with the Buddha Mahāvairocana, the Great Sun Buddha. Kakukai, in the opening statement of his *Discourse*, says that his tradition "affirms the two principles of the identity and difference of ordinary human nature [with Mahāvairocana]." He goes on to affirm the goal of supreme enlightenment, rather than the lesser ideal of birth in some Pure Land which others—notably Hōnen and the Amidist movement—had argued was all that humans could hope to attain during the Latter Days of the Law. The *mappō* theory was not supported by Kūkai and his school. The goal of Shingon practice was the attainment of Buddhahood here and now in this very body (*sokushin jōbutsu*; Kiyota 1978, pp. 123–27).

Early Mahāyāna could admit that its Buddhas and Bodhisattvas were "obviously productions of the mind, and without historical or factual basis" (Conze 1959, p. 150). The esoteric movements went a step further by asserting that

> . . . things and Gods are equally unreal compared with the one vast emptiness, but on the whole the data of mythology represent a kind of fiction far more worthwhile than the data of our everyday practical experience, and when properly handled, can greatly assist us in winning emancipation from the fetters of existence (Conze 1959, p. 185).

These mythical Buddhas and Bodhisattvas were dramatically represented as residing in their own Pure Lands, where a person might be born to escape transmigration through the Six Paths of existence even though he had not yet attained supreme enlightenment. The common people understood these "productions of the creative mythological imagination" quite literally, of course; and while Buddhism flourished, the easy movement between literal and figurative meaning posed few problems for those who organized their experience with its symbols.

The lot of unenlightened sentient beings is transmigration within the Six Destinies (*rokudō*): the realms of gods, men, fighting-beings (*asuras*), animals, hungry ghosts (*pretas*), and those in the hells—the last three comprising the Three Evil Destinies (*san'akudō*). The Ten Worlds (*jikkai*) include these six together with the enlightened realms of *śrāvaka* (*shōmon*) and *pratyekabuddha* (*engaku*) [i.e., the Hīnayana adepts], *bodhisattva* (*bosatsu*) and Buddha [i.e., the Mahāyāna adepts]. Buddhist cosmology is not so much geography as the dramatic representation of psychological states. The Three Worlds (*sangai*) of Desire (which includes the Six Destinies and the Six Desire Heavens; see note 270) of Form and of No-form describe in objective terminology the progressive states leading to enlightenment. [245] Within this three-part world of unenlightened beings are to be found several Pure Lands presided over by a Buddha, as Kakukai notes in support of his thesis that there is no essential difference between the various Pure Lands and our defiled world.

The Hossō monk Jōkei (see Chapter Four) sought birth in the Heaven of the Satisfied Gods (*Tosotsuten*) where the Buddha of the future, Maitreya (Miroku), is waiting until the current cycle of Gautama's teaching is complete; this Pure Land is one of the Six Desire Heavens. Late in life Jōkei also prayed for birth on Kannon's Mt. Potalaka (Fudarakusen), popularly understood to be situated in the sea south of India, on a mountain in China, or, in Japan, at sites near the Nachi Falls and at Nara's Kasuga Shrine. Holy Eagle Mount (Ryōjusen), the mythical site where Śākyamuni is said to have taught the *Lotus* (Hokkekyō, T. 262) and *Larger Pure Land* (Muryōjukyō, T. 360) sutras, is located near Rājag[r]ha in India.

The most famous of these regions is Amida's Pure Land of Supreme Bliss (*gokuraku jōdo*) as described in the *Larger Pure Land Sutra* and in the *Amida Sutra* (Amidakyō, T. 366). This is said to be in the "western direction" (*saihō*), evidently beyond our Three Worlds (Beal 1871, pp. 116–18). Of lesser importance is the Lapis Lazuli Pure Land (*jōruri jōdo*) of the Medicine Buddha, Yakushi Nyorai, which is "in the east" (T. 450, 451; Birnbaum 1979, pp. 152, 191–2). And there are others.

What is unique about Mahāvairocana's Terrace of Esoteric Grandeur (*mitsugon dōjō*) is that it is understood by Kakukai to be *identical with the immediate world in which we live*. The Terrace, described in the [*Mahāyāna*] *Sutra of Esoteric Grandeur* ([Daijō] mitsugongyō, T. 681–82), a scripture which Kūkai brought back from China, is also known as the Land of Esoteric Grandeur (*mitsugonkoku*) in the *Aspiration to Enlightenment* (Bodaishinron, T. 1665) traditionally ascribed to Nāgārjuna. (The term *mitsugon* also appears in the *Yugikyō*, T. 867.) The Terrace is the abode of the Great Sun Buddha (Dainichi Nyorai), a Buddha-land (*bukkoku*) of esoteric grandeur because it is the site of integration (*kaji*) of the Three Mysteries (body, voice and mind) of Mahāvairocana with the three parallel karmic actions (*sangō*) of sentient beings by virtue of which they attain Buddhahood in this very body (*sokushin jōbutsu*).[246]

According to Shingon teaching, both the Lotus Womb World of Grandeur (*Rengezō shōgon sekai*) of Vairocana (Birushana) as described in the *Garland Sutra* (Kegonkyō, T. 278–79, 293) and Amida's Supreme Bliss World (*gokuraku sekai*) of the Pure Land tradition are simply other names for the Pure Land of Esoteric Grandeur (*mitsugon jōdo*). In Japan the concept of the Pure Land of Esoteric Grandeur was emphasized by the founder of Neo-Shingon, Kakuban (1095–1143), whose writings include a 10-fascicle *Mitsugon shohishaku* (The

Mysteries of Esoteric Grandeur Variously Explained). Kakuban's views evidently influenced Kakukai, who was not, however, in the Neo-Shingon line of transmission (see earlier chart). Kakukai also uses the term, Esoteric Grandeur of the Lotus Womb (*mitsugon kezō=rengezō shōgon sekai*, above), whose second phrase indicates the Lotus Womb World (*kezō sekai*) which is the Garland World (*kegon sekai*) of the *Garland Sutra*. Although the Vairocana (Birushana) of the exoteric *Garland Sutra* and Mahāvairocana (Dainichi Nyorai) of the Two-part Mandala are distinguishable in some traditions, Shingon's Tōmitsu identifies them and thus views the Garland World as another name for Mahāvairocana's Pure Land (Miyasaka 1964, p. 432). The somewhat tedious exercise of tracing these distinctions to their scriptural sources helps us to appreciate the spirit of accommodation with which Kakukai and his school attempted to reconcile differences in scripture and tradition. It was taken for granted that there should be various rationalizations of religious experience, and no single formulation was uniquely true, although it might be seen as better, more adequate, than others.

Early in the *Discourse* Kakukai speaks of the Five Elements (Earth, Water, Fire, Wind, Space) which constitute material form (*shiki, rūpa*). These and Mind (*shin, citta*) together comprise the Six Elements (*rokudai*), which are "the inseparable entities of tathatā [*shinnyo*, 'suchness'], the Shingon concept of ulitmate reality" (Kiyota 1978, p 67; see also p. 81). The integration of knower (mind) and known (form) *is* Mahāvairocana. Meditation on the Six Elements comprising Suchness is facilitated by the two basic Shingon mandalas:the Womb (*taizōkai, garbhadhātu*) and the Diamond (*kongōkai, vajradhātu*), respectively signifying the known and the knower. For Kakukai the Holy Throng is nothing other than a dramatic representation of immediate experience as the known, rather than of a world of transcendent beings. The entire *Discourse* appears to be basically a reassertion of Shingon's allegorical understanding of religious imagery in the face of widespread literalmindedness.

The Discourse. The disciple who transcribed Kakukai's remarks does not tell us why he wrote in Japanese rather than in the prestigious Chinese commonly used in most Buddhist writings of the time. The *Discourse*, among the earliest of vernacular tracts (*kana hōgo*), apparently antedates Kōshin's collection of Myōe's aphorisms from 1235–1238 (see Chapter Two), but not, of course Genshin's *Yokawa Tract* (see Chapter One). It is reasonable to assume that the author responded to the wave of popular religious movements which were then flooding the country. But whatever his motivation, the author really made only one concession to easy comprehension: the technical terms are connected to each other through the medium of Japanese grammar. But he does not explain them and appears to be uneasy even with this minor accommodation, occasionally slipping back into the traditional *kambun* style. The result can only have been intended for those already familiar with Kakukai's thought.

My text is the modern printed edition of the Kempō 2 (1742) manuscript of the Kōya monk Myōzui (1696–1764) which is included in Miyasaka Yūshō, ed. *Kana hōgo shū* (Tokyo: Iwanami Shoten, 1964), volume 83 in the *Nihon Koten Bungaku Taikei* series. Miyasaka's text was compared against several other editions, notably the version in Washio 1925, pp. 37–42. (NKBT uses characters for *Myōtan,* but this may be an oversight since Washio and other standard references mention only Myō*zui*; and the dating is compatible. See Miyasaka 1964, p. 12, line 3.)

A word about the translation. Every terminology eventually turns to jargon, but those who first use its metaphors have in mind a very clear set of images, images which are inevitably lost in a translation paraphrase designed to read smoothly. And so I have chosen to be as literal as possible, even if the result is stylistically awkward.

Bridge-of-the-Law Kakukai's Discourse on the Dharma
(Kakukai hōkyō hōgo)

This is what was said by Bridge-of-the-Law Kaku[kai]:

The tradition of the mantra (Shingon) teaching affirms the two principles of the identity and difference of ordinary human nature [with Mahāvairocana]. If we genuinely seek Unexcelled Enlightenment,[247] we will be completely unconcerned about where we may have our being or in what form. By constantly purifying our Mind[248] we will come to the understanding of the identity of phenomena with absolute reality,[249] in which the apparent world is thought-construction.[250]

The Pure Land I look forward to as [Mahāvairocana's] Terrace of Esoteric Grandeur (*mitsugon dōjō*) is [this present world of] Nine Mountains and Eight Seas surrounding Mount Sumeru. Through the externally manifest bodies of the Buddhas,[251] the Ten Worlds [from the Buddhas to the denizens of hell (see p. 94)] are all represented as the Holy Throng (*shōju*) in the mandalas. Kaku[kai] may have a bodily form, but it cannot be other than the body of Buddha [since the Six Elements comprising all things are nothing other than the true reality (*shinnyo, tathatā,* "suchness") personified as Dharmakāya Mahāvairocana]. Since one whose mind [the sixth element, the knower] is transformed is called a Buddha, then if we carefully investigate his external forms consisting of the Five Elements [the known], we find that they are truly the Holy Throng [of beings represented in the Womb] mandala. Distinctions between the Nine Worlds [from the hells through the bodhi-sattva realms] and the world of the Buddha with respect to the formal continuities of phenomena (*sōzoku no eshin*) are [only made within the realm of *saṃsāra*, within] the interval of transmigration through birth-and-death. But to think that such distinctions between the worlds of sentient beings and that of the Buddha [are real] is due to attachment to fixed views.

When we are enlightened to the "original non-production" (*honshō fushō*)[252] of all things, then the ridge-poles and pillars of grass hut [or palace][253] are all as timbers of [Mahavairocana's] Palace of the World of Dharmas.[254] To see [Vairocana's] Lotus Womb World of Grandeur[255] [in this present world of] Nine Mountains and Eight Seas surrounding Mount Sumeru is to construct in this very world [Mahavairocana's] Terrace of [the Palace of] the World of Dharmas in which phenomena are identical with absolute reality (*sokuji nishin*; see note 249). [Thus symbolizing my everyday life in terms of the two mandalas] I see the monastic quarters where I live in terms of the absolute as the Pure Land of Esoteric Grandeur (*mitsugon jōdo*; see p. 95). I prepare myself with the Four Wisdoms[256] and the [parallel] Four Disciplinary Processes[257] to my left and right, in front and in back. [To identify with] the Nine Assemblies [of the Diamond World],[258] the Thirteen Great Assemblies [of the Womb World][259] and the Mandala of the Womb World [as representing the phenomenal] World of Dharmas (*hokkai, dharmadhātu*),[260] I contemplate the perfect enlightenment [symbolized as "the moon-disc of self-realization" (*jishō no gachirin*)] of each of the Thirty-seven deities in all the worlds of the Diamond Mandala[261] [representing the known].

While at the causal stage (*inni*) of enlightenment [i.e., during the period of practice before its attainment] it is during the practice of meditation (*kanbō zazen*) on the mind (*shin, citta*) and its functions (*shinjo, caitta,* "mentals," objects) that, as we enter into the Diamond World, the various wisdom signs (*chiin*) of Mahāvairocana, Lord of Mind, will be revealed. I should truly rid myself of deep attachments and be aware that reality arises through causes and conditions.

My! How many people there are who delight in the prospect of the afterlife! It is because none of them are yet liberated from attachments to *this* world that they discuss the difference between the "easy" and "difficult" paths to realize birth in [Maitreya's] Heaven of the Satisfied Gods (Tosotsu, Tusita) or [Amida's Pure Land of] Supreme Bliss (Gokuraku). And not a single one of them opts for [Mahāvairocana's] World of Esoteric Grandeur of the Lotus Womb (*mitsugon kezō*) by putting a stop to their delusive ruminations. The followers of the Shingon sect who emphasize the practice [without understanding the theory] of the mantras fall into the error of Eternalism (*jōken*),²⁶² while those who stress the theory fall into the error of Annihilationism (*kūken*).²⁶³ Lately there seems to be no one who is convinced that practice and theory are one and inseparable.

In response to private questioning [Kakukai] said:

You ask me, good people, what Buddha I hope to see and in what Pure Land I expect to be born. And you tell me to state unequivocally if I have realized my religious objective and abide in the Truth. Indeed, it is difficult for me to extricate myself from the miserable attachments to this world of transmigration through birth-and-death. I regret not having clarified my mind through the levels of practice to enlightenment, and I think of this matter constantly. My reason for thus seeking to realize the profound purpose for entering the Dharma-gate [to the Truth], and for inquiring into your own state of realization, is not for the sake of making a livelihood. It is solely to attain supreme enlightenment [i.e., enlightenment both for myself and for others]. Were this insignificant monk to deceive you, then surely he would receive retribution from our Great Teacher [Kūkai] and [Kōya's Guardian] Deities.²⁶⁴ It is because from the beginningless past and into the future we are obsessed by the distinction between self [power] and other [power]²⁶⁵ that the world of sentient beings and the world of the Buddha are forever separate. Even if we live through countless aeons, it will be difficult to dispel this view.

Nan[shōbō] said:

Truly, one should always be concerned with liberation (*shutsuri tokudatsu*), and it saddens me to have to be reminded of this time and time again. Even if he does not purify his mind [of ratiocination], a person who thinks in this manner will certainly have a wholesome mind; and with such an attitude he will escape the Three Evil Destinies. He will then be blessed with the essence of the teaching. Because we are all common people who have not yet realized enlightenment, we need to depend on the development of such an attitude.

When we quietly contemplate the origin and extinction of phenomena, we cannot be attached either to [Maitreya's] Heaven of the Satisfied Gods, to [Amida's Pure Land of] Supreme Bliss, or to [Mahāvairocana's] World of Esoteric Grandeur, giving no thought to where we shall be born or what we shall become as we purify our mind. If we simply purify the mind, we shall not feel pain even if we were to assume the forms of such creatures as dragons and *yaksas* [among the lowest of heavenly beings]. The realms occupied by clever beings[266] [within the Nine Worlds] are not always like the places in which we live; they are all in Pure Lands. Our partiality for the human form and our bias against the strange forms of other creatures is due to our lack of understanding. Regardless of transmigration we shall suffer no discomfort.

Nor do I consider what kind of *mudrā (in)* to make at the moment of death.[267] Depending on my state of mind I can constantly abide in the Four Dignified Postures [*shūgi:* walking, standing, sitting, lying]. What kind of deportment is not samadhi (*zammai*)? Every thought and every word are meditations (*kannen*) and mantras (*shingon*) leading to Enlightenment (*shitsuji, siddhi*). Indeed, should delusive thoughts arise in my heart, I take no notice of them even though [conventional wisdom says that] I should lament this state of affairs and put a stop to those thoughts. And what about the [other] two karmic actions of body and voice? The same also applies to them. The devotee should simply take care always to intone (*tonae*) the letter "A" (*A-ji*; see note 252) and in his heart to meditate (*kannen*) on the Reality of everything as co-arising (*enshō jissō*). The circumstances of our final moments are by no means known to others, and even our Good Friends[268] in the faith will then be no help to us. Since each maintains his own distinctions of self [power] and other [power], even though we meditate (*kannen*) on the same [object of worship] it is only to be expected that another's thinking is not identical with my own. And as for those who do *not* share a common ideal with me, it would be better to have no one at all [around at the moment of death]. If we just tranquilize our thoughts, the mind itself will be our Good Friend. I think it quite splendid to die as did the likes of Gochibō,[269] abiding in a correct state of mind with his final moments unknown to any others. These were people who calmly sought [birth in] the Pure Land of Esoteric Grandeur (*mitsugon jōdo*). But, in response to people's questioning, of none of these people can it be stated with certainty with which Buddha they were born.

Privately [Kakukai] remarked:

All beings within the Ten Worlds are essentially without attachments. But transmigration is endless; and we should understand how it is that some receive the karmic retribution of birth in the human world or as devas, while others are born into [Maitreya's Heaven of] the Satisfied Gods, the [Pure Land of] Supreme Bliss, or into the realms of demons, hungry ghosts and asuras.

Nan[shōbō] said:

Because we are essentially without attachments to the Ten Worlds, we roam through the Nine Worlds [beneath that of the Buddha] with our states of being determined by changes in our mental state. Therefore we say that we abide in the Ten Worlds without abiding in any of them (*jikkai jūbujū jizai*). It is entirely as a consequence of our attitude of attachment to things (*shūjakushin*) that our feelings conjure up the variety of forms in the Nine Worlds. And since it is through the power of karma that our feelings effect this, our lives in this world are determined according to whether or not our karma is exhausted. For man, with his sustained recollection (*okuji fumō*) of the sites of rebirth, the human and heavenly worlds are all Pure Lands. If we understand the nature of the Shingon mantra and the meaning of what the name [Amida] stands for, then even the realms of demons, animals and asuras [beneath the human and heavenly worlds] are all Pure Lands of Esoteric Grandeur.

Just as when two people sleep with pillows side by side and one may have a bad dream while the other has a good one, so also we may learn the same scripture with a single teacher in the same discipline and same tradition (*dōgyō dōhō*) but the benefit will vary depending on differing states of mind. Although within the Six Desire Heavens beings are attached to pleasure and for some [e.g., Māra] the Buddha's Law does not exist,[270] there also within the Heaven of the Satisfied Gods is the Pure Land of the Bodhisattva He-Who-Will-Be-Buddha-in-his-Next-Life (*Isshō fusho*; i.e., the future Buddha, Maitreya). Although this World-to-be-Endured (*shaba sekai, sahā-loka-dhātu*) is the Region of the Five Defilements,[271] it is also [Amida's] Pure Land of the West (*saihō jōdo*). It is said that when we purify the mind it is the land of the Buddha's Dharma.[272] Turn around the thinking of the ordinary person and the physical form bound by karma (*gobaku no eshin*) is the Pure Land of True Reward (*shōbō*) for how we have lived. Our present abode in this life is just like this. During the Three Long Aeons (*sansōgi*) [which we must spend until we attain Enlightenment] we pass the time in spiritual practices just in order to understand this principle.

Thus did Kakukai reaffirm the basic Mahāyāna principle of the identity of our phenomenal world of transmigration (*rinne, saṃsāra*) through the Six Destinies with the absolute (*nehan, nirvāṇa*). The Pure Lands of Mahāvairocana, Maitreya, or Amida were thought-constructs, "fingers pointing at the moon," expedient means to help us realize the Dharma beyond speech, the Suchness transcending forms. And this traditional interpretation of the limits and uses of reason challenged the dogmatic literalism of the extreme faction of the new Amidist Pure Land movement.

Kakukai's views no longer appealed to the people of his time and they were largely replaced by simpler, but often narrower, explanations of the religious life. Nevertheless, popularity is no sure guarantee of value. We who live in other times and circumstances may judge Kakukai differently than did most of his contemporaries. His language may be unfamiliar, but his message is clear enough. Many of us today are unable to accept a single formulation of religious experience with dogmatic certainty but quite prepared to admit a variety of mythical explanations. Moreover, for us to accept the necessity as well as the possibility of conceptual variety is to provide a firm basis for the accommodation of Eastern and Western modes of religious expression.

A P P E N D I X

Zeami's Kasuga ryūjin
(Dragon God of Kasuga),
or Myōe Shōnin

=======

I n the early decades of the Kamakura period travel between Japan and China
was hazardous, but not uncommon. The dangers of the journey had made
diplomatic missions to the continent unpopular some centuries earlier, and
the last official voyage to China was undertaken in 838.[273] Merchants and
priests, however, continued to travel to China in significant numbers for material
profit or spiritual guidance. In 987, for example, the Sanron monk Chōnen (d. 1016)
of Tōdaiji returned to Japan with the Sung edition of the Buddhist scriptures. But
only in the latter half of the twelfth century were official relations between the two
countries tentatively resumed by Taira Kiyomori (1118–1181).

Ch'an, or Zen, was at the time the most vigorous of the Chinese sects, and
Japanese students of Buddhism, seeking new methods of religious practice in China
suitable to the needs of society in those Latter Days of the Law, generally made their
way to its monastic centers. Myōan Eisai (1141–1215), the first of these Zen
pioneers, went to China twice, in 1168 and 1187, and returned in 1191 from his
second visit with a transmission of the Lin-chi (Rinzai) school. His example was
followed by Dōgen Kigen (1200–1253), the founder of the Sōtō tradition of Zen in
Japan, who visited China 1223–1227, and by the Rinzai monk Enni Ben'en
(1202–1280), who spent the years 1235–41 on the mainland.[274] Among the
students of other schools were Hōnen's disciple Chōgen (Shunjōbō 1121–1206),
who journeyed to China between 1167 and 1176[275], and the Ritsu monk Shunjō
(Gazen, 1166–1227; see Chart 1), who lived in China from 1199 to 1211 and whom
tradition credits with introducing Chu Hsi's Neo-Confucianism to Japan.

But the idea of travel to India bordered on fantasy. Although both Chōnen and
Eisai had considered making a pilgrimage to the birthland of the Buddha, nothing
came of their plans. The well-known Chinese travelers to India—Fa-hsien
(Hokken, 340?–420?), Hsüan-tsang (Genjō, 600–664), and I-ching (Gijō,
635–713)—provided their readers in both China and Japan not only with the most
authoritative geographical information about the region, but also with a vivid sense
for the rigors of the journey.[276] It was difficult enough for the Japanese in the

Kamakura period to reach neighboring China, let alone distant India. There are indications that an occasional Japanese found his way to India, but there are no prominent examples on record.[277] Bodhisena (Bodaisenna, 704–760) was the rare case of a priest taking the reverse course from India to Japan, where he helped to dedicate the Daibutsu at Tōdaiji in 752, remaining until his death.

Myōe Shōnin (Kōben, 1173–1232) first began planning a pilgrimage to India during the winter of 1202–1203; he was thirty at the time, and was living at the residence of his maternal uncle, Yuasa Munemitsu, in Kii province.[278] Myōe had lost both his parents in separate incidents in 1180 when he was only eight years old, and was supported by Yuasa connections for the rest of his life. In 1181, the young boy went to live with another maternal uncle, the monk Jōgaku Gyōji,[279] at Jingōji, a Shingon temple on Mount Takao, northwest of the capital and south of Toga-no-o. After receiving orders and the religious name Jōben at the age of sixteen, Myōe applied himself to the study of both Shingon and Kegon theory at Sonshōin, a sub-temple of Tōdaiji. In the autumn of 1195, when he was twenty-three years of age, Myōe left Jingōji and Tōdaiji for a hermitage on Mount Shirakami, where he stayed for three years before returning to Takao. Here conditions were unsettled, and so he went back to Kii, this time to Ikadachi, upstream on the Arita River from Shirakami. From his twenty-sixth to his thirty-fourth year, 1206, when Retired Emperor Go-Toba commissioned him to restore Kōzanji, Myōe lived at various places in the Yuasa estates in the Arita district.

Late in 1212, the year of Hōnen's death, Myōe composed *An Attack on the Bad Vehicle* (Saijarin), his celebrated criticism of Hōnen's *Collection of Passages* (Senjakushū), and this was supplemented by his *Record of Moral Adornment* (Shōgonki) in the following year. Whether or not Myōe properly understood Hōnen's advocacy of the Sole-practice Calling upon the Name of the Buddha (*senju nembutsu*)—and Shinran's *Teaching, Practice, Faith, Attainment* (Kyōgyōshinshō) is an elaborate rebuttal to show that he did not—he earnestly believed that the new Pure Land movements were undermining the assumptions held in common by every Mahāyāna sect.[280] In Myōe's opinion, such movements appeared to reject the need to kindle the desire for enlightenment (*hotsu bodaishin*) preliminary to any religious practice,[281] and also to deny that methods other than the *nembutsu* were viable routes to salvation during the period of the Decline of the Law (cf., Jōkei's *Kōfukuji Petition*, Chapter Four). Myōe insisted that once believers had made an initial commitment to enter the Way of the Buddha, they might pursue any of the myriad methods to spiritual realization, which for centuries had included devotion to the Buddha Amida.[282] According to Myōe, it was erroneous to teach that one particular method was the sole route to salvation and that all other practices were to be rejected. From the new Amidist point of view, however, any attempt to awaken a desire for enlightenment smacked of egocentric self-power (*jiriki*), which prevented the devotee from totally surrendering to Amida's other-power (*tariki*), and even today this fundamental issue has yet to be completely resolved.

During the period when Myōe was making plans to travel to India, he was not yet regarded as one of the most distinguished clerics of his day, a reputation later thrust on him as a result of his religious controversy, his success at Kōzanji, and the patent sincerity of his practice and preaching. In his declining years he became a favorite of the socially prominent. His confrontation and discussion with Hōjō Yasutoki (1183-1242) about the military government clashing with the imperial forces during the Jōkyū Disturbance in 1221 belongs to the last decade of his life. [283] But temperamentally Myōe was a recluse given to visions, [284] not a politician in the mold of Mongaku, Jien, or Musō Kokushi. Although he was widely respected, even by his critics, he lacked the common touch, and the Kegon revival for which he labored so diligently died out with his immediate disciples. Myōe's call for a return to the rigorous practice of earlier Buddhism fell on deaf ears and must be accounted a failure.

Myōe made two attempts to organize a small expedition to India, the first during the winter of 1202-1203 and the second in the spring of 1205. It was on this second occasion that he calculated the distance and the time it would take to walk from the Chinese capital of Ch'ang-an (Chōan) to Rājagṛha (Ōshajō)in India. A note believed to be in his own hand summarizes his conclusions (see Figure 3).

From Ch'ang-an, capital of the Great T'ang, to Rājagṛha in [India's Ma]gadha province is a distance of 50,000 *ri*. (According to the records, it is more than 50,000 *ri*. [285] I do not know whether a long *ri* or a short *ri* is meant, but the scriptures usually employ the short *ri* as a unit of distance.) Nowadays, this makes a distance of 8,333 [long] *ri* and 12 *chō*. [286] (The long *ri* is fixed at 36 *chō*.)

A man walking a little more than 8 [long] *ri* a day could reach Rājagṛha in 1,000 days. 100 short *ri* equal 16 long *ri* and 24 *chō*. By this reckoning, 100 [short] *ri* will be a two-day journey. (Using the long *ri*, this is equivalent to 8 *ri* a day.) 1,000 *ri* will take 20 days, 10,000 *ri* will take 200 days, and 50,000 *ri* will take 1,000 days.

Let us take the number of days in a year as 360. [287] If we left Ch'ang-an on the first day of the first month of the year, we would reach Rājagṛha on the 10th day of the tenth month of the third year.

I am unable to contain my affection and longing for India, the land where the Buddha was born, and so I have drawn up plans for the journey thither. Oh, how I wish to go there! If I walked 7 [long] *ri* a day, I could reach India in 1,130 days, arriving on the 20th day of the second month of the fourth year [of my travels]. And if I walked 5 *ri* a day, I could at long last arrive on the 10th day of the sixth month of the fifth year, for a total of 1,600 days. (*Dainihon shiryo* VII, pp. 427–428)

This document is mentioned in the *Biography of Venerable Myōe of Toga-no-o* (Toga-no-o Myōe Shōnin denki), perhaps written by Myōe's colleague and disciple, Kikai (Girimbo, d. 1250), but not in the form in which we know it today[288] (Tanaka 1961, pp. 203–204). This work is not so factual as the *Acts of Venerable Myōe of Kōzanji* (Kōzanji Myōe Shōnin gyōjō), known to have been written by Kikai, but its wider circulation and imaginative content accord it an important place in the Myōe legend. According to the *Biography*,

In the spring of Genkyū 2 [1205], Myōe decided to make a journey to India, his earnest desire for many years. He and five or six like-minded colleagues shared this ambition and had already made their plans. They investigated the records of those who had made the journey concerning the number of *ri* along the route from Ch'ang-an to Rājagṛha in Central India, and Myōe recorded the results of this research. The document is now kept in his personal library of the scriptures.

When they were already outfitted for departure after careful deliberation, Myōe suddenly contracted a grave and unusual illness. He was physically well and could eat and drink as usual without any discomfort. It was only when he discussed the journey to India that he suffered in both body and mind. Sometimes he would feel a searing pain on the left side of his abdomen; at other times the right side would trouble him. And when he became deeply preoccupied with his plans, he would faint from the pain that pierced both sides of his abdomen right through to his back.

This was not all that Myōe had to suffer. Some years earlier when he was making plans to go to India, he had given up the project in compliance with various oracles from the Great Deity of Kasuga. Although he abandoned the idea for the time being, he could not give up the plan completely, and he once again began to make preparations. But after several days he was so exhausted in body and mind from the illness that he was unable to travel any great distance. To divine his prospects, he made pairs of ballots to be placed before three objects of worship: Śākyamuni, the Great Deity of Kasuga, and Sudhana with other "Good Friends" in the faith.[289] One ballot read, "Go to India"; the other "Do not go." Thoroughly carrying out his ablutions, observing the tabus, and praying, he deposited the ballots with the determination that if even one of them opted for his going, his resolution would not waver.

Myōe sent messengers with the ballots to the "Good Friends" and the Great Deity, but he himself took those for Sākyamuni, placing two ballots on the altar before the image of the Buddha. Suddenly one of the ballots tumbled over and fell beneath the altar. Myōe searched for it, but it had vanished. In astonishment he opened the remaining ballot, which read, "Do not go." The ballots from Sudhana and the Great Deity also opposed his going.

That morning the Shōnin remarked: "In a dream last night I saw two white herons flying in the sky. Above the birds stood a layman dressed in a white robe who I thought was a messenger from the Great Deity of Kasuga. I saw him take a bow and arrow and shoot down one of the herons." In retrospect he noted with curiosity that this corresponded to the disappearance of the ballot. (Washio 1925, V [Denkibu 1], pp. 269–270)

We can assume that Kikai was among those "like-minded colleagues" who were planning to accompany Myōe to India. The two monks were in the midst of an exhaustive study of commentaries on the *Garland Sutra*, a project that would last more than a decade.[290] Myōe's ambition was to revive the Kegon sect as a focus for leading Buddhism back to the original teachings and practices of Sākyamuni. Hence the proposed pilgrimage to India and the appeal to the pilgrim Sudhana.

But it is the drama surrounding Myōe's first attempt to go to India that is featured in the nō play, *The Dragon God of Kasuga* (Kasuga ryūjin), by Zeami Motokiyo (1363–1443). Myōe and his small band of followers made their preparations during the winter months of 1202 for a departure in spring or early summer. Then on the 26th day of the first month of 1203, Munemitsu's wife was possessed by the spirit of the Kasuga deity, who declared that the group should not proceed to India. Myōe made a pilgrimage to the Kasuga Shrine in Nara where, on the 11th day of the second month, he had a vision of Sākyamuni on Mt. Gṛdhrakūta. He then journeyed to Kii, where he saw the Kasuga deity in a vision on the 22nd day, and returned to the Kasuga Shrine on the 25th. Two days later he visited his friend Jōkei at Kasagidera.

The legend now provides embellishments. Composed only two decades after the *Biography* (Denki), the *Kokonchomonjū* (1254, cf., Chapter Three) is usually cited as the literary source of Zeami's *Kasuga ryūjin*, but at best it appears be only one of several.

When Myōe was planning to cross over to India in the company of more than ten disciples, he came to take leave of the Great Deity of Kasuga. As he walked to the shrine, sixty deer bowed to the ground on bended knee to pay homage to the holy man. Later, when he returned to the Yuasa district of Kii, where he was born, the Great Deity took possession of a woman who was the holy man's aunt, and made this pronouncement through her: "In order to protect the Buddha's Law, I assume familiar guises[291] in this land. Where, then, would the Shōnin go after abandoning my country?"

"I find this hard to believe," replied the Shōnin. "If this is a genuine revelation, please manifest some sign."

"You must not doubt me! When you came to my mountain, sixty deer bent their knees in adoration; this was because I was present six feet above you in the air and never left your company. It was in order to worship me that they faced in your direction and bent their knees."

"That did happen," admitted the Shōnin, "but I am still not convinced. Quickly now, show me something that an ordinary person could not do."

At this, the woman vaulted up onto a beam of the thatched roof, where she seated herself. The color of her countenance was pale blue like lapis lazuli, and from her mouth trickled a white foam, whose fragrance was beyond description.

So the Shōnin believed. "This is quite extraordinary," he said. "In recent times I have come across many puzzling statements in the *Garland Sutra*. Will you resolve them for me?"

The deity consented. Taking ink and paper, the Shōnin wrote down questions on a variety of issues, and one by one the answers were clearly given. The Shōnin was moved to tears of gratitude and gave up his plans to go abroad.

When the fragrance of the white foam spread to neighboring villages, people came out of curiosity and vied with one another for a place in the crowd, such was their boundless reverence and awe. This went on for three days, and it was a profound marvel to see the woman sitting there on the beam. (Nagazumi and Shimada 1966, pp. 100–101)

Myōe's discussion with his aunt and her gymnastic feats are not mentioned in *Kasuga ryūjin*. The *Collection of Sand and Pebbles* (Shasekishū, 1279–1283) alludes briefly to Myōe's plans, including the remark (spoken by the Kyōgen in Zeami's play) that the Kasuga Deity considered Myōe and Jōkei (Gedatsubō)to be his "Tarō and Jirō," that is, his elder and younger sons.

"I regard Myōebō and Gedatsubō as my Tarō and Jirō," declared the Great Deity of Kasuga Shrine. When the two men were once on a pilgrimage to the great shrine, all the deer on Kasuga Plain bent their knees and knelt out of respect for them. When the venerable Myōe was merely thinking of making a journey to India, the Kasuga Deity communicated with him through an oracle at Yuasa to prevent his departure. Indeed, I hear that there is a written record of this communication.

The deity explained that he would be sad if they were to be separated by such a distance, and Myōe was impressed that the god dissapproved of his leaving.

"But if I should decide to go," he inquired, "would I reach India safely?"

"If I am protecting you, what could go wrong?" replied the deity.

At that time he touched the holy man's hand, which is said to have remained fragrant for the rest of his life. (S&P 1:5; Watanabe 1966, p. 70; Morrell 1985).

Stories Old and New is believed to have been compiled as a collection of themes to be portrayed visually, and the *Illustrated Record of the Miracles of the Kasuga Avatars* (Kasuga gongen genki-e, 1309) is just such a portrayal.[292] The illustrations of this picture scroll are accompanied by a text which can be treated separately as a literary work. Its approach is more sober than that of *Stories Old and New* and reveals a surer grasp of Myōe's life and religious views.

For Myōe Shōnin of Toga-no-o the winds of the Ten Profound Interdependent Relationships[293] had dispersed the dust of the passions, and the moon of the Six Characteristics of the Dharmas[294] shone brightly through the window of his meditation. People put their trust in him, regarding him as a spiritual treasure of the nation. During the period of his seclusion on [Jingōji's Mount] Takao, he stayed for a while at Shirakami in Kii, where he suddenly determined to go abroad. Now beginning on the 19th day ot the first month of Kennin 2 [1202], during the reign of Tsuchimikado, a daughter of the Tachibana family abstained from all food and drink for eight days, and her family wondered whether she was suffering from the fasting malady.[295] But there was no change in her appearance; if anything, she appeared even more robust than usual. Every day she took a bath, read the sutras, and recited the name of Buddha. People were puzzled and asked what was going on.

She replied, "Without any distractions my heart has entered the realm of the Three Treasures, unsullied by worldly concerns."

Then on the 26th day, during the hour of the Ox [11 a.m.–1 p.m.], she attached a new straw mat to the lintel over a sliding door. Climbing up and seating herself on it, she made the following declaration: "I am the Great Deity of Kasuga. Greatly distressed at hearing that the Shōnin is going to China, I have come to prevent his departure. Because your eminence is a man of unsurpassed wisdom, I extend my protection to all those who place their trust in you. From time to time, please come to visit me in the Southern Capital."

They say that after Myōe had been vouchsafed this divine request, he gave up the plan of going abroad. (*Gunsho ruijū* II, pp. 47–48)

Myōe Shōnin left [Kii] province on the 5th day of the second month of Kennin 3 [1203] to make a pilgrimage to Kasuga. On the 7th day, while he was resting at Sonshōin at the Tōdaiji, more than thirty deer bowed down to him in unison on bended knee, while an exotic perfume filled the air.

He visited the shrine on the 11th day. While nodding off somewhat in the presence of the Divine Treasure, he was transported in a dream to Mt. Gṛdhrakūṭa,[296] where he venerated the Great Teacher Śākyamuni five or six times. Later, on his return journey to Kii, the Great Deity and his entourage appeared to him nightly in dreams. And there were those who noticed that a rare fragrance emanated from his person. (*Gunsho ruijū* II, p. 51)

The *Lives of Esoteric Masters* (Shingonden, 1325) is even more restrained.[297] Although its account is concise, it includes all the major themes developed in Zeami's production: the Kasuga Deity's prohibition, the worshipping deer, the visit to Kasuga, and the appearance of Śākyamuni on Mt. Gṛdhrakūṭa.

Myōe had a special affection for India. During the winter of the second year of the same [Kennin] period [1202], he discussed plans to travel there. On the 26th day of the first month of the third year [1203], the Great Deity of Kasuga addressed him through a certain woman.

"Abandon your plan to cross over to India. Although all the gods protect you, I and the Great Deity of Sumiyoshi are especially close. If you would consider our wishes, then you would not leave our country to make this long journey. I have come to you in order to prevent this."

"In accordance with your instructions," replied the Shōnin, "I will immediately give up all thought of it."

Again he was addressed. "It is imperative that you make a pilgrimage to Mt. Kasuga and remain there for three days."

As Myōe was traveling to the shrine in compliance with the divine command, deer knelt facing the Shōnin on bended knee. And while he was sleeping, seated in the presence of the Divine Treasure, the shrine was suddenly transformed for him into the Pure Land of Mt. Grdhrakūta (Ryōzen jōdo), and he saw the Tathāgata Śākyamuni appear before him with a great retinue . . . (Washio 1928, V [Denkibu], pp. 280–281)

There is little question that Zeami is the author of *Kasuga ryūjin*, although the date of compilation is not known. A play titled *Myōe Shōnin* is reported to have been performed in 1465,[298] and this is taken to be the first reference to a presentation of the work that we know today as *Kasuga ryūjin*.

The play can be read as an assertion of religious independence from foreign influences, much as Zeami's *Hakurakuten* is an affirmation of the native Japanese literary sensibility (see Waley 1950, pp. 248-257). In the latter work, the poet who most profoundly influenced Heian literature, Po Chü-i (Hakukyoi, 772-847), is symbolically returned to China. In *Kasuga ryūjin*, Myōe is dissuaded from visiting India on the grounds that the gods of Japan are manifestations of the eternal Buddha specifically adapted to the needs of that country. Enlightenment can be realized at any time or place, and is not a mere function of geography, for the Buddha is present in Nara just as surely as in Rājagrha.

The Dragon God of Kasuga
(Kasuga ryūjin)[299]
by Zeami

PERSONS		
	Myōe Shōnin	*Waki*
	Two Clerical Attendants	*Waki-tsure*
	Elder Official of Kasuga Shrine	
	(Tokifū Hideyuki)	*Mae-shite*
	Minor Deity of Kasuga Shrine	*Kyōgen*
	The Dragon God of Kasuga	*Nochi-shite*

PLACE   Kasuga village, Yamato province

TIME   The Second Month of a year in the early Kamakura period

I

While the shidai *entrance music is being played, Myōe Shōnin enters the stage wearing a pointed hood, an informal kimono under a broad-sleeved robe, a white divided skirt with waistband, and holding a fan and rosary. His two clerical attendants are similarly attired and stand facing Myōe.*

MYŌE AND ATTENDANTS
shidai

>Westward the moon,
>There would we travel.
>Westward the moon,
>There would we travel
>Seeking the country
>Where the sun sets.[300]

 *As the chorus takes up the refrain (*jidori*), Myōe faces the front of the stage.*

MYŌE
nanori

I am priest Myōe of Toga-no-o. Since it is our intention to travel to China and cross over to India, we now come to Nara to make a farewell visit to the Gracious Deity of Kasuga.

Myōe and Attendants face each other.

MYŌE AND ATTENDANTS
michiyuki

> Over Shikimi Plain beneath Mt. Atago,
> Over Shikimi Plain we have cast our eyes,
> Behind the pines in a row on Narabi Hill,
> Leaving behind the blue and tranquil sky
> Of the serene Capital. Here on a road
> To another capital, the Southern Capital,
> We cross the Nara Slope to arrive
> At Kasuga village on Mt. Mikasa. [301]

At the phrase, "Here on a road," Myōe turns to the front of the stage, takes two or three steps forward and then returns to his original position, indicating arrival at Kasuga. At the end of the travel song, Myōe again faces front.

MYŌE

Having traveled quickly, we have now reached the village of Kasuga. Now, quietly, I would pay homage.

ATTENDANTS

Indeed we would also.

Myōe and Attendants walk to the waki seat and are seated.

II

While the entrance music issei is being played, the Elder Official comes on stage and stands at the shite seat. He wears a Koushijō Old Man mask, an old man's wig, and an old man's cap; his collar is light yellow on a heavy silk kimono woven in a small plaid design, with a figured silk garment. He is wearing a white divided skirt with a waistband and carries a fan.

ELDER OFFICIAL
issei

As we face the clear void of sky, the brightness of the gods who soften their light [302] is revealed to us.

sashi

And the mountain is motionless, expressing the persistence of the Way of the Gods through past and present. The village is a scene of peace and tranquility, ringing with the sounds of happiness and longevity, flourishing indeed since those ancient days when they called this deity the "Heavenly Little-Roof Lord." [303]

sage-uta

> Though we only glimpse by moonlight
> The two pillars of the shrine's torii,
> We cannot mistake this fact:

age-uta

> The vows of its Four Deities,[304]
> The vows of its Four Deities,
> From the Age of the Gods until now,
> Have been unwavering.
> And so by virtue of divine intent
> To mingle with the human dust—
> Including also the lesser shrine
> Of cleansing Mizuya, the Water God—
> It is so peaceful here that even the wind
> Blowing through the pines of Mikasa grove
> Makes no sound in its branches,
> Makes no sound in its branches.

At the phrase, "the pines of Mikasa grove," the Elder turns right and takes two or three steps, returning to center stage at the phrase, "make no sound through its branches."

III

Myōe stands and faces the Elder.

MYŌE

I would have a word with this official.

ELDER OFFICIAL

Why, it's Priest Myōe of Toga-no-o, just now come on a pilgrimage! The gods will certainly be pleased to see you.

MYŌE

My reason for this journey is really nothing special. I am planning to travel to China and then cross over to India, so I have come to the shrine for a farewell visit.

ELDER OFFICIAL

Such may be your determination, but what will the gods think of this? It is your wont to visit the shrine from the year's beginning through all the four seasons. And although you may miss an occasion, the gods can hardly wait for your arrival. They call you their Tarō, and rely on Priest Gedatsu as their Jirō, for you are like a pair of eyes and a pair of hands to them. How could it please them for you to leave Japan to travel to China and cross over to India? Please abandon the idea.

MYŌE

What you say is certainly true. But how could it be contrary to the wishes of the gods for us to cross China to India in order to venerate the sites associated with the Buddha's life?

ELDER OFFICIAL

This is unworthy of you. Were the Buddha living in the world today, then surely would it avail you to see and to hear him. But nowadays the mountain of Kasuga is our Eagle Peak. Moreover, when you come to visit the shrine, not only "along Nara Slope with palms joined" [305] do people pay their respects.

CHORUS
age-uta

> The plants and trees in Mikasa Grove,
> The plants and trees in Mikasa Grove,
> Bend down their branches
> Although there is no wind.
> And as morning breaks
> On Kasuga's hills and plains,
> Even the deer turn to you.
> Paying respect with bended knee
> And tilted antlers.
> To seek elsewhere
> For the real Pure Land
> Even while witnessing such marvels
> Is to have a longing for
> "The endless autumn of Musashi plain." [306]
> It is better just to submit freely
> To the gods on whom we depend,
> And to venerate the divine will,
> To venerate the divine will.

The Elder proceeds to stage center and is seated; Myōe sits beside him.

IV

MYŌE

Now then, please relate to me the facts about this shrine.

ELDER OFFICIAL

sashi

In this regard, I would remind you that the purpose of your trip to China and India is to visit the old ruins . . .

CHORUS

. . . made famous by the Buddha's propagation of the Law. But if you would venerate Mt. T'ien T'ai, you should journey to our own Mt. Hiei; and if you have a desire to visit Mt. Wu-t'ai, then pray at Yoshino or Tsukuba.[307]

ELDER OFFICIAL

Of old it was on Holy Eagle Mount,

CHORUS

But nowadays the Buddha is manifest at the shrine on this mountain as a Great Deity for the sake of all sentient beings,

ELDER OFFICIAL

So just as you would at the Mountain of the Eagle,

CHORUS

Pay homage at the Mountain of Kasuga.

kuse   The divine poem clearly states:

> Know who I am!
> Now that Śākyamuni Buddha
> Has appeared,
> Think of me as the clear moon
> Shining over the land.[308]

Thus, He has vowed that by means of the power of the gods through which the Bodhisattvas work their myriad acts of compassion, He will shine His light on our illusions. Distressed that His Perfect Teaching was of no benefit to those of small capacity, he "removed his necklace and fine garments, put on a coarse, disheveled robe,"[309] and taught the Four Noble Truths. And the Deer Park where this transpired was this very site. On Kasuga Plain where the animals rouse themselves or recline—is this not the Deer Park?

ELDER OFFICIAL
There are other aspects of this shrine:

CHORUS
Moonlight envelops Mikasa Hill
And the spring sun[310] appears from there,
Sending beams of promise to the four directions.
And the shrine roads through Kasuga Plain—
Do they ever reach an end?
In this capital where the Buddha's Law
Flourishes like its double-flower cherry blossom,
From the great temple in the cloudless west,[311]
First touched by the rays of the moon,
To all Seven Great Temples[312] with increasing splendor,
Spring on Kasuga Plain is sheer tranquility.

V

MYŌE
Yes, it is quite wonderful! I have decided that this is the god's message to
me, and I will think no more of making a trip to China at this time. But who
are you, may I ask? Please give me your name.

ELDER OFFICIAL
If you cancel your trip to China and India, you shall see the five regions of
India reflected on Mt. Mikasa, Māyā's delivery of Śākyamuni, his attaining
enlightenment at Bodh-gaya, and his preaching the Law on Eagle Peak,

CHORUS
. . . even to the Buddha's entering Nirvāṇa beneath the dual teak trees[313]—I
will show you all these things. Please wait here a short while.

The Elder rises.

It is the gods' wish.[314] I am Tokifū Hideyuki.[315] . . . And at this, he vanishes
into thin air, vanishes into thin air.

At the shite *seat the Elder gestures and quietly retires.*

—INTERLUDE—

During an agitated orchestral prelude the Kyōgen, deity of a subsidiary
Kasuga shrine, proceeds to the Name-announcing seat. He wears a Kyōgen's
pointed hood, a "climbing beard" mask, a heavy silk kimono, a figured silk
garment, knickers, leggings, waistband, and he carries a fan and a cane.

MINOR DEITY

The person who stands before you is god of a subsidiary shrine serving the Dragon God of Kasuga. The reason for my being here is simply this. Myōe Shōnin of Toga-no-o, having planned a trip to China so as to cross over to India, made a pilgrimage to this shrine for a farewell visit. But we had Hideyuki dissuade him with various arguments. This is because the Great Deity considers Myōe Shōnin and Gedatsu Shōnin of Kasagi to be like his eyes and hands, and He would not know what to do if they went away even for a short time.

Since Gedatsu Shōnin is somewhat conceited, the Deity communicates with him only indirectly, relying on him as his Jirō, his younger son. But Myōe Shōnin is such a straightforward person with such a compassionate heart that the Deity speaks to him directly, depending upon him as his Tarō, his first son. When Myōe first made a pilgrimage to the shrine, as the Deity came out in person to greet him on Nara Slope, even the insensible grasses and trees, and every variety of bird and beast paid their respects to him by kneeling down and folding in their wings—such a noble man is he. Wondering what he would do if Myōe were no longer in attendance, He dissuaded him with various arguments.

The Shōnin, having wholeheartedly decided to make the trip to India, considered what lay before him. The distance from the capital of Ch'ang-an in the Great T'ang empire to Rājagṛha in India's Magadha province is said to be 50,000 *ri*. Feeling that the land route was endlessly long, he examined the route by sea, only to find that it was 100,000 *ri* of waves; and the perils of wind and wave are fearsome. And on the land route were steep and deserted mountain roads, where he was sure to encounter devils and venomous beasts. We are told that long ago priest Hsüan-tsang Tripiṭaka on seven occasions lost his life to serpents in the desert, but each time was revived and finally reached Rājagṛha, where he was presented with a wonderfully illustrated copy of the *Great Wisdom Sutra*, which has become a treasure for later generations.[316]

Myōe wondered how he would be able to traverse the four places of peril between China and India: the Takla Makan desert, the Pamir mountains, the Iron Gate, and the Jo River.[317] But the Shōnin sincerely wished to be like Priest Tripiṭaka of old. In order to give rein to his irrepressible longing to visit the land of India where the Buddha lived, he prayed, using the esoteric ritual of the Three Mysteries, that his aspirations would be realized. At the worldly level he measured the distances of his route over mountains and rivers. Exhausting all his energies, he vowed to worship in the footsteps of the Buddha.

The Great Deity is sympathetic toward his desire to worship in the footsteps of the Buddha, even though this means going to India. If the Buddha were alive in the world today, Myōe would be able to see and to hear Him, though it meant going to India. But under the present circumstances, what would this accomplish? Since Myōe has abandoned his plans, the Deity will reveal to him during the night the five regions of India reflected in Mikasa Mountain. Inasmuch as Hideyuki dissuaded him with various arguments, promising to show him in detail Māyā's delivery of Śākyamuni, His attaining Enlightenment at Bodh-gayā, His preaching the Law on Eagle Peak, and even His entering Nirvāṇa beneath the dual teak trees; and inasmuch as Myōe has agreed to cancel his plans, the marvels tonight are of great importance.

The Minor Deity directs his gaze above center stage.

Now the five regions of India will gradually appear. The rivers and the earth tremble. Let everyone keep calm and pray, aware of what is taking place.

The Deity withdraws

VI

MYŌE AND ATTENDANTS
age-uta (machiutai)

> Truly wondrous is this
> Divine proclamation,
> Truly wondrous is this
> Divine proclamation.
> From within the voice
> A light shines forth.
> Kasuga plain and mountain
> Become a golden world,
> While trees and grasses
> Miraculously take the form
> Of the Buddha.

VII

While the entrance music haya-fue *is being played, the Dragon God enters wearing a "black beard" mask, a red wig, a coronet with a dragon crest, a gold brocade headband, and a dark blue collar. His costume consists of a striped heavy silk kimono, a gold brocade robe with a broad divided skirt of red brocade, and a waistband. Holding a fan and a staff, he stands by the first pine tree on the bridgeway.*

CHORUS
> Now the earth trembles. Is it because the Dragon Gods of the world have convened for worship?

DRAGON GOD
> Yes, here are the Eight Great Dragon Kings.[318]

CHORUS
>> Dragon King Nanda

DRAGON GOD
>> Dragon King Upananda

CHORUS
>> Dragon King Sāgara

DRAGON GOD
>> Dragon King Vāsuki

CHORUS
>> Dragon King Taksaka

DRAGON GOD
>> Dragon King Anavatapta

CHORUS
> Hundreds of thousands of followers accompany them, attend on them,

The Dragon King enters the stage.

In waves upon the plain, all come to the Buddha's assembly

He steps back.

To hear the promulgation of the Buddha's Law.

DRAGON GOD
> In addition to these, *kinnara* King Fine Law

CHORUS
>> *Kinnara* King Law-Holder[319]

DRAGON GOD
>> *Gandharva* King Pleasant

CHORUS
>> *Gandharva* King Pleasant Sound[320]

DRAGON GOD
>*Asura* King Balin

CHORUS
>*Asura* King Rāhu [321]

>Each is accompanied by followers as numerous as the sands of the Ganges, the sands of the Ganges; and these likewise sit down in a row.

>*Holding the cane in his hand, the Dragon God mimes while the following lines are being chanted.*

VIII

CHORUS
>The billowing sleeves of the dancing Dragon Girl, [322]
>The billowing sleeves of the dancing Dragon Girl,
>Bright as whitened hemp, sweep the waves of the sea,
>Breaking them into white jewels which roll in from the offing
>Where the sea reflects the colors of the azure sky;
>While the boat of the crescent moon
>Floats on the surface of the River Sao. [323]

DRAGON GOD
>The Eight Dragon Kings,

>>*The Dragon God executes an animated dance.*

>The Eight Dragon Kings

CHORUS
>Incline their coronets and ascend into the clouds
>Over moon-lit Mikasa by Kasuga Plain.
>"Come and see, watchmen of the signal fires
>On Kasuga Plain." [324] Māyā's delivery of Śākyamuni,
>His preaching the Law on Eagle Peak,
>His entering Nirvāṇa beneath the dual teak trees—
>All are here revealed in their entirety.
>Now then, Myōe Shōnin, about your plans to go to China?

>>*[The Dragon God looks intently at Myōe.]*

MYŌE
>I abandon them.

CHORUS

And your trip to India?

MYŌE

I shall not go.

CHORUS

And the vestiges of the Buddha?

MYŌE

I shall not search for them.

CHORUS

However you inquire after them,
Majestically they fly from you
Riding the storm clouds.

The Dragon God gestures to suggest flying off in the clouds.

And as the Dragon Girl flies away to the south,[325]

He walks to the right.

The blue ripples of Sarusawa Pond[326]
Are splashed and thrashed about
As the Dragon God transforms into a serpent
Six thousand feet in length,
Coils extending from earth to sky,
And vanishes into the waters of the pond.

The Dragon God leaps up in time with the phrase, "splashed and thrashed about"; at "from earth to sky" he stands at the waki *seat and points upward. At the phrase, "vanishes into the waters," he moves along the bridgeway and leaps to the edge of the curtain to suggest entering the pond. Raising his sleeves, he stands motionless.*

Bibliography and Abbreviations

Andrews, Allan A. *The Teachings Essential for Rebirth: A Study of Genshin's Ōjōyōshū.* Tokyo: Sophia University Press, 1973.

Aston, W.G. *Nihongi: Chronicles of Japan from the Earliest Times to A.D. 697.* London: George Allen and Unwin, 1956.

Bandō Shōjun. "Myoe's Criticism of Honen's Doctrine," *The Eastern Buddhist,* New Series, 7:1 (1974), pp. 37–54.

Beal, Samuel. *A Catena of Buddhist Scriptures from the Chinese.* London: Trubner & Co., 1871.

————. *Buddhist Records of the Western World.* New York: Paragon, 1968 (reprint of 1884 original).

Birnbaum, Raoul. *The Healing Buddha.* Boulder: Shambala, 1979.

Borgen, Robert. "The Japanese Mission to China, 801–806," *Monumenta Nipponica* 37/1 (1982), pp. 1–28.

Brock, Karen. "Awaiting Maitreya at Kasagi," in *Maitreya the Future Buddha,* eds. Allan Sponberg and Helen Hardacre. Princeton: Princeton University Press, (in press).

Brower, Robert H. "Ex-Emperor Go-Toba's Secret Teachings: *Go-Toba no in Gokuden,*" *Harvard Journal of Asiatic Studies* 32, pp. 5–70.

Brower, Robert, and Earl Miner. *Japanese Court Poetry.* Stanford: Stanford University Press, 1961.

Brown, Delmer M,. and Ichirō Ishida. *The Future and the Past: A Translation and Study of the Gukanshō, an Interpretative History of Japan written in 1219.* Berkeley: University of California Press, 1979.

Brownlee, John. "Crisis as Reinforcement of the Imperial Institution: The Case of the Jōkyū Incident, 1221," *Monumenta Nipponica* 30:2, 1975, pp. 193–201.

Bukkyō daijiten. See Mochizuki Shinko, ed.

Chang, Garma C.C. *The Buddhist Teaching of Totality: The Philosophy of Hwa Yen Buddhism.* University Park and London: The Pennsylvania State University Press, 1971.

Ch'en, Kenneth. *Buddhism in China: A Historical Survey.* Princeton: Princeton University Press, 1964.

Coates, Harper Havelock, and Ryūgaku Ishizuka. *Honen the Buddhist Saint: His Life and Teaching.* Kyoto: The Chionin, 1925.

Collcutt, Martin. *Five Mountains: The Rinzai Zen Monastic Institution in Medieval Japan.* Cambridge: Harvard University Press, 1981.

Conze, Edward. *Buddhism: Its Essence and Development.* New York: Harper and Row, 1959.

————. *The Large Sutra on Perfect Wisdom with the divisions of the Abhisamayālaṅkāra.* Berkeley: University of California Press, 1975.

Cook, Francis H. *Hua-yen Buddhism: The Jewel Net of Indra.* University Park and London: The Pennsylvania State University Press, 1977.

DeBary, Wm. Theodore, ed. *The Buddhist Tradition in India, China & Japan.* New York: The Modern Library, 1969.

DeVisser, M.W. *Ancient Buddhism in Japan: Sutras and Ceremonies in Use in the Seventh and Eighth Centuries A.D. and Their History in Later Times.* Leiden: E.J. Brill, 1935. 2 volumes.

Dainihon shiryō, comp. Tōkyō Daigaku Shiryō Hensanjo, 1930 (reprint 1970), V:7.

Dutt, Nalinaksha. *Aspects of Mahāyāna Buddhism in its Relation to Hīnayāna.* London: Luzac and Co., 1930.

Eliot, Charles. *Hinduism and Buddhism: An Historical Sketch, Volume II.* London: Routledge & Kegan Paul, 1954 (reprint of 1921 edition).

Fontein, Jan. *The Pilgrimage of Sudhana: A Study of Gaṇḍavyūha Illustrations in China, Japan and Java.* The Hague: Mouton & Co., 1967.

Gunsho kaidai VIII, ed. Zoku Gunsho Ruijū Kanseikai. Tokyo, 1961.

Gunsho ruijū, ed. Hanawa Hokiichi. Tokyo: Zoku Gunsho Ruijū Kanseikai, 1959–1960 (reprint of 1928–1931 edition).

Hakeda, Yoshito S. *Kūkai: Major Works.* New York and London: Columbia University Press, 1972.

Harich-Schneider, Eta. "The Music of Japan, Record IV: Buddhist Music," vol. 15 in Alain Danielou, ed. UNESCO Collection—A Musical Anthology of the Orient; Barenreiter Musicaphon BM 30 L 2015, 1967(?).

_____. *A History of Japanese Music*. London: Oxford University Press, 1973.

Hisamatsu Senichi, et al., eds. *Shinkokinwakashū. Nihon koten bungaku taikei*, vol. 28. Tokyo: Iwanami Shoten, 1958.

Hori Ichirō. "Shakkyōka seiritsu no katei ni tsuite," *Indogaku bukkyōgaku kenkyū* 3:2 (1955).

Hori Ichirō. *Folk Religion In Japan*. Chicago: The University of Chicago Press. 1968.

Hurvitz, Leon. *Chih-I (538-597): An Introduction to the Life and Ideas of a Chinese Buddhist Monk*. Melanges Chinois et Bouddhiques 12. Bruges, 1963.

_____. *Scripture of the Lotus Blossom of the Fine Dharma*. New York: Columbia University Press, 1976.

Inoue Mitsusada. "Eizon, Ninshō and the Saidaiji Order," *Acta Asiatica* 20 (1971), pp. 77-103.

Inoue Mitsusada, and Ōsone Shōsuke, eds. *Ōjōden; hokkegenki. Nihon shisō taikei*, vol. 7. Tokyo: Iwanami Shoten, 1974.

Ishida Mizumaro, ed. *Genshin. Nihon shisō taikei*, vol.6. Tokyo: Iwanami Shoten, 1970.

Iwano Shin'yū ed. *Kokuyaku issaikyō*, vol.91. Tokyo: Daitō Shuppansha, 1961.

Kageyama Haruki. *Shintō no bijutsu*. Tokyo: Hanawa Shobo, 1965.

_____. *Nihon no bijutsu* 18: *Shintō bijutsu*. Tokyo: Shibundō, 1967.

Kamata Shigeo and Tanaka Hisao, eds. *Kamakura kyūbukkyō. Nihon shisō taikei*, vol. 15. Tokyo: Iwanami Shoten, 1971.

Kaneko, Sachiko, and Robert E. Morrell. "Sanctuary: Kamakura's Tōkeiji Convent," *Japanese Journal of Religious Studies* 10:2/3 (1983), pp. 195-228.

Kawabata Yasunari. *Japan the Beautiful and Myself*. Tokyo: Kodansha, 1969.

Kawaguchi Hisao and Shida Nobuyoshi eds. *Wakan rōeishū; ryōjin hishō. Nihon koten bungaku taikei*, vol. 73. Tokyo: Iwanami Shoten, 1965.

Kern, H. *The Saddharma Pundarīka, or The Lotus of the True Law*. Oxford: Clarendon Press, 1909. Sacred Books of the East XXI. Also Dover reprint.

Kitagawa, Joseph M. *Religion in Japanese History*. New York: Columbia University Press, 1966.

Kitagawa, Hiroshi, and Bruce T. Tsuchida, trs. *The Tale of the Heike*. Tokyo: University of Tokyo Press, 1975.

Kokka taikan, ed. Matsushita Daizaburō. Tokyo: Kigensha Shoten, 1924–1925 (Second Series). In 2 volumes.

(*Kōchū*)kokka taikei, ed. Kokumin Tosho Kabushiki Kaisha. Tokyo: Kodansha, 1975–1976 (reprint of 1930–1931 edition). 28 volumes.

Kiyota, Minoru. *Shingon Buddhism: Theory and Practice*. Los Angeles and Tokyo: Buddhist Books International, 1978.

⸻, ed. *Mahāyāna Buddhist Meditation: Theory and Practice*. Honolulu: The University Press of Hawaii, 1978.

⸻. *Gedatsukai: Its Theory and Practice*. Los Angeles and Tokyo: Buddhist Books International, 1982.

Konishi Jinichi. "Shunzei no yūgenfū to shikan," *Bungaku* 20, pp. 12–20.

Kubota Jun. "Allegory and Thought in Medieval *Waka*—Concentrating on Jien's Works Prior to the Jōkyū Disturbance," *Acta Asiatica* 37 (1979), pp. 1–28.

Kubota Jun and Yamaguchi Akio, ed. *Myōe Shōnin shū*. Tokyo: Iwanami Shoten, 1981.

Legge, James. *Travels of Fa-hsien*. Oxford University Press, 1886.

Li Yung-hsi. *A Record of the Buddhist Countries*. Peking: Chinese Buddhist Association, 1957.

Lieteau, Haruyo. "The Yasutoki-Myōe Discussion," *Monumenta Nipponica* 30/2 (1975), pp. 203–210.

Luk, Charles, tr. *The Vimalakīrti Nirdeśa Sutra*. Berkeley and London: Shambala, 1972.

Manaka Fujiko. *Jichin oshō oyobi Shūgyokushū no kenkyū*. Tokyo: Mitsuru Bunko, 1974.

Matsunaga, Alicia. *The Buddhist Philosophy of Assimilation: The Historical Development of the Honji-Suijaku Theory.* Tokyo: Sophia University, 1969.

Matsunaga, Daigan and Alicia. *Foundation of Japanese Buddhism. Vol. 1: The Aristocratic Age.* Los Angeles and Tokyo: Buddhist Books International, 1974.

_____. *Foundation of Japanese Buddhism, Vol.2: The Mass Movement (Kamakura and Muromachi Periods).* Los Angeles and Tokyo: Buddhist Books International, 1976.

McCullough, William H., and Helen Craig. *A Tale of Flowering Fortunes: Annals of Japanese Aristocratic Life in the Heian Period.* Stanford: Stanford University Press, 1980. In 2 volumes.

Mikkyō daijiten, ed. Mikkyō Jiten Hensankai. Kyoto: Hōzōkan, 1970. Six-volume reprint and expansion of the 3-vol. encyclopedia published by Naigai Press, 1931-1933.

Miyasaka Yūshō. *Kana hōgoshū. Nihon koten bungaku taikei,* vol. 83. Tokyo: Iwanami Shoten, 1964.

Mizuno Kōgen, ed. *Shin bukkyō kaidai jiten.* Tokyo: Shunjūsha, 1966.

Mochizuki Shinko, ed. *Bukkyō daijiten;* revised and enlarged by Tsukamoto Zenryū.. Kyoto: Sekai Seiten Kankō Kyōkai, 1954-1963 (Ten-volume enlargement of the 3-volume dictionary of 1909-1931, with its 1932-1936 supplement.)

Morrell, Robert E. "The Buddhist Poetry in the *Goshūishū,*" *Monumenta Nipponica* 28/1 (1973), pp. 87-100.

_____. "Jōkei and the Kōfukuji Petition," *Japanese Journal of Religious Studies* 10/1 (1983), pp. 6-38.

_____. "Kamakura Accounts of Myōe Shōnin as Popular Religious Hero," *Japanese Journal of Religious Studies* 9/2-3 (1982), pp. 171-198.

_____. "Mirror for Women: Mujū Ichien's *Tsuma Kagami,*" *Monumenta Nipponica* 35/1 (1980), pp. 45-75.

_____. "Mujū Ichien's Shintō-Buddhist Syncretism: *Shasekishū* Book 1," *Monumenta Nipponica* 28/4 (1973), pp. 447-488.

_____. "Passage to India Denied: Zeami's *Kasuga Ryūjin,*" *Monumenta Nipponica* 37/2 (1982), pp. 179-200.

_____. "Shingon's Kakukai on the Immanence of the Pure Land," *Japanese Journal of Religious Studies* 11/2–3 (1984), pp. 195–220.

_____. *Sand and Pebbles (Shasekishū): The Tales of Mujū Ichien, A Voice for Pluralism in Kamakura Buddhism.* Albany: State University of New York Press, 1985.

Müller, F. Max, ed. *Buddhist Mahāyāna Texts.* Delhi: Motilal Banarsidass, 1965 (reprint of 1894 edition).

Murti, T. R. V. *The Central Philosophy of Buddhism: A Study of the Mādhyamika System.* London: Unwin Paperbacks, 1980.

Nakamura, Hajime. *Ways of Thinking of Eastern Peoples: India-China-Tibet-Japan.* Honolulu: East-West Center, 1964.

Nakamura Hajime, Hayashima Kyōshō, and Kino Kazuyoshi, eds. *Jōdo sambukyō.* Tokyo: Iwanami Shoten (Iwanami Bunko series), 1963, 1964. In 2 volumes.

Nagazumi Yasuaki and Shimada Isao, eds. *Kokonchomonjū. Nihon koten bungaku taikei,* vol 84. Tokyo: Iwanami Shoten, 1966.

Nihon emakimono zenshū VII: *Kegon engi.* Tokyo: Kadokawa Shoten, 1959.

Noma Seiroku. *Kasuga gongen genki-e. Nihon emakimono zenshū* XV. Tokyo: Kadokawa Shoten, 1963.

Nippon Gakujutsu Shinkōkai, ed. *The Manyōshū: One Thousand Poems Selected and Translated from the Japanese.* Tokyo: Iwanami Shoten, 1940.

Oda Susumu. *Nihon no kyōkishi.* Tokyo: Shisakusha, 1980.

Okazaki Jōji. *Pure Land Buddhist Painting.* Tokyo: Kodansha, 1977. Translation of Nihon no bijutsu 43: *Jōdokyōga.*

O'Neill, P.G. *Early Nō Drama: Its Background, Character and Development 1300– 1450.* London: Lund Humphries, 1958.

Petzold, Bruno. *Buddhist Prophet Nichiren—A Lotus in the Sun.* Ed. by Shotaro Iida and Wendy Simmonds. Tokyo: Hokke Janaru, 1978.

Ponsonby-Fane, R.A.B. *Studies in Shintō and Shrines* (Rev.Ed.). Kyoto: Kenkyūsha, 1953.

Rasmus, Rebecca, tr. "The Sayings of Myōe Shōnin of Togano-o," *The Eastern Buddhist, New Series* 15/1 (1982), pp. 89–105.

Reischauer, A.K. "Genshin's Ojo Yoshu: Collected Essays on Birth into Paradise," *The Transactions of the Asiatic Society of Japan, Second Series*, vol. 7 (1930), pp. 16–97.

Reischauer, Edwin O. "The *Heiji Monogatari*," in Edwin O. Reischauer and Joseph K. Yamagiwa, eds. *Translations from Early Japanese Literature.* Cambridge: Harvard University Press, 1951.

Rhodes, Robert F., tr. "Saichō's *Mappō Tōmyōki*: The Candle of the Latter Dharma," *The Eastern Buddhist, New Series* 13/1 (1980), pp. 79–103.

Rhys Davids, Caroline. *The Book of Kindred Sayings (Sanyutta-nikāya)* or *Grouped Suttas*, Vol. 1. London: Luzac, 1917 (reprinted 1950). Vol. II. London: Luzac, 1922 (reprinted 1953).

Rosenfield, John M., and Fumiko E. and Edwin A. Cranston. *The Courtly Tradition in Japanese Art and Literature: Selections from the Hofer and Hyde Collections.* Cambridge: Fogg Art Museum, Harvard University, 1973.

Ruch, Barbara A. "Otogi Bunko and Short Stories of the Muromachi Period," unpublished Ph.D. dissertation, Columbia University, 1965.

Sakamoto Yukio and Iwamoto Yutaka eds. *Hokkekyō*, vols I–III. Tokyo: Iwanami Shoten (Iwanami Bunko), 1962, 1964, 1967.

Sanari Kentarō, ed. *Yōkyoku taikan.* Tokyo: Meiji Shoin, 1930. In 7 volumes.

Sato Hiroaki and Burton Watson, eds. *From the Country of Eight Islands: An Anthology of Japanese Poetry.* Garden City, N.Y.: Doubleday, 1981.

Satō Seijun, tr. in Tsukamoto Zenryū, ed. *Nihon no meicho: Hōnen; Myōe.* Tokyo Chūō Kōron, 1971.

Sansom, George. *A History of Japan to 1334.* Stanford: Stanford University Press, 1958.

Saunders, E. Dale. *Mudrā: A Study of Symbolic Gestures in Japanese Buddhist Sculpture.* Bollingen Series LVIII. New York: Pantheon Books, 1960.

Seiten. Buddhist Churches of America, ed. *Shinshū Seiten: Jōdo Shin Buddhist Teaching.* San Francisco, 1978.

Sekiguchi Shindai, ed. *Maka shikan.* Tokyo: Iwanami Shoten (Iwanami Bunko series), 1966. In 2 volumes.

Shimazu Isamu. "'Takaoka, Prince Imperial Shinnyo," *Transactions of the Asiatic Society of Japan, Third Series*, V (1957), pp. 1–35.

Shirahata Yoshi. *Shōzōga.* Nihon no bijutsu 8. Tokyo: Shibundō, 1966.

Shiseki zassan, ed. Kokusho Kankōkai. Tokyo: Zoku Gunsho Ruijū Kanseikai, 1974 (reprint of 1911–1912 edition), vol. 1.

Sieffert, Rene. *Nô et Kyôgen,* I: *Printemps Été.* Paris: Publications Orientalistes de France, 1979.

Suzuki, Daisetz Teitaro. *Essays in Zen Buddhism (Third Series).* London: Luzac and Co., 1934.

Tada Kōryū, Ōkubo Ryōjun, Tamara Yoshirō, and Asai Endō, eds. *Tendai hongaku ron.* Nihon shisō taikei 9. Tokyo: Iwanami Shoten, 1973.

T. Takakusu Junjirō, et al., eds. *Taishō shinshū daizōkyō.* Tokyo: Taishō Shinshū Daizōkyō Kankōkai, 1962; reprint of 1924–1932 edition. 100 volumes. Numbering through vol. 55 in Paul Demieville, et al., eds. *Hōbōgirin: Fascicule Annexe.* Tokyo: Maison Franco-Japonaise, 1931.

Tada Kōryū, Ōkubo Ryōjun, Tamara Yoshirō, and Asai Endō, eds. *Tendai hongaku ron. Nihon shisō taikei 9.* Tokyo: Iwanami Shoten, 1973.

Taga Munehaya. *Jien. Jimbutsu sōsho* series 15. Tokyo: Yoshikawa Kōbunkan, 1959.

————. "Jien no shakkyōka," in Bukkyō Bungaku Kenkyūkai, ed. *Bukkyō bungaku kenkyū* 6. Kyoto: Hōzōkan, 1968, pp. 117–149.

————. *Kōhon shūgyokushū.* Tokyo: Yoshikawa Kōbunkan, 1971.

————. *A Record of the Buddhist Religion as Practised in India and the Malay Archipelago (A.D. 671–695).* Delhi: Munshiram Manoharlal, 1966 (reprint of 1896 edition).

Takatori Masao, Akai Tatsurō and Fujii Manabu, eds. *Zusetsu nihon bukkyōshi.* Kyoto: Hōzōkan, 1980, 1981. In 3 volumes.

Tanaka Hisao. *Myōe. Jimbutsu sōsho* series 60. Tokyo: Yoshikawa Kōbunkan, 1961.

Thomas, Edward J. *The History of Buddhist Thought.* London: Routledge & Kegan Paul 1933.

Bibliography and Abbreviations 1 3 1

Ury, Marian. "Recluses and Eccentric Monks: Tales from the *Hosshinshū* by Kamo no Chōmei," *Monumenta Nipponica* 27/2 (1972), pp. 149–173.

Washio Junkei, ed. *Kokubun tōhō bukkyō sōsho*, Series One, 10 vols. Tokyo: Kokubun Tōhō Bukkyō Sōsho Kankōkai, 1925–1927; Series Two, 8 vols. Tokyo: Tōhō Shoin, 1927–1933.

_____. *Zōtei ihon bukke jimmei jisho*. Tokyo: Tokyo Bijutsu, 1979 (reprinted and enlarged from the 1903 edition).

Watanabe Tsunaya. *Shasekishū. Nihon koten bungaku taikei* 85. Tokyo: Iwanami Shoten, 1966.

Watson, Burton. *Japanese Literature in Chinese, Volume 1: Poetry & Prose by Japanese Writers of the Early Period*. New York and London: Columbia University Press, 1975.

Watters, Thomas. *On Yuan Chwang's Travels in India*. Delhi: Munshiram Manoharlal, 1961 (reprint of 1904 edition).

Waley, Arthur. *The Real Tripitaka and Other Pieces*. London: George Allen and Unwin, 1952.

Weinstein, Stanley. "The Kanjin Kakumushō," unpublished Ph.D. dissertation, Harvard University, 1965.

_____. "Rennyo and the Shinshū Revival," in John W. Hall and Toyoda Takeshi, eds. *Japan in the Muromachi Age*. Berkeley/Los Angeles/London: University of California Press, 1977.

Yamada Shōzen and Miki Sumito, eds. *Zōtanshū*. Tokyo: Miyai Shoten, 1973.

Yamagishi Tokuhei, ed. *Hachidaishūshō*. Tokyo: Yūseidō, 1960. In 3 volumes.

Zoku kokka taikan, ed. Matsushita Daizaburō. Tokyo: Kigensha, 1925–1925; 1958 reprint. In 2 volumes.

Zoku shiryō taisei, ed. Takeuchi Rizō. Kyoto: Rinsen Shoten, 1967.

Table of Translations

A.D.

594 *Mo-ho chih-kuan* (*Maka shikan*; Great Cessation and Insight) by Chih-i (Chigi, 538–597) / Kuan-ting (Kanjō, 561–632); selection from 1:2:1, p. 14.

ca. 983 *Nihon ōjō gokurakuki* (Accounts of Japanese Born into Paradise) by Yoshishige Yasutane (ca. 931–1002); chapter 17 (on Kūya Shōnin), pp. 15–16.

ca. 985–1017 *Yokawa hōgo* (The Yokawa Tract) by Genshin (Eshin 942–1017), pp. 17–18. Complete.

1205 *Tenjiku riteisho* (Calculations on the Distance to India) by Myōe (Kōben, 1173–1232). pp. 105–106. Complete.

1205 *Kōfukuji sōjō* (The Kōfukuji Petition) by Jōkei (Gedatsubō, 1155–1213). pp. 75–88. Complete.

ca.1208 *Gedatsu shōnin kairitsu saikō gammon* (The Venerable Gedatsu's Written Vow for the Restoration of the Precepts) by Jōkei / Kainyo (Chisokubō, d. 1213), pp. 7–9. Complete.

1213 *Kanjin'i shōjōemmyō no koto* (On the Purity and Clarity for Contemplating Mind) by Jōkei, p.71. Selection.

ca. 1223 *Kakukai hōkyō hōgo* (Bridge-of-the-Law Kakukai's Discourse on the Dharma) by Kakukai (Nanshōbō, 1142–1223) through a disciple, pp. 97–101. Complete.

1235–38 *Toga-no-o Myōe shōnin ikun* (Final Injunctions of the Venerable Myōe of Toga-no-o) by Myōe / Kōshin (ca. 1193–1250), pp. 53–65. Complete.

ca. 1232–1245 *Toga-no-o Myōe shōnin denki* (Biography of the Venerable Myōe of Toga-no-o) by (?) Kikai (Girimbō, d. 1250), pp. 106–107. Selection.

1254 *Kokonchomonjū* (Stories Old and New) by Tachibana Narisue (dates unknown). Selections from 2:53 (Ryōnin), pp. 18–20; 2:61 (Jōkei), p. 10; 2:64 (Myōe), pp. 47–48, 109–10.

1279–1238 *Shasekishū* (Collection of Sand and Pebbles) by Mujū Ichien (1226–1312). Selections from 1:5, pp. 69, 109; 2:10, p. 92; 3:5, p. 9; 3:8, pp. 50–52; 5B:9, p. 30.

1309 *Kasuga gongen genki-e* (Illustrated Record of the Miracles of the Kasuga Avatars), pp. 109–110 (selections on Myōe).

1325 *Shingonden* (Lives of Esoteric Masters) by Eikai (1268–1348), pp. 110–111 (selection on Myōe).

15c. *Kasuga ryūjin* (The Dragon God of Kasuga) by Zeami Motokiyo (1363–1443), pp. 112–122. Complete.

Shakkyōka ("Poems on Śākyamuni's Teachings") and associated verse in the royal anthologies of waka (*chokusenshū*): *Kokinshū, Gosenshū, Goshūishū, Senzaishū, Shinkokinshū, Shinchokusenshū, Shokugosenshū, Shokukokinshū, Shokushūishū, Shingosenshū, Gyokuyōshū, Shokusenzaishū, Shokugoshūishū, Fūgashū, Shinsenzaishū,* and *Shinshokukokinshū.* Also poems in *Kokin rokujō* and *Fubokushū*; and cross-references to Jien's *Shūgyokushū.* See index for page number of specific poems.

1. Weinstein 1977, p. 331ff.

2. Matsunaga 1976, p. 134. Matsunaga 1974, pp. 218–223, provides a useful survey of the *mappō* theory. See also Morrell 1985, n. 1.

3. Ch'en 1964, p. 298, indicates that the 500/1000 pattern was the most prevalent among four possibilities in his discussion of Hsin-hsing and the Sect of the Three Stages.

4. Since the year 1 A.D. immediately follows 1 B.C.

5. Is it mere coincidence that the *Chronicles of Japan* (Nihon shoki, 720; Aston II, pp. 65–67) gives 552 as the year of the first official introduction of Buddhism to Japan?

6. Nichiren's position is condensed in his slogan, *Ritsu koku zoku* (Ritsu is the Traitor to the Country); Petzold 1978, pp. 107–109.

7. Matsunaga 1974, pp. 47–64, discusses the Hīnayāna precepts and the founding of the Japanese Ritsu sect in detail.

8. Ch'en 1964, p. 301. This Tao-hsüen is not to be confused with Ganjin's disciple (702–760) having the same romanized name, but different characters.

9. Dommutoku-bu; also Hōzōbu. A branch of the Sarvāstivādins, the Dharmagupta school (ca. 184–84 B.C.) was one of the traditional twenty Hīnayānist sects. For additional fragmentary information see Thomas 1951, passim; Beal 1871,pp. xiii, 204–244.

10. North of today's Tokyo, near Nikkō.

11. These are conveniently summarized in Matsunaga 1969, pp. 152–155; cf. Inoue 1971, p. 87ff.; Dutt 1930, pp. 290–322.

12. Also Jitsuhan or Jippan; Inoue 1971, pp. 77–78; Coates and Ishizuka 1925, p. 168. The *Honchō kōsōden* (1702) says that Jitsuban wrote a book called *The Ordination Platform Procedures* (Kaidan shiki; Iwano 1961, p. 889), but the work is not listed in standard bibliographies and is presumably lost.

13. Adapted from Washio 1979, introduction p. 196 (Kairitsushū); Mochizuki 1955, vol. 6, addendum p. 29 (Shibunrisshū); and Inoue 1971. Of course, the names of many monks may appear in several lines of transmission. Jōkei, for example, is also listed under the Hossō sect.

14. Translation made from the modern annotated edition in Kamata and Tanaka 1971, pp. 10–11, 304 (*kambun* original), whose text is a manuscript copy of the *Gammon* held by the Kōfukuji and believed to be a Nambokuchō copy.

15. In early Buddhism *biku* (Skt., bhiksu) and *bikuni* (Skt., bhiksuni,) designated full-fledged monks and nuns who observed the standard Hīnayānist precepts (*gusokukai*), normally 250 for monks and 348 for nuns. *Shami* (śrāmanera) and *shamini* (śrāmaṇerī) were under-age novices who observed a group of ten precepts (*jikkai*); and the *shikishamana* (śikṣāmaṇā) were advanced apprentice nuns who were preparing themselves to observe the full precepts. *Ubasoku* (upāsakā) and *ubai* (upāsikā) designated male and female laymen who merely observed the five basic regulations (*gokai*). Mahāyāna practice and local adaptations in both China and Japan considerably modified the observance of the regulations. For example, *shami* often merely referred to a householder with wife and children who shaved his head and wore clerical dress. The other terms tended to be used in Japan mainly by those concerned with the restoration of the original vinaya.

16. *Jūjuritsu* (T. 1435), the precepts of the Hīnayānist Sarvāstivādin (Setsu-issaiubu) school translated by Kumārajīva and others.

17. The three groups of scriptures constituting the "Three Baskets" (*sanzō; tripiṭaka*) of early Buddhism. In the beginning they were memorized and recited, only being committed to writing around the time of Aśoka (ca. 273–232 B.C.). The Chinese translators here use the older transliterations from Sanskrit (*bini, shutara*, and *abidon*) instead of the more familiar translations (*ritsu, kyō*, and *ron*).

18. The traditional Six Nara Sects (Kusha, Jōjitsu, Ritsu, Hossō, Sanron, Kegon) plus Tendai and Shingon from the Heian period.

19. *Sangaku.* Commonly indicating the three general characteristics of the Buddhist teaching— morality (*śīla*), wisdom (*prajñā*) and meditation (*samādhi*), the term here refers to the three parallel practices which lead to an increase in one's powers (*sōjō*) to observe the precepts (*sōjōkaigaku*), to attain wisdom (*sōjōegaku*), and to perfect meditation (*sōjōshingaku*).

20. *Jūshi*, or *sanshi shichishō* (Three Masters and Seven Witnesses) as Jōkei uses the term later on. During the ceremony conferring the Hīnayānist Precepts (*gusokukai*), three main celebrants (*sanshi*)—Preceptor (Kai wajō), Rule Reader (Kommashi), and Expositor (Kyōjushi), were accompanied by seven bhikṣus (*shichi shō[myō] shi*) as witnesses.

21. Yuima no Daie. A major ceremony held at the Kōfukuji at which nine or ten learned priests acted as expounders (*ryūgi*) to answer difficult points of doctrine. Originally seriously conducted to determine a candidate's worth, the discussion eventually degenerated into a formality. See DeVisser1935, II, pp. 596, 605; 471–472.

22. I am uncertain of the meaning of the two romanized phrases in this sentence. Jōkei appears to be saying that formerly those initiated into the priesthood could be expected to achieve a high level of spiritual realization.

23. Similar examination assemblies, with the *Lotus Sutra* as the focus, were conducted on Mount Hiei and other Tendai centers where they were known as Eight Expoundings of the Lotus (*Hokke hakkō*).

24. The distinction between difficult and easy paths (*nan'i nidō*) to salvation is traced to the *Jūjūbibasharon*, T. 1521, attributed to Nāgārjuna, and refers to attainment through one's own effort as opposed to attainment through the power of faith. The two paths are likened to walking on land and floating on the sea, and Amidism contrasts the "self-power" (*jiriki*) of works with the "other-power" (*tariki*) of faith in Amida. But faith may be directed toward objects of worship other than Amida, as we see, for example, in Jōkei's devotion to Maitreya.

25. The standard grouping of Nara's Seven Great Temples (Nanto shichidaiji): Tōdaiji (Kegon), Kōfukuji (Hossō), [Shin] Gangōji (Kegon), Daianji (Sanron; later Shingon), Yakushiji (Hossō), Saidaiji (Shingon/Ritsu), and Hōryūji (Yuishiki/Sanron; later Hossō, now Shōtokushū). See n. 312.

26. *Biku, bikuni, shami*, and *shamini*; see note 15.

27. Such as the Kaijusenji, to which Jōkei retired in 1208 and where he may have written this document.

28. Jōkei's disciple Chisokubō (d. 1213); see chart 1.

29. *Ango*, observed from the 15th day of the fourth month to the 15th day of the seventh month.

30. *pācittiya.* A lesser offense within the Complete Regulations (*gusokukai*) meriting hell but forgivable through repentance.

31. *pārājika.* One of the four most serious offenses for a monk, calling for expulsion from the order. Mujū is poking fun, of course, at the scholasticism of much of the clergy of his day; it is hard to imagine that the monk in the anecdote would not have known that killing is a major offense in both traditions.

32. Paraphrased from *Shasekishū* (1279–1283) 3:5; Watanabe 1966, pp. 154–155; Morrell 1985, pp. 130–131.

33. *Kokonchomonjū* 2:61; Nagazumi and Shimada 1966, p. 96.

34. *Fumimiru* associates *fumi-* ("to walk, step") with *fumi* ("a writing"); hence, "to walk and see" and "to read the [sacred] writings."

35. *The Collection of Ancient and Modern Times Continued* (Shokukokinshu, 1251) includes a variant on this poem (ShokuKKS VIII: 802; *Kōchū kokka taikei* 8, p. 506): When Bishop Shinken became abbot of the Sankaiji, he immediately held a Thirty-Part Discussion [of the Lotus Sutra, i.e., of the 28 chapters of the sutra itself plus the "opening" *Muryōgikyō* and the "closing" *Fugengyō*]. As snow began to fall on the people in attendance, Priest Zōben, hearing a difficult issue presented, asked how it was to be answered. Jōkei wrote the following in the snow with a rib of his cypress fan.

Inishie wa	In ancient times
Fumimishikadomo	They saw where they were walking;
Shirayuki no	But now indeed the path,
Fukaki michi koso	Covered deep in white snow,
Ato mo oboene	Shows no tracks at all!

36. *Kantō ōgenki,* in *Shiseki zassan* I, pp. 1.2 The passage in question is translated in Morrell 1985, pp. 30–32.

37. In contrast, say, to Myōe, who belonged to the Kōzanji tradition; see Mochizuki 1955, 6: supplement p. 30.

38. Cited from Harich-Schneider 1973, pp. 319–321. One of the three records (OUP 111, side 2) includes a fragment of Ubaribai. See also Harich-Schneider 1967 (?), "The Music of Japan, Record IV: Buddhist Music," vol 15 in Alain Danielou, ed. UNESCO Collection—A Musical Anthology of the Orient; Barenreiter Musicaphon BM 30 L 2015. Plates 3 and 4 show the scroll and an example of its neumatic notation.

39. C. *Pan Chou San Mei Ching*; 3 fascicles. The most popular of four extant translations of a lost Sanskrit original, this Han dynasty (A.D. 179) version by Lokaksema (Shirukasen, 147–186) is among the earliest of Mahāyāna sutras.

40. Represented in a Japanese copy of a Sung painting brought from China by Hōnen's disciple Shunjōbō Chōgen (1121–1206) and now owned by the Nison-in in Kyoto. See Okazaki 1977, pp. 16–17.

41. Also known as the Seven Eminent Founders (*shichi kōso*), or simply, the Seven Founders (*shichiso*).

42. The early Tenjukoku Mandala, for example, depicting the Land of Heavenly Longevity, is said to have been created in 623 in memory of Prince Shōtoku. It is generally believed that the Land of Heavenly Longevity is the Land of the Buddha of Eternal Life (Muryōju), that is, Amida's Paradise; but the hanging may in fact depict Maitreya's Tusita Heaven.

43. *Fa-hua Hsüan-i, Hokke gengi*; T. 1716.

44. *Fa-hua Wen-chü, Hokke mongu*, T. 1718.

45. Hori Ichirō (1910-1974), the eminent scholar of Japanese folk religion, prefers the reading, Kōya. See Hori 1968, pp. 83-139, especially pp. 106-107. He also distinguishes between the popular religious dance, *odori-nembutsu*, traditionally said to have been initiated by Kūya, and *nembutsu-odori*. Originally the two may have had the same meaning. "Later, however, odori-Nembutsu meant professional dancing originally under the leadership of Nembutsu-hijiri. Nembutsu-odori meant dancing, dramas, music and so on, derived from odori-Nembutsu, but which had lost religious elements." (p. 126, n. 68 ; see also Kitagawa 1966, pp. 73-82.)

46. Carved before 1207 by Unkei's son, Kōshō. See Mōri 1977, pp. 83-85.

47. The present-day Keisokuji ("Chicken Leg Temple") in Himeji.

48. Not identified.

49. Unclear. Possibly an ascetic practice related to the moxa treatment. See Hori 1968, p. 119, for similar austerities practiced by Nembutsu ascetics.

50. The identity of both individuals is uncertain.

51. Yasutane refers to the civil disorders of this and the preceding period, commonly known as the *Jōhei Tengyō no ran*, during which the government was threatened by Taira Masakado (d. 940) and Fujiwara Sumitomo (d. 941). Kūya became active shortly thereafter, enrolling on Mt. Hiei with the name Kōshō, ca. 948.

52. *Nihon ōjō gokurakuki* 17, in Inoue and Ōsone 1974, pp. 28-29.

53. Translated in Keene 1960, pp. 197-212. It is also reasonable to suppose that Yasutane's *Accounts* may have inspired Kamo's *Tales of Pious Resolution* (Hosshinshū, ca. 1214). Chōmei also had Amidist leanings, but of the Tendai variety (see Ury 1972, p. 151). In 1212 Myōe's *Saijarin* had attacked Hōnen largely on the ground that Hōnen deprecated the need for "aspiration to enlightenment," *hotsu[bodai]shin*. Chōmei's sympathies on the issue can be seen in his choice of title for the collection. For a translation of the *Chiteiki* see Watson 1975, pp. 57-64.

54. See Hori 1968, pp. 109-110, for more on Yasutane, including translation from the preface to *Accounts*.

55. See, for example, the description of the Amitābha Hall at the Hōjōji in *Eiga monogatari* 18 (McCullough 1980, II, pp. 564-580).

56. For a survey of these two schools see Ui 1959, pp. 33-74; for a selection of annotated texts, including one by Ryōgen and three by Genshin, see Tada et al. 1973.

57. *Ōjōyōshū*; translated in Reischauer 1930, pp. 16-97. See also Andrews 1973; Hori 1968, pp. 107-108; and Okazaki 1977, pp. 98-102 for Genshin's influence on Japanese art.

58. *Shingosenshū* IX: 702; *Fūgashū* XVIII:2069. See Chapter Two.

59. Translated from the modern printing of the version in the collection of Uji's Byōdōin in Miyasaka 1964, pp. 51-52.

60. Cf., Hori 1968, p. 121: "This idea [of the wicked who attained paradise and of the good who failed to] . . . indicates that the state of one's mind at the moment of death is paramount in determining one's destiny in the future life, just as the possibility of deification or of becoming a *goryō* was believed to have depended primarily upon a determined mind in the last moment of life. The common belief, and the foundation of the belief in *goryō*, was that nothing was impossible to a determined mind at the moment of death."

61. Translated from the modern printing of the version in the Library Department of the Imperial Household Ministry (Kunaichō shoryōbu) in Nagazumi and Shimada 1966, pp. 89–91 (item 53).

62. By traditional count whereby Ryōnin's year of birth (1072) is already his first year, we arrive at 1117. "Twenty-four years" depends on a like calculation.

63. The tentativeness of Ryōnin's closing remarks perhaps reflects the fact that the statement was written seven years after the event.

64. Takatori et al. 1981, I, pp. 244–245, provides illustrations of the subscription list and other items associated with Ryōnin and the Yūzūnembutsu sect not readily available elsewhere.

65. *kyūyō*; also *kyūsei*. The nine stars which control human destiny according to the Yin-yang system of divination.

66. *nijūhasshuku*. Traditional grouping of stars into twenty-eight clusters.

67. *jōbon jōshō*. The highest of nine grades of birth in Amida's Pure Land as described in the *Kammuryōjukyō*, Part III. See Müller 1965, p. 188; Seiten 1978, pp. 39–40.

68. "Ryōnin (1072–1132) was a pioneer of Tendai *shōmyō* who invented the notation system *meyasu-hakase* ('notation easy on the eye'), recording the melodic unit in the form of florid neumes" (Harich-Schneider 1973, p. 316.) A manuscript entitled *Eulogy of the Four Wisdoms* (Shichi-no-san) in Ryōnin's hand dated 1110 is the oldest surviving example of *shōmyō* notation (ibid., pp. 318–319; plate 12a and accompanying recording).

69. A 5-fascicle version held by the Shōren'in was completed in 1346 by Son'en (1298–1356) and later augmented by two books to make the 7-fascicle popular edition (*rufubon*) of 1594, which is numbered among the "Six Private Collections" (*rokkashū*). Taga 1971 uses its own numbering system, 1-6117; but references in this article to the *Shūgyokushū* (hereafter, SGS) will retain the standard *Zoku kokka taikan* numbering. The 7-fascicle version is also to be found in *K.taikei* x.

70. More or less. Yamagishi 1960, 111, p. 89, states that Jien has two *shakkyōka* in the *Shokugosenshū*, but at least one text (*K. taikei* v, pp. 284–286) attributes five to him. Such discrepancies will slightly affect the total count.

71. However, Jien's Buddhist poems provide us with one direct reference (*Fūgashū* XVIII: 2092, see below) to a building called Hannyadai ("Wisdom Heights") which Jōkei dedicated in 1195 at Kasagidera, 12 km NE of the Kōfukuji (Morrell 1983, pp. 10–11).

72. For additional details see Reischauer and Yamagiwa 1951, pp. 375–457; Sansom 1958, pp. 210–11, 255–63; Brown and Ishida 1979, pp. 94–120.

73. Inasmuch as the detailed analysis of court titles and their English equivalents in McCullough 1980, II, pp. 787–831, is likely to be the standard reference for some time to come, I have adopted their usage even where it conflicts with Brown and Ishida 1979. The *Gukanshō* translation, for example, distinguishes between *Sesshō* ("Regent") and *Kampaku* ("Chancellor"), the names for the official appointed to govern during the ruler's minority. The former title was used before the emperor's Coming-of-Age ceremony (*gempuku*), the latter employed subsequently. McCullough II, p. 795, uses the term "Regent" for both; "Chancellor" translates Daijō Daijin in place of Brown and Ishida's "Prime Minister." With clerical ranks, however, I have been less consistent.

74. By Japanese count (*sai*), here and later. Western usage would require the circumlocution, "in his tenth year."

75. SZS XVII: 1134; Yamagishi 1960, II, p. 472. The fourth line, *waga tatsu soma ni* ("Upon this hall of timbers hewn from the mountain") is an allusive variation on the Saichō poem composed when he built the Central Hall on Mt. Hiei (*Shinkokinshū* XX: 1921, tr. below). It also alludes to an anonymous poem in the *Gosenshū* (II:64):

Ōzora ni	Would that I
Oou bakari no	Might have a sleeve to cover
Sode mo ga na	The entire sky:
Haru fuku hana wo	Then the spring-blown blossoms
Kaze ni makaseji	Would not be routed by the wind.

76. SZS XIX: 1222; Yamagishi 1960, II, p. 492.

77. SZS XIX: 1223. One of two poems in the imperial anthologies by this obscure monk, who is not to be confused with the later Abbot of the Shōren'in (see note 69), although both use the same characters.

78. *Gunsho ruijū* XIII, pp. 365–83 (Book 218) has the text; for the complex problem of dating see *Gunsho kaidai* VIII, pp. 50–53.

79. cf., Brower 1967, p. 124. This poem is also mentioned in *Shasekishū* 5A:12 (Watanabe 1966, p. 224) in a slight variation.

80. Famous mountain in Tottori Prefecture off the Sea of Japan, east of Matsue. This poem also appears among the *shakkyōka* of the *Shokushikashū*, private collection by Shunzei's conservative rival, Fujiwara Kiyosuke (1104–77); see Gunsho ruijū X, p. 84 (Book 148).

81. According to Yamagishi 1960, II, p. 801. Chien has not been identified.

82. Mitsu (no) dera, "The Temple of the Three Crossings," now commonly called Daifukuin. Founded by Gyōgi Bosatsu (668–749) in Naniwa (Ōsaka), it enshrines an Eleven-faced Kannon said to have been carved by him.

83. According to tradition, Saichō erected the Komponchūdō on Mt. Hiei in 788 and enshrined within it an image of the Buddha Yakushi. See also note 75 and associated text for Jien's allusive variation on this poem.

84. In the spring of 850 and again in the spring of 851, Chishō Daishi (Enchin 814–891), founder of Tendai's Onjōji (Miidera), prayed to the Sannō deity, Shintō protector of Mt. Hiei, that he might be permitted to go to China in search of the Law. Having received a favorable sign in a dream, he made the journey in the fall of 853, shortly after Ennin's return to Japan. Selections from his travel diary are translated in Waley 1952, pp. 159–68.

85. Bodaiji. This is the early name for Nara's Tachibanadera, one of seven notable temples founded by Prince Shōtoku. However, Hisamatsu et al. 1958, p. 389, suggests that the word is not a proper noun; hence, "ancestral temple." Yamagishi 1960, II, p. 802, hints at a site in Tamba Province.

86. Gokuraku. Amida's Pure Land of "Supreme Bliss."

87. Name of a cave on Mt. Kimpu in Yamato Province, Shō no Iwaya. The *shō* is a musical instrument with a grouping of vertical pipes, a shape perhaps suggesting the natural formation. *Shasekishū* 8:22 (Watanabe 1966, p. 360–61) also places Nichizō Shōnin (d. 985) at this site.

88. Gratitude for the good fortune that the serenity of his retreat approaches the inner peace of the Buddha.

89. Amidist Pure Land devotees often attached one end of a five-colored cord to the hands of an image of Amida and placed the other end in the hands of a person at the time of death, who would then symbolically be drawn up to the Western Paradise. When Hōnen (1133–1212) died, however, he is said to have declined this consolation (Coates and Ishizuka 1925, p. 636).

90. Little is known of this monk who lived early in the eleventh century and also has a poem in the *Goshūishū* (1086).

91. Eshin (942–1017), the noted Tendai Amidist, author of the *Essentials of Salvation* (Ōjōyōshū, 985).

92. The Temple of the Four Heavenly Kings (Shitennōji) founded by Prince Shōtoku in Naniwa (Ōsaka). Jien was the temple's abbot from 1207 to 1209.

93. Michinaga's daughter, the Empress Shōshi (988–1074). She appears prominently in the *Eiga monogatari*; see McCullough 1980, I-II. Jōtōmon'in was the title given to her when she took the tonsure in 1026. The poem also appears in the *Shokushikashu* (see note 80).

94. Presumably as the serpent became a Buddha. The reference is to the eight-year-old daughter of the dragon king Sāgara who attained instant Buddhahood, as described in Chapter 12 (Devadatta) of the *Lotus Sutra*. See Hurvitz 1976, pp. 199–201; also the conclusion of *Kasuga ryūjin* in Appendix.

95. Fujiwara Tadamichi (1097–1164), Jien's father and founder of the Hosshōji.

96. *Lotus Sutra*. Chapter XIII. Sakamoto and Iwamoto II 1964, p. 238; Hurvitz 1976, p. 206:
> We, venerating and believing the Buddha,
>   Will don the armor of forbearance,
> And, to preach this scripture,
>   Will endure these troubles, etc . . .

97. Fujiwara Tadanobu (967–1035). See McCullough I 1980, p. 162, *passim*.

98. Enlightenment Lectures (*bodaikō*) on the *Lotus Sutra* were held at the Urin'in in Kyoto's Murasakino ("Purple Field") district. *Afuchi* (*ōchi*, "bead-flower") associates with *afu* ("to meet, encounter," e.g., the Buddha's Law). Moreover, Amida and his retinue were thought to lead to Paradise those who trusted in him. Urin'in was a famous literary site in the Heian Period; see McCullough II 1980, p. 513, n. 72.

99. Biographical details are skimpy on this poetess (fl. ca. 1100) whose name derives from the fact that she was a daughter of the Governor of Higo Province, Fujiwara Sanenari. Fifty-nine of her poems are included in the imperial anthologies.

100. The Mahāyānist account of Sākyamuni's death in the *Daihatsu nehangyō* ("Northern text," T. 374) stresses his eternal nature, as does Chapter XVI of the *Lotus Sutra*, both works being especially important to the Tendai sect. The historical Buddha is said to have died on the fifteenth day of the second month in the garden at Kusinagara, and his passing is a popular literary and pictorial motif with prominent moon and falling flower imagery. See *Goshūishū* XX: 1181–85 (Morrell 1973, pp. 92–94); ShokuSIS XIX: 1365, translated below.

101. This poem also appears in Kiyosuke's *Shokushikashū* (cf, SKKS XX: 1919, 1927) with some variation (*Gunsho ruijū* X, p. 84): "When Higo was reciting the *Nirvana Sutra*, a divine youth who appeared to be just over ten years of age wrote this verse and gave it to her: 'In the spring wind,/Even the ice . . . etc.' In her dream she replied: 'Valley stream: . . . etc.'"

102. So also the essentially unsullied Buddha-nature immanent in all sentient beings is revealed when the agitation of the stream of human consciousness is quieted.

103. Go-Toba includes this among Jien's "best liked poems that people are constantly quoting" (Brower 1972, pp. 37, 58–59).

104. Allusive variation on a poem by the Tendai Priest Sosei (fl. ca. 890), *Kokinshu* XI: 470.

Oto ni nomi	Knowing you only by report,
Kiku no shiratsuyu	I feel my lot to be like the white dew
Yoru wa okite	Resting on the chrysanthemums:
Hiru wa omou ni	We both arise during the night
Aezu kenubeshi	And do not survive the noon sun.

Jien quotes the second and third lines. The interest of Sosei's "Love" poem turns on several pivot-words. *Kiku*, "chrysanthemum," associates with its homonym, "to hear"; okite, "put, place, rest," with "to arise." And the *(h)i* of *omo(h)i*, "to think," suggests "sun."

105. *gokuraku*. Although this term usually refers to Amida's Pure Land, which Hōnen's movement saw as attainable solely by the Other Power (*tariki*) of Amida's forty-eight vows, Jien here writes in the context of Tendai's Self-Power (*jiriki*) meditation (*kannen*) on Amida through which one attains the supreme bliss (*gokuraku*) of Buddhahood in this very body (*sokushin jōbutsu*).

106. *Lotus Sutra*. Chapter II (Sakamoto and Iwamoto I 1962, p. 106; Hurvitz 1976, p. 34). The *Lotus Sutra*'s, and Tendai's, claim that there is only One Vehicle, One Law, means that all sentient beings will eventually attain the *same* religious realization; it is equally insistent that the Buddha employs a *variety* of "expedient devices" to accomplish this.

107. cf., *Lotus Sutra* XXI (Sakamoto and Iwamoto III 1967, p. 164; Hurvitz 1976, pp. 289–90): ". . . As the wind in the midst of space/ Is unobstructed by anything."

108. *Lotus Sutra*, Chapter VIII (Sakamoto and Iwamoto II 1964, p. 86; Hurvitz 1976, p. 7).

109. *Lotus Sutra*, Chapter XVII (Sakamoto and Iwamoto III 1967, p. 44; Hurvitz 1976, p. 247).

110. Initially Mt. Gṛdhrakūṭa (Ryōjusen) in India, where Śākyamuni proclaimed the *Lotus Sutra*; then by association, Japan's Mt. Hiei, headquarters of the Tendai sect, for whom this is the basic scripture. Scholars working from Sanskrit sources (e.g., Kern 1909) frequently render the name as "Vulture Peak." But since Chinese and Japanese know the place through Kumārajīva's use of the character for "eagle" (J. *washi, ju*), Hurvitz's rendering as "Numinous Eagle Mount" seems entirely appropriate, and certainly less forbidding, than "Vulture Peak."

111. To the six realms of transmigration. Again, as in SKKS XX: 1942, this poem is not to be construed as an assertion of dogmatic exclusiveness. *All* are included in the One Vehicle of the Mahāyāna, however different may be the expedient devices they employ. Only those who are deluded into thinking that there are Three Distinct Vehicles, as did the earlier Hīnayānists, are subject to return until such time as they realize that there is one equal salvation for all.

112. *Lotus Sutra*. Chapter XXV (Sakamoto and Iwamoto III 1967, p. 260; Hurvitz 1976, p. 160.) This chapter is sometimes treated independently as the *Kannon Sutra*.

113. Amida, Kannon and an assembly of divine beings on purple clouds were said to meet (*raigō*) the devotee at the time of death to escort him to the Western Pure Land. Cf., SKKS XX: 1930 and n. 98.

114. *Lotus Sutra*. Chapter VIII (Sakamoto and Iwamoto II 1964, P. 102; Hurvitz 1976, p. 160).

115. Pūrṇa (Furuna), noted for his eloquence as a preacher and one of Śākyamuni's original Ten Great Disciples who heard the teaching at the Deer Park near Benares, is represented in the

Lotus Sutra as adopting the guise of a mere "voice-hearer" (*shōmon, śrāvaka*). He "inwardly concealed his bodhisattva-conduct" as an expedient teaching device even though he actually understood the profound teaching of the Mahāyāna.

116. Texts for the translations from this collection and those which follow are in *K. taikei* V-VIII.

117. *Shari hōonkō*: also *sharie, sharikō*. The Sarīra Service to honor the temple's relics; instituted by Tendai's Ennin (Jikaku Daishi, 794–864) in 860.

118. A follow-up from the preceding poem. When the clouds of our illusion are dispersed, we can see the moon of the Buddha's Law shining on the summit of Eagle Peak and/or Mt. Hiei.

119. *gobu*, literally "five parts." The central Karma Assembly of Diamond Mandala (*kongōkai; vajradhātu*) consists of five moon-circles: a central circle in which is represented Mahāvairocana (Dainichi nyorai) surrounded by encircled Buddhas in the four directions. See Kiyota 1978, pp. 93–98.

120. Allusive variation on a poem in the *Goshūishū* (VII:449) by Ōe no Yoshitoki (fl. early XI century). Yamagishi I 1960, p. 739 provides the *furigana*, Yoshinobu; Hisamatau et al. 1958, p. 480 suggests Yoshitoki or Yoshikoto.

Kimi ga yo wa	May your reign last
Chiyo ni hitotabi	Until the dust which settles once
Iru chiri no	In every thousand years
Shirakumo kakaru	Grows to be a mountain
Yama to naru made	Ringed with white clouds.

121. *jikkai*. The ten worlds of beings, or "stations of being" (Kiyota 1978, pp. 51–52): hells, hungry-beings, beasts, fighting beings, men, gods, *śrāvaka, pratyekabuddha, bodhisattva*, Buddha.

122. *mitsu* ("fulfill, realize one's prayers, hopes") associates with mitsu ("full, broad, high," as a tide, current, flood). A probable geographical reference to the Yodo River flowing west to Naniwa (Ōsaka) Bay, as well as a metaphorical reference to Amida's Western Paradise. Hence "...I pledge my efforts and pray that I may be born in Amida's Pure Land." Cf., Kubota 1979, pp. 12–13.

123. Hie (popularly, Hiyoshi) Shrine in Sakamoto consists of "Twenty-one Shrines of the Sannō God" (*Sannō nijū issha*), the Shintō protector of Tendai's Enryakuji; and among these is the Jūzenji Shrine. This partly explains the inclusion of a shrine poem among *shakkyōka*. Moreover, in the Kamakura period Jūzenji Gongen was identified as a "manifest trace" (*suijaku*) of the bodhisattva Jizō.

124. Some versions of the poem have *satori* ("understanding, enlightenment") instead of *tayori* ("news, tidings") in the third line.

125. This is preceded in the collection by a poem by Princess Senshi (Senshi Naishinnō, 964–1031), daughter of Emperor Murakami and High Priestess of the Kamo Shrine, 975–1031. Its headnote, "Stopping to lodge at a grass hermitage," suggests that Jien's poem may be an allusive variation.

Kusa no io ni	Over the years
Toshi heshi hodo no	Spent in this grass retreat
Kokoro ni wa	Have you perhaps thought
Tsuyu kakaran to	In your heart: "My stay here
Omoikakeki ya	Will be as brief as the falling dew"?

Taga 1971 No. 2652, however, has the same headnote but a somewhat different hermitage poem, not ascribed to Senshi.

126. *Lotus Sutra* XVIII, "The Merits of Appropriate Joy" (*Zuikikudokubon*); Sakamoto and Iwamoto 1967, p. 84; Hurvitz 1976, p. 261:

> If a man in the Dharma-assembly
> Can hear this scriptural canon
> And, even for a single gāthā,
> Rejoice appropriately and preach it to others,
> *And if in this way it is taught by turns*
> Till it reaches the fiftieth,
> The happiness obtained by the last person
> I will now set forth with discrimination: . . .

127. See n. 100 and Higo's poem (SKKS XX: 1931) on the *Nirvana Sutra*, above. Śākyamuni died on the fifteenth day of the second month at the time of the full moon and was then cremated. The garden in which he died is also known as the Grove of Cranes because at that time "the trees are said to have turned white as cranes" (McCullough II 1980, p. 514, n.77); see also Morrell 1973, pp. 92–94. Śākyamuni's final moments are also described in the Mahāyānist *Buddhacarita* (Acts of the Buddha; Busshogyōsan. T. 192), of which several versions are available in English.

128. *Onriedo*; also, *enriedo*. Title of the first of ten divisions of the *Essentials of Salvation* (Ōjōyōshū, 985) by the Tendai Amidist, Genshin (Eshin, 942–1017). See Ishida 1970, pp. 10–11, 485; Reischauer 1930, pp. 25–27.

129. *Lotus Sutra* XXIII, "The Former Affairs of the Bodhisattva Medicine King"; Sakamoto and Iwamoto III 1967, p. 208; Hurvitz 1976, p. 301: "After my passage into extinction, within the last five hundred years, broadly proclaim and propagate it in Jambudvipa, never allowing it to be cut off..." In what is obviously a misprint, *K. taikei* VI, p. 594, gives the name as Jihō rather than Jichin; but see Taga 1971, no. 2735.

130. On the Hie Shrine and its relationship to the Enryakuji, see note 123.

131. *Onriedo*, see note 128 and associated poem. The fifth line of the *Shūgyokushū* version (SGS 5978) has: *Aki no yo no tsuki* ("Moon of an autumn night").

132. cf., SKKS XX: 1944, SCSS X: 596–597. See also notes 110 and 118.

133. That is, the world during the period of the Decline of the Law (*mappō*)—a notion which obsessed Jien and many, but not all, of his contemporaries. ZKT places this poem in the private collection, the *Akishino gesseishū*, of Jien's nephew, Yoshitsune; Taga 1971 lists it as SGS No. 2001. Both versions begin with *saritomo to* instead of *saritomo na*.

134. The famous *Commentary on the Lotus Sutra* (Hokkekyō gisho, ca. 614–15) by Prince Shōtoku (573–621) was said to have been written during his meditations in the Hall of Dreams (Yumedono) at Nara's Hōryūji. In 1195 the Hossō monk Jōkei (Gedatsubō, 1155–1213) consecrated a great sutra repository called Hannyadai ("Wisdom Heights") at Kasagidera, whose centerpiece was a new copy of the voluminous *Great Wisdom Sutra* (Morrell 1983, pp. 10–11). A prelate of Jien's eminence would no doubt have had access to both copies and so could make the comparison. Mention of the Hall of *Dreams* permits Jien to play on the well-worn dream/reality polarity.

135. The Mahāyānist Two Truths maintain that although the Absolute (*shintai, paramārtha satya*) is ultimately beyond every conceptual formulation or system, a variety of conventional

truths (*zokutai, saṃvṛti satya*) ʼcan be employed as means (*hōben, upāya*) to lead up to it (see Murti 1980, pp. 244–55), as "fingers pointing at the moon." Jien appears to be saying that one can arrive at Enlightenment by a variety of paths and our only real problem is indecisiveness. In the fifth phrase of the poem I have followed Taga's *tōrazarurame* instead of *tomarazarurame* as given in K. taikei VII, p. 615.

136. However, this poem is preceded by one which the compiler of the collection evidently thought was similar in spirit. It is by Seal-of-the-Law Chōshun (fl. ca. 1348) and based on a phrase from the *Shikan bugyō denguketsu* T. 1912), a commentary on Chih-i's *Great Cessation and Insight*, by Chan-jan (Tannen, 711–782).

On the meaning of "Returning to the Original Principle: the Three Thousand Dharmas in One Moment of Consciousness"

Furusato ni	Truly we do not
Kaeru wa yasuki	Realize the simple principle
Kotowari wo	Of return to our old home,
Shirade ya yoyo ni	And so we will have lost our way
Mayoikiniken	From one world to another.

[SSZS IX:855]

137. *Lotus Sutra* I, "Introduction"; Sakamoto and Iwamoto I 1962, p. 62; Hurvitz 1976, p. 21:

"I saw how the Buddha Torch-Burner's (Dīpamkara)
Former signal ray was of the same sort."

138. *Lotus Sutra* I; Sakamoto and Iwamoto I 1962, p. 24; Hurvitz 1976, p. 5:

When the ray from between his brows
Illuminates the east,
Eighteen thousand lands
Are all the color of gold.

139. Shukaku Hōshinnō, Cloistered Prince Shukaku (1150–1202). Son of Emperor Go-Shirakawa and brother of the poetess, Princess Shikishi (d. 1201), Shukaku was abbot of Ninnaji from 1169.

140. This obscure priest, whose name literally means "Bright Sound," may have belonged to a family of flute players. Motokata's father was the famous music historian, Motomasa (1077–1138). See Harich-Schneider 1973, pp. 253–62.

141. A notation at the top of Jōnin's famous painting of Myōe meditating in a tree (Figure 2) states that the location was "in the Rope-Seat Tree on Meditation Rock at Kōzanji's Mount Ryōga ('Lanka')." See Bandō 1974, frontispiece; Shirahata 1966, Plate 4; *Kegon engi* 1959, text p. 9.

142. *eju myōju*. Possibly a reference to the Parable of the Hidden Jewel in the *Lotus Sutra* (Ch. 8) in which the inherent Buddha-nature of which worldly men are unaware is likened to a precious stone sewn in a garment.

143. K. *Taikei* 5, p. 92. Cf., Sato and Watson 1981, p. 191.

144. According to one view expressed in the *Great Treatise on Wisdom* (Daichidoron, T. 1509) a short kalpa is the time required to empty a hundred square mile (40 *li*^{2}) city enclosure filled with poppy seeds if one seed were removed every three years.

145. There is no general agreement on Kōshin's dates. If he were 71 *sai* in 1263 (Tanaka 1961, p. 235), then he would have been born in 1193, and thirty-nine in 1232, the year of Myōe's death. Other records, however, indicate that he was twenty-nine that year (Tanaka 1961, p. 251). And at

least one modern source (Mizuno 1966, p. 268) lists his dates as 1219–1250, which would mean that Kōshin was still in his teens when he compiled the *Final Injunctions.*

146. Shallow, medium, and deep understanding are represented by the metaphor of a rabbit, a horse, and an elephant crossing a ford. The rabbit skims the surface, the horse is half-submerged, while the elephant makes the crossing with his legs firmly planted on the river-bed. Miyasaka finds this metaphor in the *Ubasokukaikyō* (T. 1488) and in the *Bibasharon* (T. 1547). As depicted in the *Kokonchomonjū*, Myōe was an avid reader. A tabulation of such relatively obscure references would help define the extent of his erudition.

147. The literature of Buddhism frequently stresses the good fortune of our having been born in human form, where we have the opportunity of following the Buddha's teaching. See, for example, the opening statement of Mujū's *Tsuma kagami* (Morrell 1980, p. 51). A defiled mind will lead to rebirth in one of the Three Evil Destinies beneath the human realm: the world of the animals, the world of the hungry-ghosts, and the hells.

148. *susuki hōshi. Dengaku* ("Field Music") began as a rustic entertainment but toward the end of the Heian period was performed by a class of entertainers who shaved their heads and attached themselves to temples in order to avoid taxation and labor service (O'Neill 1958, pp. 4–8). I have not been able to identify the specific sub-class called "Eulalia Priests."

149. *Agongyō,* "Sutras of the Tradition." The four *āgamas* in Chinese translation roughly correspond to the five Nikāyas ("Discourses") of the Pali *Sutta-piṭaka.* Miyasaka identifies four among a number of possible early sources for this statement. As for the somewhat brusque ending of this section, Kōshin records the aphorisms as Myōe's verbatim statements to his immediate disciples rather than as general moral admonitions. The order is not directed at us, but at someone who was present when Myōe made the remark.

150. References to the Hell Chapter (Jigokubon) of the *Sutra of Meditation on the True Law* (Shōbōnenjokyō, T. 721).

151. The pagoda is located just west of the intersection of Ōmiya and Ninth Avenue on Kyoto's southern edge of town, east of the Rajōmon Gate. Myōe presumably walked down Ōmiya, which runs north-and-south just east of the original side of the Imperial Palace.

152. Hashinoku-ō (Pali, Pasenadi), King of Kosalā. The source of this story is the *Zōagongyō* (T. 99, Samyuktāgama), the Chinese translation of the *āgama* (cf., note 149) parallel to the Pali *Samyutta-nikāya.* The Pali version is about King Pasenadi and his grandmother (Rhys Davids 1917, p. 122).

153. The central Mahāyāna doctrine that not only is the phenomenal world empty (*kū*) of any abiding self or substance (*muga*), but that the elements (*hō,* dharmas) postulated by the Sarvāstivāda and other Hīnayāna schools are equally empty. Myōe's Kegon sect views the phenomenal world as the "interdependent arising of the realm of elements" (*hokkai engi*), Emptiness being defined as Dependent Origination.

154. *Tennin(no)shi.* One of the Ten Epithets (*jūgō*) of the Buddha, a concept developed in early Buddhist writings. There is also a *Jūgōkyō* (T. 782), Sutra of the Ten Epithets, which may have been known to Myōe.

155. *shintai.* The multiplicity of the world viewed as arising interdependently (cf., note 153) is Empty of any self or substance; this is the Ultimate or Absolute Truth. The same world viewed empirically, however, has a provisional existence (*ke*); this is the complementary Conventional Truth (*zokutai*).

156. *Daihatsunehangyō.* Both "Northern Text" (T 374), Ch. 15, and "Southern Text" (T. 375), Ch. 14, differ slightly from Myōe's citation.

157. *Dengaku, sarugaku.* Both are precursors of the nō drama. See note 148.

158. *jōhari no kagami.* Mirror at Emma'a court in hell in which is reflected the good and evil karma produced by the deceased during his lifetime.

159. *Engakukyō* (T. 842).

160. The *Engakukyō ryakusho* (T. 1795) by Kuei-feng Tsung-mi (Keihō Shūmitsu, 779–841). The influential Tsung-mi was fifth patriarch of the Chinese Hua-yen (Kegon) sect in addition to being the last representative of the Ch'an transmission from Hui-neng's noted disciple Shen-hui (Kataku Jinne, 668–770). Traditionally there has been a close rapport between Kegon philosophy and Zen practice.

161. *shōken.* Originally, Right Views, a step in the Eightfold Path; but here probably "the man with discrimination."

162. *Hōshakkyō* (T. 310). The reference is not in the extant version of the sutra.

163. The commendable but inferior vehicles of śràvaka (*shōmonjō*) and pratyeka-buddha (*engakujō*) focused upon the attainment of nirvana, which the Mahāyāna contrasts with the way of the bodhisattva, whose wisdom (bodhi) leads to selfless compassion (karuna) for all sentient beings.

164. *Shutsugen monki.* The work is no longer extant.

165. Unlike Kegon, the Hossō sect of Myōe's friend Jōkei (1155–1213) teaches that a certain class of sentient being does not have the nature (*mushō*) to attain Buddhahood. Myōe seems to be saying that such a notion might be provisionally useful in motivating people to religious practice, whereas the theoretically correct view might lead to complacence and egoistic attachment.

166. *Dengaku no nō* and *Sarugaku no nō.* Myōe has already expressed a lack of enthusiasm for these entertainments in items 3 and 17.

167. That is, they are wolves in sheep's clothing (?). The force of the comparison is unclear.

168. *Zōagongyō* (T. 99, Samyuktāgama); cf., *Samyutta-nikāya* 16:10. The Pali account does not say that the nun was Ānanda's sister, nor that she fell into hell (Rhys Davids 1922, p. 146).

169. Presumably to be distinguished, at least in the matter of degree, from the decisive commitment of "awakening the desire for enlightenment" (*hotsubodaishin*) which was central to Kegon, and Myōe's, thought.

170. At least as far as the devotee is concerned; cf., Mujū's *Shasekishū* 2:6.

171. *Mandara shaku.* The work is no longer extant.

172. Kōzanji on Mount Toga-no-o.

173. *shinji.* The substratum of undifferentiated Consciousness to which the various forms of meditation would penetrate. "This mind-ground is the locus of religious practice promoted by the Four Houses of the Mahayana, together with the Zen sect." (Morrell 1980, p. 70).

174. As new sects developed in Japan they were eventually included in a standard grouping of recognized teachings, from the Six Nara Sects (Kusha, Jōjitsu, Sanron, Ritsu, Hossō and Kegon) to as many as thirteen, with numerous sub-schools, in recent times. In early Kamakura the Eight Sects, mentioned by Jōkei in his Petition, included Tendai and Shingon in addition to the Nara group.

175. Chōken is noteworthy as the founder of the Agui school of popular preachers from which emerged the *Shintōshū* (Collection of the Way of the Gods, ca. 1358–61), a collection of stories which mark the transition from *setsuwa* to *otogizōshi* (Ruch 1965, p. 151). Chōken's son Shōgaku (also, Seikaku or Shōkaku, 1167–1235) is the subject of an amusing anecdote in Mujū's *Shasekishū* (Collection of Sand and Pebbles, 1279–83) 6:8; Morrell 1985, pp. 187–88.

176. The theory that the teaching of the present Buddha, Śākyamuni, would progressively decline through three periods until its final extinction had several interpretations in China and Japan, and strongly colored Kamakura Buddhist thought. Hōnen's authority, and that of many others, was the *Mappō tōmyōki* (Record of the Lamp during the Latter Days), traditionally but doubtfully ascribed to Tendai's Saichō (767–822). (Article 8 of Jōkei's Petition—see p. 86—includes a statement attributed to Hōnen's followers which seems to refer to this document.) Among several views proposed in the *Record* for the beginning of *mappō*, the one which eventually gained popularity in Japan placed the death of Śākyamuni at B.C. 949 and assumed that each of the two early periods lasted for a millennium. This would place the start of the Decline of the Law at A.D. 1052, which was compatible with Fa-shang's view (see Rhodes 1980, p. 91).

177. An'yō, The Land of Peace and Rest, is another name for Amida's Pure Land. In spite of Jōkei's opposition to what he regarded as the excesses of the popular Pure Land movements, writings from his last years show Amidist leanings in addition to his devotion to Maitreya (Miroku) and Kannon.

178. Kanezane, brother of the Tendai prelate Jien (1155–1225) and author of the *Gyokuyō* diary, became a *senju nembutsu* convert in 1177 and was the impetus behind Hōnen's composing the *Senjakushū*. The Kōfukuji was the Fujiwara clan's family temple; Kanezane, as head of the clan, was responsible for its restoration.

179. Parallel to Amida's Western Paradise is Maitreya's Pure Land, the Tusita Heaven (*tosotsuten*). With the overwhelming success of the *nembutsu* movements, the term Pure Land (*jōdo*) has virtually come to refer to Amida's; but some representations of other paradises survive, such as Maitreya's Tuṣita Heaven and Kannon's Mount Potalaka (Fudarakusen). (See Okazaki 1977, pp. 29–36, 75–82; Brock 1985).

180. In Shintō-Buddhist syncretic thought Maitreya is identified at different times as the Original Ground (*honji*) of which Kasuga's Ninomiya, Wakamiya and Sanjū-hassho-daimyōjin are viewed as the Manifest Traces (*suijaku*). See Kageyama 1965, pp. 51, 137; Matsunaga 1969, p. 232, 240–43.

181. The *Mahāprajñāpāramitāsūtra*, J. *Daihannyaharamittakyō*; T. 220.

182. *Rishubun*, T. 220 (10), 578; the Adhyardhasatika (Conze 1960, pp. 79–80). Although this sutra is a tantric work, Jōkei unlike Myōe who developed a synthesis of Kegon and Shingon, had little training in esotericism (Tanaka 1987, p. 461).

183. Myōe visited Kasuga Shrine in the second month of 1203 during his first attempt to mount an expedition to visit India. It was at this time that the deer knelt to him, but the sequence of events suggests that Jōkei is not included in the depiction of this event in the *Kasuga Gongen genki-e* (Noma 1963, color plate 9; see also Appendix A).

184. Verse included in the *Gyokuyōshū* (Collection of Jeweled Leaves), XX: 2720, with this headnote: "When Jōkei Shōnin moved to a place called Wisdom Heights, he wanted to invite the Great Deity of Kasuga, which caused the god to respond with this poem" (K. Taikei 6, p. 604).

185. Verse included in the *Shokukokinshū* (Collection of Ancient and Modern Times Continued, 1265) VII: 691, with a short headnote ascribing the poem to the Great Deity of Kasuga (K. Taikei 5, p. 491); also *Kasuga ryūjin*, n.308.

186. Myōe's visit to Jōkei at Kàsagidera late in the second month of 1203 (see note 183) is represented in *maki* 17.3 of the *Kasuga Gongen genki-e* (Noma 1963, illustration p. 82, text p. 58).

187. Myōe's attack on Hōnen's *Senjakushū* (1198; made public 1212) came in two installments: the *Saijarin* (An Attack on the Bad Vehicle, 1212) and the *Shōgonki* (Record of Moral Adornment, 1213). Unlike Jōkei's Petition, which was composed as a concise summary of common complaints against the *senju nembutsu*, Myōe's works are an elaborate rebuttal directed against the movement's claim to be the sole religious method appropriate to the *mappō* period, and to its rejection, or at least downgrading, of the need to kindle the desire for enlightenment (*hotsu bodaishin*). See Bandō 1974; for additional recent information about Myōe, see Rasmus 1982 and Appendix A.

188. *Fudarakusen.* Among several scriptural sources for Kannon's Potalaka Pure Land are the three Chinese translations of the *Garland Sutra* (Kegonkyō, T. 278, 279, 293; Avatamsaka). The pilgrim Sudhana's visit to Avalokitesvara (Kannon) is 28th of the 54 stages. Potalaka was said to be in the sea south of India, but its translation to a Japanese setting placed it near Nachi Falls or even (as Jōkei may have viewed it) at the Kasuga Shrine. Kaijusenji owns a Kamakura wall painting of Mt. Potalaka (Okazaki 1977, pp. 82–83) as well as a statue of Jōkei. See Fontein 1967, pp. 10, 101, 211; Brock 1985.

189. For the history of *sange* and related terms, see deVisser 1935, I: 249–56.

190. The idealist philosopher Vasubandhu (5th century) is traditionlly credited with the *Sukhāvatīvyūhôpadeśa* (Treatise on the Pure Land; Jōdoron, T. 1524). For a translation and commentary on this work and its influence on Chinese and Japanese Pure Land Buddhism, see Kiyota 1978, pp. 249–296.

191. For an alternate (but much older) translation of this passage by the venerable Nanjō Bunyū (1849-1927) see Muller 1965, p. 73. Professor Kiyota notes that "In the popular Pure Land tradition, this line [i.e., what follows the double hyphen] is omitted" (Kiyota 1978, p. 274). But cf., Seiten 1978, p. 11.

192. These two items comprise what is known as the Seven-Article Injunction (*Shichikajō seiki*) and are included in Shunjō's life of Hōnen, from which they have been rendered into English (Coates and Ishizuka 1925, pp. 550–554).

193. In spite of his help to Hōnen during the last year of his life, Jien regarded his behavior to have been the result of possession by a "deceptive demon" (*jumma*); Brown and Ishida 1979, pp. 171–73.

194. Statement inscribed on the front page of the *teihon*, but not part of Jōkei's text. The editor has attached the *kambun* addenda without transcription or annotation (Tanaka 1971, pp. 316-17).

195. Jōkei's praise of Saichō is all the more striking when we remember that four centuries earlier the Tendai founder's great opponent was the Hossō monk, Tokuichi.

196. Because of the criticism it provoked (see also Bandō 1974, p. 49), this early variety of Pure Land picture lost favor and was replaced by the *kōmyō honzon*, a central column of 8–10 characters emitting rays which fall on a Pure Land assembly, without others being represented. No examples of this genre survive, and the *Petition* is our main source of information about it (Okazaki 1977, pp. 167–171). *Shasekishū* 1:10 mentions the mandala and also apparently refers to the *Petition* (Morrell 1985, p. 102).

197. The scriptural authority is the *Meditation Sutra*: ". . . each ray extends so far as to shine over the worlds of the ten quarters, whereby Buddha embraces and protects all the beings who think upon him and does not exclude (any one of them)." Müller 1965, p. 180; cf., Nakamura et al. 1964b, p. 56; *Seiten* 1978, p. 34.

198. A biography of the great Vasubandhu, the *Basohanzu hōshiden* (T. 2049) mentions Buddhamitra (Kakushin Ronshi, V century A.D.) as a disciple. His offense is described in Article 6. The case of Dharmapriya (Hōai, or Dommabi, IV century) is unclear.

199. (*Ōjō)raisan(ge)*, T. 1980. Shan-tao (Zendō, 613–681), fifth of the seven Pure Land patriarchs, was a crucial influence on Hōnen by his emphasis on recitation over meditation (Matsunaga 1976, pp. 26–27, 59, 69). Throughout the *Petition* Jōkei appeals to the very sutras and authorities accepted as basic by the Pure Land movement. Kyoto's Chion-ji owns a splendid portrait of Shan-tao from the Kamakura period (Okazaki 1977, pp. 172–173).

200. The 28 chapters of Kumārajīva's translation of the *Lotus Sutra* (Myōhōrengekyō, T. 262) are grouped into eight "scrolls" (*kan*). The *Sutra of Innumerable Meanings* (Muryōgikyō, T. 276) and the *Sutra of Meditation on the Bodhisattva Universal Vow* (Fugengyō, T. 277) were traditionally seen as its "opening" and "closing" sutras, for a total of ten scrolls.

201. Seven decades later Mujū relates such an episode in *Shasekishū* 1:10 (Morrell 1985, pp. 97–103).

202. *Kegonkyō*. See note 188.

203. Hsin-hsing founded the Sect of the Three Stages. Unlike the view prevalent in Jōkei's day (see note 176) the combined span of the first two periods of the Law tended to be seen by the Chinese as 1500 years. This, then, would place *mappō* not at 1052 by the Western calendar, but at A.D. 552 (Ch'en 1964, pp. 297–300).

204. This story appears to combine two incidents recorded in the *Shakumon jikyōroku* (Personal Record of Followers of the Buddha, T. 2083): vol. 51, p. 806 tells of one Hsiao-Tz'u who lost his ability to speak, and also of a certain Shen-fang (Shimbō), who saw Hsin-hsing take the form of a serpent with an enormous mouth.

205. *gogyakuzai*. The five offenses which cause rebirth in the lowest hell: 1. Killing one's mother; 2. Killing one's father; 3. Killing an arhat; 4. Spilling a Buddha's blood; 5. Causing dissention in the community. (This is the original Indian order, but in China and Japan the order of 1 and 2 is reversed—revealing Confucian influence?) Slander of the Mahāyāna is not included, unless perhaps subsumed under 5.

206. Vow 19 of Amida's 48 vows enumerated in the *Larger Pure Land Sutra* (Muryōjukyō) is called the *injō higan* ("compasionate vow to lead and receive"); Nakamura 1963, p. 136. (This compares to Vow 18 of the Sanskrit version; Müller 1965, pp. 15, 73.)Cf., *Seiten* 1978, p. 11.

207. *hibō shōbō*, a phrase appearing in the all-important 18th Vow (Nakamura 1963, p. 136). See also note 191 and related text for translation.

208. *sōbyō*. Especially, the Ise and Iwashimizu Hachimangū, which enshrine ancestors of the Imperial line. The sun goddess, Amaterasu, is venerated at Ise; and Hachiman was identified with Emperor Ōjin. The Iwashimizu Shrine was also associated with Ōjin's mother, Empress Jingū (Ponsonby-Fane 1953, p. 78).

209. This is likely to be an error for the Kaharu Shrine in Buzen Province. Saichō visited both Usa and Kaharu shrines in Kyūshū just before his trip to China in 805 and again on his return to Japan the following year (Matsunaga 1969, p. 182).

210. The Buddhist Priest Gyōkyō was instrumental in having the Iwashimizu Shrine constructed so that the Shintō deity Hachiman could be worshipped near the capital. See Matsunaga 1969, p. 222; Ponsonby-Fane 1953, p. 78.

211. Jingōji temple records in Mongaku's handwriting state that Kūkai there enshrined the likeness of Hachiman Daibosatsu drawn by himself.

212. *hotsubodaishin*. The question of the need to "raise the desire for enlightenment" became a central issue in Myōe's attack on the *Senjakushū*. See note 187 and Chapter Three.

213. From the *Kammuryōjukyō*. Nakamura 1964, p. 44; Muller 1965, p. 167.

214. From the *Brief Discourse on the Pure Land of Peace and Rest* (Ryakuron anrakujōdogi, T.1957, v. 47, p. lc). The wording of the *Petition* varies slightly from the current modern edition.

215. From the *Compendium on the Land of Peace and Rest* (Anrakushū, T. 1958).

216. According to the biographical sketch of Shan-tao in the *Auspicious Biographies of Those who Attained Birth in the Pure Land of the West* (Ōjōsaihōjōdo zuiōden, T. 2070, v. 51, p. 105).

217. Anecdotes about the following ten individuals—from T'an Jung through Hsing Yen—were probably included in the *New Collection of Birth in the Pure Land according to the Vows* (Shimpen zuiganōjōshū) by Fei-cho (d. 1063), a work probably known to Jōkei but now lost. However, the items also appear in the Shimpukuji manuscript of the *Ōjōjōdoden* (cf., T. 2071?) by the Ch'an monk Chieh Chu (Kaishu, 985–1077), a work believed to have been based on Fei-cho's.

218. Asaṅga's noted *Mahāyāna-samgraha (Shō[daijō]ron*, T. 1592–94).

219. The story of Tao-chün's refusal to copy the Great Wisdom Sutra is to be found in another work by Fei-cho, the *Records of Spiritual Response from the Three Treasures* (Sambō kannōroku, T. 2084).

220. *sokuō anraku. Lotus Sutra*, Chapter 23. See Sakamoto and Iwamoto 1967, p. 204; cf., Hurvitz 1976, p. 300.

221. The source of this phrase has not been identified, but its proximity to the Tao-chün reference and the lost *Shimpen zuiganōjōshū* may not be accidental. See notes 217, 219.

222. The argument is obscure, but Jōkei seems to be saying that no provisional means used to attain undifferentiated Mind is to be made into an absolute.

223. Yung-ming Yen-shou (Yōmyō Enju, 904–975), who attempted to harmonize Ch'an with the Pure Land movements in China (Ch'en 1963, pp. 404–405), was also the author of *The Mirror of Sectarian Differences* (Sugyōroku), a work promoted shortly after Jōkei's time by the Zen syncretist, Enni Ben'en (1202–80).

224. Phrase from the 18th Vow as related in the *Larger Pure Land Sutra*. See p. 101 and Nakamura et al. 1963, p. 136; Seiten 1978, p. 11.

225. Possibly a reference to the "blind turtle and the floating log" (*mōki fuboku*) metaphor found in the *Lotus Sutra* and elsewhere.

226. The *Meditation Sutra* says: "Thou shouldst apply thy mind entirely to close meditation upon those who have already perfected the pure actions necessary for that Buddha country." (Takakusu, tr.; Müller 1965, p. 167; Nakamura et al. 1964, p. 44; *Seiten* 1978, p. 25.

227. In addition to being included in the 18th Vow (see p. 101 and note 224), the expression *jūnen*, "ten thoughts/invocations", is found in the description of the sixteenth, and lowest, of the classes of meditation described in the *Meditation Sutra* (Müller 1965, pp. 198–99; Nakamura et al. 1964, p. 71; *Seiten* 1978, p. 46.)

228. Sources as above, note 226. The sutra continues: "Let him do so serenely with his voice uninterrupted; let him be (continually) thinking of Buddha until he has completed ten times the thought . . ."

229. The *Kuan-ching-su* (Kangyōsho, T. 1753), one of the most influential works on Hōnen's thought (see Coates and Ishizuka 1925, *passim*)

230. Sincerity, profundity, and aspiration, according to the *Meditation Sutra*; but a parallel triad is also described in the *Larger Pure Land Sutra*. See Matsunaga 1976, pp. 98, 319 (note 101).

231. Four rules for the practice of the *nembutsu* set forth in Shan-tao's *Ōjōraisange* (cf., note 119). See Coates and Ishizuka 1925, p. 410.

232. The *Completion of Mere Ideation* (Jōyuishikiron, T. 1585) lists six sutras and eleven commentaries considered canonical by the sect.

233. Sembu no Ronshi. The thousand items were thought to have been 500 which Vasubandhu (Seshin) wrote as a Hinayānist and 500 as a Mahāyānist.

234. The ten philosophers mentioned in the *Jōyuishikiron* and enumerated by K'uei-Ch'i in his *Ch'eng wei-shih lun shu-chi*, T. 1830).

235. Jien makes a similar complaint in the *Gukanshō* (1219): "The *nembutsu* priests went so far as to make such promises as these: 'If you become a practitioner of this teaching, Amitābha Buddha will not consider you the lease bit sinful, even if you lust after women and eat fish or fowl . . ." (Brown and Ishida 1979, p. 171).

236. Metaphor appearing in the *Mappō tōmyōki* (Rhodes 1980, p. 92).

237. Part of the description of the Pure Land as found in the *Amida Sutra*. See Müller 1965, pp. 93–94; Nakamura et al. 1964, p. 90; *Seiten* 1978, pp.52–53.

238. Possibly a reference to Hōnen, whom Jōkei sees as upright, but misguided (cf., Article 4).

239. Hotsushamitsu-ō. In 184 B.C. Puṣyamitra overthrew the Mauryan dynasty, whose outstanding representative had been the Buddhist King Aśoka (ca. 273–232 B.C.). Puṣyamitra favored the Brahmans and Buddhist historians tell of his severe persecutions (Eliot 1954, pp. 68–69).

240. That is, by Emperor Wu-tsung who, in Hui-ch'ang 5 (845) initiated the great persecution in China witnessed by Ennin (Ch'en 1964, pp. 226–233).

241. Shunkai. A rather unusual compound, but this is perhaps the most plausible interpretation. The character *shun* is that used to transliterate the *śūn-* of *śūnyatā*, Emptiness, the Void. Had Jōkai used the character which usually *translates* the term (i.e., *kū*), his metaphor would have forced him to employ the compound used to identify the great Shingon leader, Kūkai; and his audience would not likely have taken the two characters as meaning literally, "Sea of Emptiness."

242. Myō-ō, the manifestation of Mahāvairocana who disperses evil. Probably an oblique reference to the Japanese monarch who is being asked to disperse the "evil" of the sole-practice movement.

243. Jōkei rounds off his *Petition* with some rather convoluted historical and theoretical allusions. Morohashi (III, p. 214) lists some nine mountains called Yao, but we cannot say to which, if any, Jōkei is referring. But it cannot be coincidence that Yao and Shun, the names of Jōkei's mountain and river, are also the names of the great legendary rulers of China known for their virtue.

244. Hōnen's submission of any letter of apology (*taijō*) prior to the *Petition* is not corroborated elsewhere (Tanaka 1971, p. 42). It is clear from what follows in the Summary that Jōkei is not confusing this with the 1204 Pledge (*kishōmon*) sent to the Tendai abbot.

245. Different sutras and commentaries provide partial descriptions of the Buddhist cosmos which we can organize into a single coherent system only with patience and ingenuity. The major scriptural source is the encyclopedic *Abhidharmakośa* (Abidatsuma-kusharon, T. 1558–59) of Vasubandhu. See Rosenfield et al. 1973, pp. 104–09, for early Buddhist maps with commentary; Coates and Ishizuka 1925, pp. 89–98, for additional explanations. Beal's pioneer *A Catena of Buddhist Scriptures* (1871), pp. 10–125, has a substantial discussion of Buddhist cosmology which is worth consulting.

246. See Kiyota 1978, pp. 69–70, 125–27. I am indebted to Professor Kiyota's lucid account of the system in which Kakukai lived and wrote, and I heartily recommend it to the reader for complementary details. In spite of his own demanding schedule, Professor Kiyota generously agreed to read this manuscript and made many valuable suggestions. I cannot, of course, hold him responsible for any errors which appear because of my own lack of understanding.

247. *mujō bodai*; anuttara-samyak-sambodhiḥ. The unexcelled wisdom of the Buddhas. The transliteration of this term from Sanskrit into Sino-Japanese is incorporated in the curious poem by the Tendai patriarch, Saichō (Dengyō Daishi, 767–822) when he established the Enryakuji on Mt. Hiei in 788 (*Shinkokinshū* XX: 1921):

Anokutara	O Buddhas
Sammyaku sambodai no	Of unexcelled enlightenment,
Hotoke tachi	Bestow your grace
Waga tatsu soma ni	Upon this hall of timbers
Myōga arase tamae	Hewn from the mountain.

248. Kakukai paraphrases the third line of the *Verse of Admonition Handed Down by the Seven Buddhas* (Shichibutsu tsūkai ge), which is thought to epitomize the Buddha's teaching. It appears in several forms in early sources, but the most popular version is found in two translations of the *Dharmapada*, the *Hokkukyō* (T. 210) and the *Shutsuyōkyō* (T. 212), as well as much later in *Shasekishū* 4:1 (Watanabe 1966, p. 179):

Shoaku makusa	Avoid all evil,
Shuzen bugyō	Cultivate every good,
Jijō koi	And purify your thoughts—
Ze shobutsu kyō	This all Buddhas teach.

249. *sokuji nishin*. At the common level of understanding, the phenomenal world of things (*ji*) is distinguished from the undifferentiated "truth" (*shin*, as it appears in this compound), i.e., the absolute (*ri*). But since there is ultimately there is no distinction between the absolute and phenomena, there is also equality among things. This is the world of the interpenetration of all things (*jiji muge hokkai*)—a concept shared by Shingon and Kegon, among others (see Cook 1977, pp. 35–36). But whereas the exoteric schools explain this identity as a temporal *return* of phenomena to the absolute which underlies their multiplicity, Shingon speaks of things *just as they are* being identical with the absolute.

250. *zuishin tenjiki;* literally, "change of form in accordance with mind." Shingon shares the Yogācāra (Hossō) doctrine of consciousness-only (*yuishiki, citta-mātra*), by which all phenomena are a function of mind.

251. *shikisō no busshin,* "the Buddha body with form (*rupa*) and characteristics (*lakśana*)." Tradition assigns 32 major characteristics (*sanjūūnisō*) and 80 minor attributes (*hachijūū shukō*) to the Enjoyment Body (*sambhogakāya, juyūjin*) of the Buddha. For the listing in the *Great Wisdom Sutra* (Daihannyaharamittakyō, T 220) see *Bukkyō daijiten* 1954, pp. 1554–60, 4212–13; cf., Conze 1975, pp. 583–587.

252. Also *hompushō, anutpāda.* Shingon's Meditation on the Letter A (*A-ji kan*) leads to the understanding that while all phenomenal things co-arise according to conditions and have conventional names, they are essentially empty. Essentially, "originally, nothing arises" or is produced because all things are essentially absent of a self-nature (*jishō, svabhāva*); at the same time, conventional truth (*zokutai*) recognizes the provisional existence of things. On *A-ji* and *anutpāda* see Kiyota 1978, pp. 71–74.

253. The *Ryōjin hishō* (Songs to Make the Dust Dance on the Beams) compiled by Emperor Go-Shirakawa (1127–1192) ca. 1169 includes this *imayō* (II:45; Kawaguchi and Shida 1965, pp. 350–51):

Shingonkyō no medetasa wa	The glory of Shingon teaching is to declare
Hōsōkuden hedatenashi	No distinction between
	mugwort hut and palace,
Kimi wo mo tami wo mo oshinabete	Equality between the lord and his subjects
Dainichi Nyorai to toitamō	Through identity with
	the Great Sun Buddha.

254. *hokkai gūden.* Dharmadhātu, the world of all elements (*hokkai*), the universe, is symbolized as a palace (*gūden*) wherein resides Mahāvairocana, the personification of true reality (*shinnyo, tathatā,* "suchness"), which is nothing other than the phenomenal world comprised of the Six Elements.

255. An abbreviation of Vairocana's *Rengezō shōgon sekai* (padma-garbha-lokadhātu) described in the *Garland Sutra* and in the *Net of Brahma* (Bommōkyō, T 1484).Both the Tōdaiji and the Tōshōdaiji in Nara represent Vairocana as being in this paradise (Fontein 1967, p. 167; Cook 1977, pp. 90–93). See also the introductory comments to this translation.

256. *shichi.* The four consciousnesses untainted by illusion (or *chihon,* types of wisdom) are important Yogācāra concepts adopted by Shingon: (1) the wisdom of perfect reflection (*daienkyōchi*), (2) the wisdom of equality (*byōdōshōchi*), (3) the wisdom of unerring cognition (*myōkanzatchi*), and (4) the wisdom for accomplishing all things through skillful means (*jōshosachi*). They are represented in the Diamond Mandala by the four Buddhas surrounding Mahāvairocana in the four directions, ESWN respectively. The Fivefold Wisdom (*gochi*) adds to these four the "wisdom that perceives the Essential Nature of the World of Dharma (*hokkai taishōchi*), represented by Mahāvairocana in the center. Cf., Hakeda 1972, pp. 83–84; Weinstein 1965, pp. 253–54.

257. *shigyō:*(1) enlightened mind (*bodai*), (2) compassion (*fukuchi*), (3) wisdom (*chie*) and (4) action, function, skillful means (*katsuma*). These *actions* parallel the four wisdoms of note 256.

258. *kue.* The 1,461 deities represented in the Diamond Mandala are grouped into Nine Assemblies. See Kiyota 1978, pp. 93–104.

259. More commonly, *jūsandai-in*, "Thirteen Halls." The standard (*genzu*, "iconographic") Womb Mandala transmitted by Kūkai comprised only twelve halls (Kiyota 1978, pp. 83–93). A rare older form, the so-called "Womb Representation" (*taizō zuzō*) brought back from China by Tendai's Chishō (Enchin, 814–91), has an additional thirteenth outer enclosure of Thunderbolt Deities (*kongōjin*) in the Hall of the Four Great Protectors (*shidaigo-in*). But it seems curious that Kakukai would refer to this form. On the other hand, the problem may simply depend on how one counts the halls (see Kiyota 1978, p. 143, notes 8 and 10).

260. The "known" represented by the Womb Mandala is the *dharmadhātu* (*hokkai*), "the world of the infinite co-arising (continuity) of dharmas based on the doctrine of the emptiness of a dharma-essence" (Kiyota 1978, p. 110).

261. *kongōkai sanjūshichison*. The Five Buddhas and thirty-two Bodhisattvas of the central Karma Assembly of the Diamond Mandala.

262. *jōken*. The notion that there is a permanent substratum, a self, to individuals and dharmas. This violates the basic Buddhist principle of *anātman* (*muga*), "no-self." See following note.

263. *kūken*. The Mahāyāna has always been careful to distinguish its central notion of Emptiness (*kū*) from the extreme view of Annihilationism which would deny all continuity and thus render impossible the workings of karma. Buddhism proposes to teach the Middle Way, maintaining a kind of continuity without postulating a permanent self for persons or things.

264. Among four deities (*shisho myōjin*) associated with Kōya, Nibu(tsuhime) Myōjin and Kōya Myōjin are the most prominent. According to legend, Nibu Myōjin provided Kūkai with the site for the Kongōbuji (of which Kakukai was 37th Superintendent) in 816. See Ponsonby-Fane 1953, pp. 272–73; Kiyota 1982, p. 33.

265. The *Sutra on the Stages of Bodhisattva Practice* (Bosatsujijikyō, T. 1581), a major exposition of the Mahāyāna disciplinary code, describes four powers (*shiriki*) through which one may attain Enlightenment: (1) self power (*jiriki*), (2) other power (*tariki*), (3) the power of past good karma (*inriki*), and (4) the power of skillful means (*hōbenriki*), i.e., the good offices of friends in the faith (*zenchishiki*). In Kakukai's day the Amidist Pure Land sects emphasized their reliance on the efficacy of the Other Power of Amida's Vows, in opposition to the traditional sects of the Holy Path (*shōdōmon*) which promoted the teaching and practice of Self Power.

266. Those with *naishō*, the inner realization of *satori* which is outwardly manifest (*geyū*) in enlightened action. Within the scheme of Ten Worlds (*jikkai*), they operate in the nine beneath the formless world of the Buddha.

267. One's posture and state of mind at the moment of death were often considered to have a critical bearing on favorable birth. ("And the time of death is every moment"? Kakukai, Genshin and Hōnen would probably agree with Eliot, but not Shinran and the subsequent Pure Land Movement.) A traditional posture was that assumed by Śākyamuni when he entered Nirvāṇa, head to the north while lying on the right side facing west. See Coates and Ishizuka 1925, pp. 637–38; Hori 1968, p. 121.

268. *zenchishiki*. See note 265. Kakukai here uses the term in the simple sense of religious colleague or spiritual mentor, although it frequently refers to the fifty-three "Good Friends" (*kalyāṇamitra*) in the *Garland* (*Kegon*) *Sutra's* account of Sudhana's pilgrimage.

269. Yūgen (d. 1147), disciple of Kakuban.

270. Beneath the heavens of Form (*shikikaiten*) and of No-form (*mushikikaiten*) are the Six Desire Heavens (*rokuyokuten*) which include, in ascending order, the heavens of (1) the Four Heavenly Kings (*shitennō*), (2) the Thirty-three (*tōri*), (3) Yama, (4) the Satisfied Gods

(*tosotsu*), (5) Self-providing Pleasures (*keraku*) and (6) Other-providing Pleasures (*takejizai*). Within this last heaven is the abode of Mara (Maō) who obstructs the practice of Buddhism (cf., *Shasekishū* 1:1; Morrell 1985, p. 73).

271. *gojoku.* The five sources of defilement in our present world. Our evils arise because of (1) the times in which we live, (2) deteriorating views, (3) the passions, (4) declining capacities, and (5) decreasing life span. Among a variety of scriptural sources to express this notion are the *Lotus Sutra* (T. 262; Hurvitz 1976, p. 31) and the *Amida Sutra* (T. 366; Müller 1965, p. 102;Seiten 1978, p. 56.)

272. A reference to the *Vimalakirti-nirdeśa Sūtra* (Yuimakitsu shosetsukyō, T. 475), Chapter 1: ". . . if a Bodhisattva wants to win the pure land he should purify his mind, and because of his pure mind the Buddha land is pure." Luk 1972, p. 13.

273. Reasons for the termination of these official voyages are discussed in Borgen 1982, pp. 24–25.

274. For the early Tendai affiliations of all three, see Chart 2.

275. The Sung painting mentioned in note 40 and accompanying text would have come to Japan around this time.

276. For Fa-hsien, see Legge 1886 and Li 1957. Hsüan-tsang's own account of his travels is titled *Hsi-yü chi* (Saiikiki, T. 2087), and is completely translated in Beal 1884 (reprinted 1968), and partially translated with commentary in Watters 1904 (reprinted 1961). A biography of Hsüan-tsang based on accounts by three disciples is included in Waley 1952. I-ching's account of his travels (T. 2125) is translated in Takakusu 1896 (reprinted 1966).

277. A curious case is Emperor Kammu's grandson, Prince Takaoka (799–865), who took the religious name Shinnyo. In 864 he left Ch'ang-an for India via Canton; it is assumed that he died en route in 865, but he may have reached Singapore. See Shimizu 1957, pp. 1–35. According to Chinese sources, a Japanese called Kongō Sammai had traveled to Central India (Shimizu, p. 34, note 63).

278. Tanaka 1961 is an invaluable guide to Myōe's life and works. See also Kamata and Tanaka 1971 for Japanese renderings of selected works and a condensed biographical sketch.
Munemitsu makes a brief appearance in *Heike monogatari* X:10, where he meets Taira Koremori just after the latter has received the tonsure. Munemitsu, Myōe's mother, and Jōgaku were children of Yuasa Muneshige, the pivotal figure in the fortunes of the Yuasa clan in those unstable times. During the Heiji Disturbance, 1159 (cf., Chart 3), he urged Taira Kiyomori to attack the forces of Minamoto Yoshitomo, the father of Yoritomo. Jien records the incident in the *Gukanshō* (see Brown and Ishida 1979, p. 110 ff.). Muneshige later won Yoritomo's confidence and was awarded the Yuasa manor.

279. Jōgaku was also in the thick of political intrigue and took part in his father's meeting with Kiyomori (Brown and Ishida 1979, p. 110). Later, he seems to have accompanied Mongaku into exile in Izu in 1179, where Yoritomo raised troops against the Taira.

280. An annotated Japanese version of the *kambun* text of the first of the three books of *Saijarin* is given in Kamata and Tanaka 1971, pp. 43–105; complete *kambun* text, pp. 317–390.
Hōnen may have completed his *Senjakushū* as early as 1198, but it was not made public until the ninth month of 1212, two months before Myōe's reply. For an analysis of the issues, see Bando 1974, pp. 37–54. The first draft of Shinran's *Kyōgyōshinshō* was completed in 1224 and later revised.

281. The crucial importance of the concept of *bodaishin* in the *Garland Sutra* (Avatamsaka; Kegonkyō, see note 290), and for Mahāyāna thought in general, is discussed in Suzuki 1934, pp. 137–185, "The Desire for Enlightenment (Bodhicittotpāda)."

282. Myōe's view was founded on the classic doctrine of accommodation (*hōben*). The buddhas and bodhisattvas apply various "skillful means" or "expedients" to the specific needs of the devotee, rather than prescribing the same remedy for different spiritual ailments.

283. A discussion of the issues, with a translation from the *Denki* (see note 288), is to be found in Brownlee 1975, pp. 193–201, and Lieteau 1975, pp. 203–210. For the *Denki's* account of Myōe's using the Kōzanji as a sanctuary for military stragglers and his confrontation with Yasutoki, see Kaneko and Morrell 1983, pp. 206–209.

284. Myōe kept an account of these experiences, 1191–1230, in his *Record of Dreams* (Yume no ki). See Bandō 1974, p. 40ff.; also, Oda 1980, pp. 94–108, provides a current psychological anaylsis of these visions.

285. Presumably a reference to Hsüan-tsang's *Hsi-yü chi* (see note 276), although I have been unable to locate therein a single reference to the total number of *ri* between Ch'ang-an and Rājagṛha. Perhaps this is Myōe's own composite figure.

286. Myōe calculates the long *ri* employed in Kamakura Japan as exactly six times the short *ri*. If the long *ri* is about 4 kilometers, or 2.44 miles, then the distance from Ch'ang-an to Rājagṛha would be, by Myōe's calculation, 20,333 miles!

287. Since the lunar month could be 29 days long but not more than thirty, the lunar year would be less than 360 days unless there was an intercalary month, which occurred about once every three years.

288. For a comparison of manuscripts and modern printings, see Lieteau 1975, p. 209. This is supplemented by the recent printing of the 1665 *rufubon* in Kubota and Yamaguchi 1981. In the following translation I have followed the *rufubon* text in Washio 1925, pp. 239–332. *Dainihon shiryō* VII, pp.430–432 and 435–437, also includes excerpts from the *Acts* (Gyōjō), Book 2, for the period under consideration.

289. *Zenzai dōji*, the youth in the *Garland Sutra* who visited 53 "good friends" (*zenchishiki*), beginning and ending with the bodhisattva Mañjuśri (Monju), who guided him on his religious quest to the abode of the bodhisattva Samantabhadra (Fugen) at the 54th stage. Myōe was the major patron of this theme in Japanese art. See Fontein 1967, pp. 78–115.

290. They began around 1198 with an investigation of the *T'an hsüan chi* (Tangenki, T. 1733), a long commentary by the philosopher Fa-tsang (Hōzō, 643–712),and completed their studies in 1210. The *Garland Sutra* (Kegonkyō, T. 278, 279, 293) refers to three translations of the *Avataṃsaka Sutra* in 60, 80, and 40 fascicles, respectively. The title *Avataṃsaka* is applied to all three; but the third version comprises merely the final chapter, Sudhana's pilgrimage, of the two earlier translations, and is also referred to as *Gaṇḍavyūha*. See Suzuki 1934, p. 49. The *Garland Sutra* is the basic scriptural authority for the Kegon sect and was also influential in Zen.

291. *ato wo tareri*. The buddhas as "original ground" (*honji*) "manifest their traces" (*suijaku*, the *on* reading for *tareri-ato*) as local Japanese deities.

292. Noma 1963, color plates 8 & 9, & monochrome plate 45, pp. 82–83. The scroll painting also includes several illustrations of Jōkei (Gedatsubō).

293. *jūgen engi*. One of the two central formulations of the Kegon sect to explain the interdependence of all phenomenal beings, which thus have no persisting "self" or "substance,"

independent of the totality, the *dharma-dhātu (hokkai)*, the "world of the *dharmas.*" See Matsunaga 1974, I, pp. 103–105.

294. *rokuso en'yū.* The second of the formulations of the Kegon sect, noted in n. 293, above. Matsunaga 1974, I, pp. 105–107; Chang 1977, p. 168ff.; Cook, 1977, p. 76ff.

295. *fushoku no yamai,* also *fushokubyō.* A condition, regarded as a specific illness, in which the invalid refused all food (anorexia nervosa?). Myōe also suffered from this condition just before he died.

296. Ryōjusen, "Mount of the Numinous Eagle," where the *Lotus Sutra* (and also the *Kammuryōjukyō*) was proclaimed. The mountain is northeast of Rājagṛha, Myōe's destination. See also note 110.

297. Composed by Eikai (1268–1348), who was associated with the Jison'in, where Myōe, at the age of nineteen, had received the transmission of several esoteric rituals. Tanaka 1961, p. 17.

298. The reference appears in *Chikamoto nikki* by Ninagawa Chikamoto (1433–1488); see *Zoku shiryō taisei* X, p. 231.

299. The text for this translation appears in Sanari 1930, pp. 667–680; *Japanese Noh Drama* II, pp. ix–xxvi, has been helpful in providing English equivalents for the specialized vocabulary of *nō* costuming. Readers are referred to both collections for additional information on technical terms that are retained in the translation without explanation. A French translation of *Kasuga ryūjin* is available in Sieffert 1979, pp. 267–279. The play is a dramatic dream *nō* included in the repertory of all five current schools of *nō*.

300. Gesshi, literally "Moon Branch" (although the word is a transliteration for a non-Chinese name), refers to the Yüeh-chih, some of whom settled in Bactria in Central Asia as the Kushans, known for their great Buddhist king, Kanishka (r. ca. 120–144). The moon reference thus vaguely conjures up regions west of China, i.e., Central Asia and India. Along the way the party would pass through the "country where the sun sets," i.e., China, in Prince Shōtoku's phrase; see Aston 1956, II, p. 139.

301. The travel song begins at Mount Atago, northwest of Kyoto and visible to the west from Myōe's Kōzanji. On their way to Nara, the party would pass Narabigaoka in the Hanazono district of west Kyoto, south of Ninnaji. Narazaka and Mount Mikasa (Wakakusayama) are both just north of Kasuga Shrine in east Nara.

302. *wakō (dōjin),* the gods who "soften their light (and identify with the dust)", i.e., the Shintō deities who "manifest the traces" *(suijaku)* of the Buddhas and Bodhisattvas who are their "original ground" *(honji);* cf., note 291.

303. Ama no Koyane, ancestor of the Nakatomi clan, of which the Fujiwara was a branch; Kasuga was the family shrine of the Fujiwara. See Philippi 1968, pp. 456–457. Sanari, p. 670, notes that the pillow word *hisakata* associates (through *hisashi,* "eaves") with *koyane,* "little roof," thus inferring that Zeami's audience was aware of the literal meaning of the deity's name.

304. Kasuga enshrines four principal deities—Kashima Takemikazuchi, Katori-iwainushi, Hiraoka-amakoyane, and Aidonohime—as well as a number of subordinate gods including Mizuya Daimyōjin. These are all identified more or less consistently with specific Buddhas as their Original Ground, and are graphically represented in outstanding pictorial scrolls from the period, perhaps the most famous being the *Kasuga Miya Mandala* (1300) owned by the Nezu Museum, Tokyo. See Kageyama 1965, pp. 121–142; Kageyama 1967, pp. 28–35 and Plate 8; Matsunaga 1969, pp. 231–233.

Sanari notes that the phrases at this point in the text contain a number of associations with water, and he refers us to a verse in *Fubokushō* (ca. 1310):

Kasugayama	Until the waters
Mizuya no mizu no	Of Mizuya on Mount Kasuga
Sue made mo	Are all expended,
Kami ni makasete	I rely upon the god,
Mi wo tanomu kana	Entrusting myself to his care.

Kōchū kokka taikei XXII, p. 259

305. This phrase, with "mountain" (*yama*) replaced by "slope" (*saka*), suggests a poem in the *Man'yōshū* (XVI: 3836); cf., *Kokin rokujō* (Six Quires of Ancient and Modern Poetry, 987) VI: 35146.

Narayama no	In the hills of Nara
Konotegawashi no	There grows the *child's-hand* cypress
Futaomo ni	With leaves double-faced.
Ka nimo kaku nimo	On either side of me I see
Nejikebito no tomo	A swarm of rascals

Nippon Gakujutsu Shinkōkai 1940, p. 227.

Further, *Narazaka no konote* (*wo awasete*) associates with *Narayama no konote gawashi* ("child's-hand cypress") of the *Man'yōshū* poem. Sanari p. 672.

306. An allusion to *Shinkokinshū* IV: 378.

Musashi no wa	I came to see Musashi Plain,
Yukedomo aki no	But its autumnal scenery
Hate zo naki	Is without limit.
Ikanaru kaze ka	What wind can be blowing
Sue ni fukuran	In its far extremity?

307. T'ien-t'ai and Wu-t'ai-shan were both sites of great monastic establishments in China often visited by Japanese students of Buddhism. Japan's Mt. Hiei and Yoshino would be probable counterparts. Tsukuba is mentioned perhaps because of its proximity to Kashima, where Takemikazuchi (see note 304, above) is worshipped as well as at Kasuga.

308. The verse, ascribed to Kasuga Daimyōjin, appears in the *Shokukokinshu* (VII: 691). *Shasekishū* I:5 states that the verse was spoken to Jōkei at Hannyadai (see Chapter Four, note 185 and associated text).

309. An allusion to the Parable of the Prodigal Son in the *Lotus Sutra*, Chapter 4: "Straightway he removed his necklaces, his fine outer garments, and his ornaments, and put on instead a rough, torn, dirty, tar-stained garment . . ." Hurvitz 1976, p. 87.
   The story is a metaphor for the principle of accommodation and is not part of the historical record of Śākyamuni's first sermon at the Deer Park in Benares, near Sarnath.

310. *harubi*, the characters usually read as "Kasuga."

311. Saidaiji, lit., "Western Great Temple." Eizon was its restoring founder (see Chapter One).

312. The Seven Great Temples of Nara are Tōdaiji, Kōfukuji, Gangōji, Daianji, Yakushiji, Saidaiji, and Hōryūji. Kōfukuji, adjacent to and associated with Kasuga Shrine, is noted for its double-flower cherry blossoms. Cf., n. 25. The passage contains a numbering pattern which may be of interest: *Mikasa* suggests "three", there are four directions, seven temples, and the double-flower cherry blossom, *yaezakura*, is written with the character for "eight."

313. Śākyamuni's death at Kuśinagara in an enclosure formed by a brace of teak trees at each of the four directions has provided a popular genre of picture, the *Nehan-zu*.

314. The text here pivots the meaning, "strips of folded white paper made of tree fiber" (*yuu shide no kami*), an appropriate shrine image outside the logic of the sentence.

315. According to *Teiō hennenki* (ca. 1300), when Kasuga Daimyōjin—in this case Takemikazuchi (see note 304, above)—left Kashima in Hitachi to go to Mt Mikasa, he was accompanied by two attendants, Tokifū and Hideyuki. Zeami treats the names as that of a single individual. See *Shintei zōho kokushi taikei* 12, p. 166.

316. Hsüan-tsang's monumental translation of the *Mahāprajñāpāramitā sūtra* (Daihannyaharamitakyō, T. 220) in 660 after his return to China is described in the last chapter of the biography (T. 2053) written by his disciple Hui-li. See Waley 1952, pp. 124–127; Li 1959, pp. 260–265.

317. The Iron Gate (Tetsumon) was a fortified pass south of Samarkand and north of the Oxus River. (Watters 1904, pp. 100–102). I have been unable to locate Jakusui, Jo River (?), in Hsüan-tsang's account. In any case, such place names were used by Zeami for their exotic sounds only, since his audience had little knowledge of geography west of China.

318. The Eight Dragon Kings were part of the vast assembly on Holy Eagle Mount to hear Śākyamuni preach the *Lotus Sutra*, as described in its introductory chapter. Zeami mentions only six of the kings. See Sakamoto and Iwamoto 1962, I, p. 14; Hurvitz 1976, p. 3. When Kumārajīva *transliterated* the Indian name into Chinese, Professor Hurvitz gives us the Sanskrit reading; when the name is *translated*, he gives an English translation.

319. Zeami mentions two of the four *kinnara* ("mythical being, half horse, half man") kings: Myōhō and Jihō; Hurvitz 1976, pp. p.3.

320. Again, Zeami selects two of the *gandharva* ("musician-demigod") kings: Gaku and Gakuon; Hurvitz 1976, p. 3.

321. Again, two of the four *asura* ("titan") kings: Bachi and Rago.

322. The famous story of the Dragon King's eight-year-old daughter who suddenly attains Buddhahood before the eyes of the assembly is told in the *Lotus Sutra*, Chapter 12; Hurvitz 1976, pp. 199–201.

323. The Saogawa flows east to north around Mt. Mikasa and then southwest through the center of the old Nara capital of Heijō.

324. An allusion to *Kokinshū* I:19:

Kasuga no no	Come and see,
Tobuhi no nomori	Watchmen of the signal fires
Idete miyo	On Kasuga Plain!
Ima ikuka arite	How many days is it now
Wakana tsumiten	Till we pluck the young shoots?

325. *Lotus Sutra* 12: ". . . the assembled multitude all saw the dragon girl . . . go southward to the world-sphere Spotless . . ." (Hurvitz 1976, p. 201).

326. A small pond west of Kasuga Shrine and just south of the Kōfukuji. The stage directions reflect the geography of the area: if the Dragon King faces south at Kasuga Shrine to watch the departure of the Dragon Girl and then makes a right turn, he will be looking in the direction of Sarusawa Pond.

Illustrations

Figure 1. Jien (1155–1225). Sketch attributed to Sumiyoshi Hirozumi (1631–1705).

Figure 2. Myōe (1173–1232). Painting by Jōnin (fl. early 13th c.). (See p. 48 for related text).

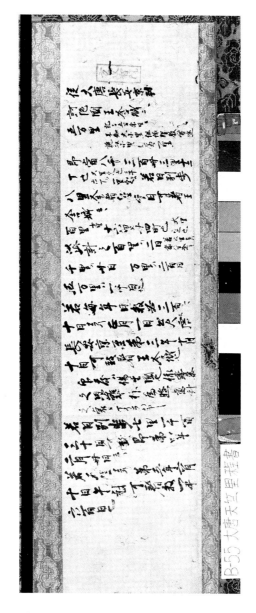

Figure 3. Myōe's *Calculations on the Distance to India* (Tenjiku riteisho, ca. 1205; holograph). Translation on pp. 105–106.

Figure 4. Jōkei (1155–1213). Anonymous sculpture in Kaijusenji collection.

Figure 5. Kakukai (1142–1223). Detail of Edo period scroll in the Zōfukuin collection, Mt. Kōya.

INDEX

Numbers in italics indicate pages
with relatively extensive coverage.
Endnotes are identified by an initial "n".

Four Practices (*shishu* 四修)85, n231
Four Universal Methods (*shishōbōgyō* 四摂
法行) 64
frog in well 83
Fubokushō 夫木抄 (The Japanese Collec-
tion) n304
Fudarakusen. See Potalaka.
Fūgashū 風雅集(Collection of Elegance)
XVIII: 2069 41, n58
XVIII: 2071 41
XVIII: 2075 42
XVIII: 2092 42, n71
Fugengyō 普賢経 (Sūtra of Meditation on
the Bodhisattva Universal Vow) n35
Fujiwara 藤原. See also Kujō.
Jien. See Jien (Jichin).
Kiyosuke 清輔 (1104–1177) n80
Michinaga 道長 (966–1024) 4
Michinori. See Shinzei.
Nobuyori 信頼 (1133–1159) 67, Chart 3
Shunzei 俊成 (or Toshinari, 1114–1204)
24, 29
Sumitomo 純友 (d. 941) n51
Tadamichi 忠通 (1097–1164) 27, 33,
n95, Chart 3
Tadanobu 斉信 (967–1035) 34, n97
Tadazane 忠実 (1078–1162) 27, Chart 3
Tameie 為家 (1198–1275) 38
Teika 定家 (or Sadaie, 1162–1241) 28,
30, 36, 45, 48
Tsunesada 経定 (12th c.) 27
Yorimichi 頼通 (992–1074) 4
Yorinaga 頼長 (1120–1156) Chart 3
Yoritsune 頼経 (1218–1256) 36
Yoshitsune 良経 (1169–1206) 30, 36,
n133
fukuchi 福智 (compassion) n257
fumimiru 䜭 (文) 見る n34

Furuna. See Pūrṇa.
fusen no sen nari 不専の専なり85
fushoku no yamai 不食病 (fasting malady)
n295
Future and the Past, The. See *Gukanshō.*

Gaen 雅縁, Abbot 70
Gaku 楽 n319
Gakuon 学音 n319
gakushō 学生 (scholars) 28; cf. *dōshō.*
Gaṇḍavyūha Sūtra. See *Kegonkyō.*
Gangōji 元興寺 n25
Ganjin 鑑真 (Chien-chen, 687–763) 1, 4, 7,
76, n8
ganshu 願主 (prayer) 9
Garland Sūtra. See Kegonkyō.
Gazen. See Shunjō.
Gedatsubō. See Jōkei.
Gedatsu Shōnin kairitsu saikō gammon.
(Venerable Gedatsu's Written Vow for
the Restoration of the Precepts) 7ff
Gembō 玄昉 (d. 746) 1
Gempei 源平 War 25, 67
gempuku 元服 (Coming-of-Age ceremony)
n73
Genjō. See Hsüan-tsang.
Genkū. See Hōnen.
gensa 験者 (adepts) 54
Genshin 源信 (Eshin 恵心, 942–1017)
12–14, 16, *17*, 33, 72, n56, Chart 2
genzu 源図 "iconographic" maṇḍala n259
Gesshi 月枝 ("Moon Branch") n300
geyū 外用 (outward manifestation) n266; cf.
naishō.
Gion Shrine 1
Gishin 義真 (781–833) Chart 2
go (*iki* 囲碁) (game) 86
gobaku no eshin 業縛の依身 101

Tuṣiṭa Heaven (*tosotsuten* 兜率天; Heaven
of the Satisfied Gods) 68, 95, 98, 99,
n179, n270
Two-fold Emptiness 55, 60
Two Truths (*nitai* 二諦) 42, *n135*, n155,
n252
Two Vehicles 58

ubai 優婆夷 (*upāsikā*) n15
Ubaribai 優婆離唄 (Song of Upāli) 11
ubasoku 優婆塞 (*upāsaka*) n15
Ubasokukaikyō 優婆塞戒経 n146
"Ulysses" (Tennyson) 45
Upāli (Ubari 優婆離) 11
Urin'in 雲林院 34, n98
uro 有漏 (tainted) 84
Usa Hachiman 宇佐八幡 Shrine 79
ushō 有性 (having nature) 58 vs. *mushō*.

Vaidehī (Idaike 韋提希) 72
Vairocana (Birushana 毘盧遮那) 95, n255;
cf. Mahāvairocana.
Vasubandhu (Seshin 世親 , Tenjin 天親 ,
5th c.) 12, 71, 72, 85, n190, n198, n233,
n245
Vehicles, Two 56
*Venerable Gedatsu's Written Vow for the
Restoration of the Precepts.* See *Gedatsu
Shōnin kairitsu saikō gammon.*
Venerable Myōe's Waka. See *Myōe Shōnin
wakashū.*
vernacular tract. See *kana hōgo.*
*Verse of Admonition Handed Down by the
Seven Buddhas.* See *Shichibutsu tsūkai
ge.*
Vimalakīrti Sūtra. See *Yuimakitsukyō.*
vinaya (*ritsu* 律; precepts) 3, *4ff,* 7, 9, 11, 73,
86

Vinaya in Ten Sections. See *Jūjuritsu.*
Vinayapiṭaka (*ritsuzō* 律蔵 ; "Basket of
Precepts") 11
Visualization of Amida Sūtra. See *Han-
jusammaikyō.*
*Votive Declaration to the Great Deity of
Kasuga.* See *Kasuga daimyōjin hotsu-
gammon.*
Vows 72, 81, 84

Wakadokoro 和歌所 (Bureau of Poetry) 30
Wakamiya 若宮 n180
waki 脇 (in *nō*) 112
waki-tsure 脇連 (in *nō*) 112
wakō-dōjin 和光同塵 ("soften the light and
identify with the dust") n302; see also
honji suijaku.
Western Paradise, Amida's. See *gokuraku
jōdo.*
Wisdom Heights. See Hannyadai.
works, good 17; see also faith vs. works.
Wu-chen Temple 悟真寺 (in China) 48
Wu-t'ai 五台山, Mount 116, n307
Wu-tsung 武宗 n240

yaezakura 八重桜 (double-flower cherry
blossom) n312
Yakushi Nyorai 薬師如来13, 95
Yakushiji 薬師寺 (Nara) n25, n312
Yakushiji 薬師寺 (Shimotsuke province) 4
Yakushin 益信 (827-906) Chart 4
Yama (Emmaten 焔摩天) n270
Yama'i 山井 (禅尼) 27
Yao 堯 (mountain) 88
Yao 堯 and Shun 舜 n243
Yasutane. See Yoshishige Yasutane.
Yearnings for the Ancient Chinese Style. See
Kaifūsō.